A COMMENTARY ON
THE CONFESSION OF 1967
AND
AN INTRODUCTION TO
"THE BOOK OF CONFESSIONS"

A COMMENTARY ON
THE CONFESSION OF 1967
AND
AN INTRODUCTION TO
"THE BOOK OF CONFESSIONS"

by
Edward A. Dowey, Jr.

Wipf and Stock Publishers
150 West Broadway • Eugene OR 97401

*A Commentary on the Confession of 1967
and An Introduction to "The Book of Confessions"*
by Edward A. Dowey, Jr.

Copyright© Westminster John Knox Press, 1968
Reprinted by Permission

Printed By *Wipf and Stock Publishers*
150 West Broadway • Eugene OR 97401

To the
Elders, Pastors, and Teachers
of the Special Committee
on a Brief Contemporary Statement of Faith
who persevered to the end!

Markus Barth
Arnold B. Come
Calvin DeVries
Janet Harbison
George S. Hendry
Cornelius Loew
John W. Meister

Kenneth E. Reeves
James D. Smart
Theophilus M. Taylor
Leonard J. Trinterud
Charles West
Gayraud S. Wilmore
Samuel M. Thompson,
Secretary

FOREWORD

Creeds and confessions generally need commentary. They are by nature highly compressed and carefully shaded in meaning. They are usually the work of more than one person and are intended for various levels of use. They arise out of diverse backgrounds and are carried into new situations unforeseen by their authors, acquiring interpretations and sometimes revisions along the way.

This book is aimed to help the average interested person understand the writings contained in *The Book of Confessions* of The United Presbyterian Church in the U.S.A. It should be especially useful to study groups and candidates for various church offices. Every reader should be equipped with *The Book of Confessions* and a Bible, preferably a study edition with notes.

The new Confession of 1967 is put first and discussed at greater length than the others by choice of the writer. This was done because it is meant to be the living edge of the church's confession and has been very much on the mind of the whole church throughout the procedures of writing, revision, and adoption. Precise reference to the numbered paragraphs required including the complete text of the Confession of 1967. Also, its Preface is a good introduction to the whole *Book of Confessions*. The material on each document, however, is independent and can be read separately from the rest. The Harmony at the end helps anyone who wants to trace a single theme through all the confessions. It will be obvious that the material in boldface is quoted from the document being commented upon.

The writer, for better or for worse, did not consult fellow members of the committee that first put forward *The Book of Confessions* and the Confession of 1967, nor members of the study and revision committee of which the Rev. Dr. W. Sherman Skinner was chairman. This book, hence, is a personal and not a consensus commentary. A lovely committee of one, Lois Montgomery Dowey, read the manuscript and made suggestions that improved the style and clarity.

Since this is not a book for professional scholars, it is not littered with notes and references. Where useful to the intended reader, such references are found within the text. In addition, I wish here to note with thanks that the remarks on the Biblical text beginning on page 104 are based on Professor Metzger's *The Text of the New Testament: Its Transmission, Corruption, and Restoration* (Oxford University Press, 1964). The words of J. N. D. Kelly on page 160 are from his *Early Christian Creeds* (David McKay Company, Inc., 2d ed., 1960), p. 425, from which much of the material on the Apostles' Creed is drawn.

E. A. D., Jr.

CONTENTS

Part Two

Appendix

Part One

Part One

THE CONFESSION OF 1967

The Confession of 1967 was prepared by the Special Committee on a Brief Contemporary Statement of Faith, first appointed in 1958 on the occasion of the union of the former United Presbyterian Church of North America and the Presbyterian Church in the United States of America. It was first published for study in the Committee's report to the General Assembly of the church in 1965. The report contained the complete proposal for the creation of *The Book of Confessions* and appropriate changes in the questions asked candidates for ordination as ministers, elders, and other officers of the church.

The report was published widely and studied extensively. A new Special Committee of Fifteen studied the proposals and received criticism and suggestions for amendment from the church at large. A somewhat revised text was then prepared by this Committee in consultation with the original Committee and approved for action by the General Assembly in 1966. During the following year presbyteries further studied and then voted as units, more than the required two-thirds majority deciding in favor of change. A third General Assembly, the 178th, meeting in Portland, Oregon, gave final approval by which the church's Constitution was altered in May of 1967.

The rather detailed commentary that follows makes it necessary to print the text of the Confession of 1967 so that its numbered paragraphs can be referred to specifically. The outline of the Confession is very helpful in showing how the whole is put together, but is awkward for precise reference.

THE CONFESSION OF 1967[1] [TEXT]

PREFACE

The church confesses its faith when it bears a present witness to **9.01** God's grace in Jesus Christ.

In every age the church has expressed its witness in words and **9.02** deeds as the need of the time required. The earliest examples of confession are found within the Scriptures. Confessional statements have taken such varied forms as hymns, liturgical formulas, doctrinal definitions, catechisms, theological systems in summary and declarations of purpose against threatening evil.

Confessions and declarations are subordinate standards in the **9.03** church, subject to the authority of Jesus Christ, the Word of God, as the Scriptures bear witness to him. No one type of confession is exclusively valid, no one statement is irreformable. Obedience to Jesus Christ alone identifies the one universal church and supplies the continuity of its tradition. This obedience is the ground of the church's duty and freedom to reform itself in life and doctrine as new occasions, in God's providence, may demand.

The United Presbyterian Church in the United States of America **9.04** acknowledges itself aided in understanding the gospel by the testimony of the church from earlier ages and from many lands. More especially it is guided by the Nicene and Apostles' Creeds from the time of the early church; the Scots Confession, the Heidelberg Catechism and the Second Helvetic Confession from the era of the Reformation; the Westminster Confession and Shorter Catechism from the seventeenth century; and the Theological Declaration of Barmen from the twentieth century.

---

[1] Reprinted with permission from *The Book of Confessions* (Philadelphia, The General Assembly of The United Presbyterian Church in the United States of America, 1966, 1967).

13

9.05   The purpose of the Confession of 1967 is to call the church to that unity in confession and mission which is required of disciples today. This Confession is not a "system of doctrine," nor does it include all the traditional topics of theology. For example, the Trinity and the Person of Christ are not redefined but are recognized and reaffirmed as forming the basis and determining the structure of the Christian faith.

9.06   God's reconciling work in Jesus Christ and the mission of reconciliation to which he has called his church are the heart of the gospel in any age. Our generation stands in peculiar need of reconciliation in Christ. Accordingly this Confession of 1967 is built upon that theme.

THE CONFESSION

9.07   In Jesus Christ God was reconciling the world to himself. Jesus Christ is God with man. He is the eternal Son of the Father, who became man and lived among us to fulfill the work of reconciliation. He is present in the church by the power of the Holy Spirit to continue and complete his mission. This work of God, the Father, Son, and Holy Spirit, is the foundation of all confessional statements about God, man, and the world. Therefore the church calls men to be reconciled to God and to one another.

PART I

GOD'S WORK OF RECONCILIATION

Section A. The Grace of Our Lord Jesus Christ

1. Jesus Christ

9.08   In Jesus of Nazareth true humanity was realized once for all. Jesus, a Palestinian Jew, lived among his own people and shared their needs, temptations, joys, and sorrows. He expressed the love of God in word and deed and became a brother to all kinds of sinful men. But his complete obedience led him into conflict with his people. His life and teaching judged their goodness, religious aspirations, and national hopes. Many rejected him and demanded his death. In giving himself freely for them he took upon himself the judgment under which all men stand convicted. God raised him from the dead, vindicating him as Messiah and Lord. The victim of sin became victor, and won the victory over sin and death for all men.

God's reconciling act in Jesus Christ is a mystery which the Scrip- **9.09** tures describe in various ways. It is called the sacrifice of a lamb, a shepherd's life given for his sheep, atonement by a priest; again it is ransom of a slave, payment of debt, vicarious satisfaction of a legal penalty, and victory over the powers of evil. These are expressions of a truth which remains beyond the reach of all theory in the depths of God's love for man. They reveal the gravity, cost, and sure achieve-ment of God's reconciling work.

The risen Christ is the savior for all men. Those joined to him by **9.10** faith are set right with God and commissioned to serve as his recon-ciling community. Christ is head of this community, the church, which began with the apostles and continues through all generations.

The same Jesus Christ is the judge of all men. His judgment dis- **9.11** closes the ultimate seriousness of life and gives promise of God's final victory over the power of sin and death. To receive life from the risen Lord is to have life eternal; to refuse life from him is to choose the death which is separation from God. All who put their trust in Christ face divine judgment without fear, for the judge is their redeemer.

2. THE SIN OF MAN

The reconciling act of God in Jesus Christ exposes the evil in men **9.12** as sin in the sight of God. In sin men claim mastery of their own lives, turn against God and their fellowmen, and become exploiters and despoilers of the world. They lose their humanity in futile striving and are left in rebellion, despair, and isolation.

Wise and virtuous men through the ages have sought the highest **9.13** good in devotion to freedom, justice, peace, truth, and beauty. Yet all human virtue, when seen in the light of God's love in Jesus Christ, is found to be infected by self-interest and hostility. All men, good and bad alike, are in the wrong before God and helpless without his forgiveness. Thus all men fall under God's judgment. No one is more subject to that judgment than the man who assumes that he is guilt-less before God or morally superior to others.

God's love never changes. Against all who oppose him, God ex- **9.14** presses his love in wrath. In the same love God took on himself judgment and shameful death in Jesus Christ, to bring men to re-pentance and new life.

Section B. The Love of God

9.15 God's sovereign love is a mystery beyond the reach of man's mind. Human thought ascribes to God superlatives of power, wisdom, and goodness. But God reveals his love in Jesus Christ by showing power in the form of a servant, wisdom in the folly of the cross, and goodness in receiving sinful men. The power of God's love in Christ to transform the world discloses that the Redeemer is the Lord and Creator who made all things to serve the purpose of his love.

9.16 God has created the world of space and time to be the sphere of his dealings with men. In its beauty and vastness, sublimity and awfulness, order and disorder, the world reflects to the eye of faith the majesty and mystery of its Creator.

9.17 God has created man in a personal relation with himself that man may respond to the love of the Creator. He has created male and female and given them a life which proceeds from birth to death in a succession of generations and in a wide complex of social relations. He has endowed man with capacities to make the world serve his needs and to enjoy its good things. Life is a gift to be received with gratitude and a task to be pursued with courage. Man is free to seek his life within the purpose of God: to develop and protect the resources of nature for the common welfare, to work for justice and peace in society, and in other ways to use his creative powers for the fulfillment of human life.

9.18 God expressed his love for all mankind through Israel, whom he chose to be his covenant people to serve him in love and faithfulness. When Israel was unfaithful, he disciplined the nation with his judgments and maintained his cause through prophets, priests, teachers, and true believers. These witnesses called all Israelites to a destiny in which they would serve God faithfully and become a light to the nations. The same witnesses proclaimed the coming of a new age, and a true servant of God in whom God's purpose for Israel and for mankind would be realized.

9.19 Out of Israel God in due time raised up Jesus. His faith and obedience were the response of the perfect child of God. He was the fulfillment of God's promise to Israel, the beginning of the new creation, and the pioneer of the new humanity. He gave history its meaning and direction and called the church to be his servant for the reconciliation of the world.

Section C. The Communion of the Holy Spirit

God the Holy Spirit fulfills the work of reconciliation in man. **9.20**
The Holy Spirit creates and renews the church as the community
in which men are reconciled to God and to one another. He enables
them to receive forgiveness as they forgive one another and to enjoy
the peace of God as they make peace among themselves. In spite of
their sin, he gives them power to become representatives of Jesus
Christ and his gospel of reconciliation to all men.

1. THE NEW LIFE

The reconciling work of Jesus was the supreme crisis in the life of **9.21**
mankind. His cross and resurrection become personal crisis and present hope for men when the gospel is proclaimed and believed. In
this experience the Spirit brings God's forgiveness to men, moves
them to respond in faith, repentance, and obedience, and initiates the
new life in Christ.

The new life takes shape in a community in which men know **9.22**
that God loves and accepts them in spite of what they are. They
therefore accept themselves and love others, knowing that no man
has any ground on which to stand except God's grace.

The new life does not release a man from conflict with unbelief, **9.23**
pride, lust, fear. He still has to struggle with disheartening difficulties
and problems. Nevertheless, as he matures in love and faithfulness
in his life with Christ, he lives in freedom and good cheer, bearing
witness on good days and evil days, confident that the new life is
pleasing to God and helpful to others.

The new life finds its direction in the life of Jesus, his deeds and **9.24**
words, his struggles against temptation, his compassion, his anger,
and his willingness to suffer death. The teaching of apostles and
prophets guides men in living this life, and the Christian community
nurtures and equips them for their ministries.

The members of the church are emissaries of peace and seek the **9.25**
good of man in cooperation with powers and authorities in politics,
culture, and economics. But they have to fight against pretensions and
injustices when these same powers endanger human welfare. Their
strength is in their confidence that God's purpose rather than man's
schemes will finally prevail.

9.26   Life in Christ is life eternal. The resurrection of Jesus is God's sign that he will consummate his work of creation and reconciliation beyond death and bring to fulfillment the new life begun in Christ.

2. THE BIBLE

9.27   The one sufficient revelation of God is Jesus Christ, the Word of God incarnate, to whom the Holy Spirit bears unique and authoritative witness through the Holy Scriptures, which are received and obeyed as the word of God written. The Scriptures are not a witness among others, but the witness without parallel. The church has received the books of the Old and New Testaments as prophetic and apostolic testimony in which it hears the word of God and by which its faith and obedience are nourished and regulated.

9.28   The New Testament is the recorded testimony of apostles to the coming of the Messiah, Jesus of Nazareth, and the sending of the Holy Spirit to the church. The Old Testament bears witness to God's faithfulness in his covenant with Israel and points the way to the fulfillment of his purpose in Christ. The Old Testament is indispensable to understanding the New, and is not itself fully understood without the New.

9.29   The Bible is to be interpreted in the light of its witness to God's work of reconciliation in Christ. The Scriptures, given under the guidance of the Holy Spirit, are nevertheless the words of men, conditioned by the language, thought forms, and literary fashions of the places and times at which they were written. They reflect views of life, history, and the cosmos which were then current. The church, therefore, has an obligation to approach the Scriptures with literary and historical understanding. As God has spoken his word in diverse cultural situations, the church is confident that he will continue to speak through the Scriptures in a changing world and in every form of human culture.

9.30   God's word is spoken to his church today where the Scriptures are faithfully preached and attentively read in dependence on the illumination of the Holy Spirit and with readiness to receive their truth and direction.

PART II
THE MINISTRY OF RECONCILIATION

Section A. The Mission of the Church

1. DIRECTION

To be reconciled to God is to be sent into the world as his recon-   **9.31**
ciling community. This community, the church universal, is entrusted
with God's message of reconciliation and shares his labor of healing
the enmities which separate men from God and from each other.
Christ has called the church to this mission and given it the gift of
the Holy Spirit. The church maintains continuity with the apostles
and with Israel by faithful obedience to his call.

The life, death, resurrection, and promised coming of Jesus Christ   **9.32**
has set the pattern for the church's mission. His life as man involves
the church in the common life of men. His service to men commits
the church to work for every form of human well-being. His suffering makes the church sensitive to all the sufferings of mankind so
that it sees the face of Christ in the faces of men in every kind of
need. His crucifixion discloses to the church God's judgment on
man's inhumanity to man and the awful consequences of its own
complicity in injustice. In the power of the risen Christ and the hope
of his coming the church sees the promise of God's renewal of man's
life in society and of God's victory over all wrong.

The church follows this pattern in the form of its life and in the   **9.33**
method of its action. So to live and serve is to confess Christ as Lord.

2. FORMS AND ORDER

The institutions of the people of God change and vary as their   **9.34**
mission requires in different times and places. The unity of the
church is compatible with a wide variety of forms, but it is hidden
and distorted when variant forms are allowed to harden into sectarian
divisions, exclusive denominations, and rival factions.

Wherever the church exists, its members are both gathered in cor-   **9.35**
porate life and dispersed in society for the sake of mission in the
world.

The church gathers to praise God, to hear his word for mankind,   **9.36**
to baptize and to join in the Lord's Supper, to pray for and present
the world to him in worship, to enjoy fellowship, to receive instruction, strength, and comfort, to order and organize its own corporate

life, to be tested, renewed, and reformed, and to speak and act in the world's affairs as may be appropriate to the needs of the time.

9.37   The church disperses to serve God wherever its members are, at work or play, in private or in the life of society. Their prayer and Bible study are part of the church's worship and theological reflection. Their witness is the church's evangelism. Their daily action in the world is the church in mission to the world. The quality of their relation with other persons is the measure of the church's fidelity.

9.38   Each member is the church in the world, endowed by the Spirit with some gift of ministry and is responsible for the integrity of his witness in his own particular situation. He is entitled to the guidance and support of the Christian community and is subject to its advice and correction. He in turn, in his own competence, helps to guide the church.

9.39   In recognition of special gifts of the Spirit and for the ordering of its life as a community, the church calls, trains, and authorizes certain members for leadership and oversight. The persons qualified for these duties in accordance with the polity of the church are set apart by ordination or other appropriate act and thus made responsible for their special ministries.

9.40   The church thus orders its life as an institution with a constitution, government, officers, finances, and administrative rules. These are instruments of mission, not ends in themselves. Different orders have served the gospel, and none can claim exclusive validity. A presbyterian polity recognizes the responsibility of all members for ministry and maintains the organic relation of all congregations in the church. It seeks to protect the church from exploitation by ecclesiastical or secular power and ambition. Every church order must be open to such reformation as may be required to make it a more effective instrument of the mission of reconciliation.

3. REVELATION AND RELIGION

9.41   The church in its mission encounters the religions of men and in that encounter becomes conscious of its own human character as a religion. God's revelation to Israel, expressed within Semitic culture, gave rise to the religion of the Hebrew people. God's revelation in Jesus Christ called forth the response of Jews and Greeks and came to expression within Judaism and Hellenism as the Christian religion. The Christian religion, as distinct from God's revelation of himself, has been shaped throughout its history by the cultural forms of its environment.

The Christian finds parallels between other religions and his own 9.42 and must approach all religions with openness and respect. Repeatedly God has used the insight of non-Christians to challenge the church to renewal. But the reconciling word of the gospel is God's judgment upon all forms of religion, including the Christian. The gift of God in Christ is for all men. The church, therefore, is commissioned to carry the gospel to all men whatever their religion may be and even when they profess none.

4. RECONCILIATION IN SOCIETY

In each time and place there are particular problems and crises 9.43 through which God calls the church to act. The church, guided by the Spirit, humbled by its own complicity and instructed by all attainable knowledge, seeks to discern the will of God and learn how to obey in these concrete situations. The following are particularly urgent at the present time.

a. God has created the peoples of the earth to be one universal 9.44 family. In his reconciling love he overcomes the barriers between brothers and breaks down every form of discrimination based on racial or ethnic difference, real or imaginary. The church is called to bring all men to receive and uphold one another as persons in all relationships of life: in employment, housing, education, leisure, marriage, family, church, and the exercise of political rights. Therefore the church labors for the abolition of all racial discrimination and ministers to those injured by it. Congregations, individuals, or groups of Christians who exclude, dominate, or patronize their fellowmen, however subtly, resist the Spirit of God and bring contempt on the faith which they profess.

b. God's reconciliation in Jesus Christ is the ground of the peace, 9.45 justice, and freedom among nations which all powers of government are called to serve and defend. The church, in its own life, is called to practice the forgiveness of enemies and to commend to the nations as practical politics the search for cooperation and peace. This requires the pursuit of fresh and responsible relations across every line of conflict, even at risk to national security, to reduce areas of strife and to broaden international understanding. Reconciliation among nations becomes peculiarly urgent as countries develop nuclear, chemical, and biological weapons, diverting their manpower and resources from constructive uses and risking the annihilation of mankind. Although nations may serve God's purposes in history, the church which identifies the sovereignty of any one nation or any one way of life with the cause of God denies the Lordship of Christ and betrays its calling.

9.46   c. The reconciliation of man through Jesus Christ makes it plain that enslaving poverty in a world of abundance is an intolerable violation of God's good creation. Because Jesus identified himself with the needy and exploited, the cause of the world's poor is the cause of his disciples. The church cannot condone poverty, whether it is the product of unjust social structures, exploitation of the defenseless, lack of national resources, absence of technological understanding, or rapid expansion of populations. The church calls every man to use his abilities, his possessions, and the fruits of technology as gifts entrusted to him by God for the maintenance of his family and the advancement of the common welfare. It encourages those forces in human society that raise men's hopes for better conditions and provide them with opportunity for a decent living. A church that is indifferent to poverty, or evades responsibility in economic affairs, or is open to one social class only, or expects gratitude for its beneficence makes a mockery of reconciliation and offers no acceptable worship to God.

9.47   d. The relationship between man and woman exemplifies in a basic way God's ordering of the interpersonal life for which he created mankind. Anarchy in sexual relationships is a symptom of man's alienation from God, his neighbor, and himself. Man's perennial confusion about the meaning of sex has been aggravated in our day by the availability of new means for birth control and the treatment of infection, by the pressures of urbanization, by the exploitation of sexual symbols in mass communication, and by world overpopulation. The church, as the household of God, is called to lead men out of this alienation into the responsible freedom of the new life in Christ. Reconciled to God, each person has joy in and respect for his own humanity and that of other persons; a man and woman are enabled to marry, to commit themselves to a mutually shared life, and to respond to each other in sensitive and lifelong concern; parents receive the grace to care for children in love and to nurture their individuality. The church comes under the judgment of God and invites rejection by man when it fails to lead men and women into the full meaning of life together, or withholds the compassion of Christ from those caught in the moral confusion of our time.

Section B. The Equipment of the Church

Jesus Christ has given the church preaching and teaching, praise **9.48** and prayer, and Baptism and the Lord's Supper as means of fulfilling its service of God among men. These gifts remain, but the church is obliged to change the forms of its service in ways appropriate to different generations and cultures.

1. Preaching and Teaching

God instructs his church and equips it for mission through preach- **9.49** ing and teaching. By these, when they are carried on in fidelity to the Scriptures and dependence upon the Holy Spirit, the people hear the word of God and accept and follow Christ. The message is addressed to men in particular situations. Therefore effective preaching, teaching, and personal witness require disciplined study of both the Bible and the contemporary world. All acts of public worship should be conducive to men's hearing of the gospel in a particular time and place and responding with fitting obedience.

2. Praise and Prayer

The church responds to the message of reconciliation in praise and **9.50** prayer. In that response it commits itself afresh to its mission, experiences a deepening of faith and obedience, and bears open testimony to the gospel. Adoration of God is acknowledgment of the Creator by the creation. Confession of sin is admission of all men's guilt before God and of their need for his forgiveness. Thanksgiving is rejoicing in God's goodness to all men and in giving for the needs of others. Petitions and intercessions are addressed to God for the continuation of his goodness, the healing of men's ills, and their deliverance from every form of oppression. The arts, especially music and architecture, contribute to the praise and prayer of a Christian congregation when they help men to look beyond themselves to God and to the world which is the object of his love.

3. Baptism

By humble submission to John's baptism Christ joined himself to **9.51** men in their need and entered upon his ministry of reconciliation in the power of the Spirit. Christian baptism marks the receiving of the same Spirit by all his people. Baptism with water represents not only cleansing from sin but a dying with Christ and a joyful rising with him to new life. It commits all Christians to die each day to sin and to live for righteousness. In baptism the church celebrates the renewal of the covenant with which God has bound his people to himself. By baptism individuals are publicly received into the church to share in its life and ministry, and the church becomes responsible for their training and support in Christian discipleship. When those baptized are infants the congregation, as well as the parents, has a special obligation to nurture them in the Christian life, leading them to make, by a public profession, a personal response to the love of God shown forth in their baptism.

4. THE LORD'S SUPPER

9.52   The Lord's Supper is a celebration of the reconciliation of men with God and with one another, in which they joyfully eat and drink together at the table of their Savior. Jesus Christ gave his church this remembrance of his dying for sinful men so that by participation in it they have communion with him and with all who shall be gathered to him. Partaking in him as they eat the bread and drink the wine in accordance with Christ's appointment, they receive from the risen and living Lord the benefits of his death and resurrection. They rejoice in the foretaste of the kingdom which he will bring to consummation at his promised coming, and go out from the Lord's Table with courage and hope for the service to which he has called them.

PART III
THE FULFILLMENT OF RECONCILIATION

9.53   God's redeeming work in Jesus Christ embraces the whole of man's life: social and cultural, economic and political, scientific and technological, individual and corporate. It includes man's natural environment as exploited and despoiled by sin. It is the will of God that his purpose for human life shall be fulfilled under the rule of Christ and all evil be banished from his creation.

9.54   Biblical visions and images of the rule of Christ such as a heavenly city, a father's house, a new heaven and earth, a marriage feast, and an unending day culminate in the image of the kingdom. The kingdom represents the triumph of God over all that resists his will and disrupts his creation. Already God's reign is present as a ferment in the world, stirring hope in men and preparing the world to receive its ultimate judgment and redemption.

With an urgency born of this hope the church applies itself to **9.55** present tasks and strives for a better world. It does not identify limited progress with the kingdom of God on earth, nor does it despair in the face of disappointment and defeat. In steadfast hope the church looks beyond all partial achievement to the final triumph of God.

"Now to him who by the power at work within us is able to do **9.56** far more abundantly than all we ask or think, to him be glory in the church and in Christ Jesus to all generations, forever and ever. Amen."

Chapter 1

THE PREFACE
(¶s 1-6)

The first confession of the church, at root its only confession, contains four words: "Jesus Christ is Lord" (Phil. 2:11; Rom. 10:9; I Cor. 12:3). Jesus was a man of a given place and time. "Christ" means "Messiah," the fulfillment of the Old Testament hope. "Lord" is part of the divine name indicating the ruler over all, especially over those who confess. In these words, epitomized, is the nature of God, the relation between God and man, salvation, obedience, the church, and the Christian hope.

It takes the whole Bible to explain the meaning of "Jesus Christ is Lord," and the history of Israel and the church to spell it out in human life. The many creeds and confessions of Christendom are occasional expanded reminders of this original act of praise and obeisance.

The verbs "to confess" and "to witness" are used in the New Testament more than are the nouns. This helps us remember that the center of confessing is not the formula, written or spoken, but the act. Confessing is a single event, both talking deed and acting word. Jesus made a "good confession" in his "testimony" before Pilate (I Tim. 6:13). Stephen and Paul did also, with their lives at stake (Acts, chs. 7 and 24). Some others failed "for fear" (John 12:42). "Witness" very early came to mean "martyr." Traditionally, "confessors" survived persecution and "martyrs" died by it, as in the quaint, grisly account of the burning of the English Reformers: "Their upper parts were Confessors, when their lower parts were Martyrs and burnt to ashes."

27

Day in, day out, dramatic or commonplace, there is confessing still to be done in words and deeds matched to the need of the time.

The historic creeds and confessions are a work of the church, not of individuals. Nor do individuals make any profession but faith in Christ to become church members. They do not sign documents by fellow believers, even those adopted into the church constitution. At least this is so among Presbyterians. However, pastors, elders, and some others must formally "subscribe" to the church's Confession and teach in harmony with it. Since these individuals make up the ruling bodies and supervise teaching, preaching, and mission, the Confession does, if conscientiously observed, direct the church, both in words and deeds.

Confessing in words produces dogma or theology—it always risks becoming a set of statements isolated from life. And action tends toward deeds without explanation, anonymous doing. There is danger when the two become separated. Recent church history in America holds a classic example of detachment. The old Westminster Confession orthodoxy became narrowly devoted to defining beliefs and building a defensive system of theology. The "social gospel" tended to empty itself in activity. Around the time of World War I there was a complete impasse. But a new start was already being made, a revival of Reformation theology modified by some aspects of liberalism. Through the middle years of the century, this new-old road was taken. The Confession of 1967 is a fruit of finding the way again, leading the church to confess both in words and deeds as the need of the time require[s].

Still, creeds and confessions come to us as a body of writings bound in books, not a set of activities. They are correctly called confessional statements. Various kinds are listed in the Preface, ¶ 2. The introductions to parts of *The Book of Confessions* in the chapters following show the circumstances in which certain ones were written. There is no single prescription for what a confessional statement should be or how it comes to be. History and influence determine its status more than formal rules about what it contains or how it is made and adopted.

Creeds have been short or long, technical or popular, general or specific, as the need of the time required. The earliest ones (see below on Apostles' Creed) instructed candidates for baptism, warded off heresy, and sometimes expressed the faith in worship. Others have clarified reform of the church, stabilized orthodoxy, or drawn up lines of opposition against threatening evil. All have been meant to draw upon the promises in Scripture for the continued guidance of the church by the Holy Spirit (John 16:13; Acts, throughout).

Present guidance is especially necessary as modern life raises problems undreamed of in the ancient or Reformation church. Neither sprawling consensus, nor makeshift pronouncements, nor stubborn traditionalism are a service to the gospel. The church should not reflect every ripple of history and every wind of doctrine, but it must respond to profound changes in life and culture, and bring about profound changes in life and culture, or suffer the fate of the Wonderful One Hoss Shay.

The ordination vow shows that confessions and declarations are subordinate standards in the church, and are subject to the authority of Jesus Christ, the Word of God, as the Scriptures bear witness to him. The promise is to teach and serve "in obedience to Jesus Christ, under the authority of the Scriptures, and under the continuing instruction and guidance of the confessions of this Church." These are cencentric circles of authority, moving from the middle outward: Christ, Bible, Confession. The structure is evangelical, Biblical, Reformed, in that order.

The theme of Christ the Word as the center of the written and spoken word is dealt with below (in discussion on ¶ 27). For the moment, we note only that some things in the Bible are central and others peripheral. The rule for measuring is nearness to the theme of salvation in Christ. This is important because some things on the fringe, or in the frame of the picture, of salvation have become antiquated and must be let go. Here the church's confession carries out a crucial function. A confession can either undermine or overstate Biblical authority. Either is a serious detriment to the gospel and a theft of Christ's authority (Matt. 28:18).

Subordinate confessional statements are go-betweens, inter-mediate between the Bible and contemporary life and language. Therefore, no one type of confession is exclusively valid, no one statement is irreformable. The Confession rejects verbatim the decree of the First Vatican Council (1870) that papal definitions are "infallible" and "irreformable." It is a far cry also from the straitjacket oath that once required Presbyterian seminary professors not to "inculcate, teach, or insinuate" anything that "directly or impliedly" appeared to them to "contradict or contravene" the Westminster Standards. Both life and dogma are to be reformed as new occasions, in God's providence, may demand.

Subordinate standards are, nonetheless, standards. They are not lightly drawn up, subscribed to, ignored, or dismissed. The discipline of the church is equipped to counsel with, admonish, and even hold trial for one ordained who seriously rejects the faith expressed in the confessions. Such action is happily both difficult and uncommon, for the church is in peril when its testimony becomes a mere test. Also, the church needs to listen to critics on every level of its life. The principle of reform is ill served by ousting reformers, and the principle of having creeds and confessions is ill served unless they are taken seriously. Christ is Lord over the Scriptures, over the confessions, and over the leaders and members of the church, but he is meant also to be Lord through them all in the church.

Obedience to Jesus Christ alone identifies the one universal church and supplies the continuity of its tradition. The obedience of faith described here and in the other Reformed confessions is a response to grace, not conformity to canonized traditions, unless, of course, they serve this obedience. The church must have institutional structures, but not one of them—creed, pastoral office, sacramental tradition, administrative provisions—can usurp the role of Christ, who is the sole bond of union in the church catholic (¶s 34-40).

This obedience is the ground of the church's duty ... to reform itself in life and doctrine. It is self-evident that part of the obedience described is the duty to reform, a very important, continuing activity in the history of the church. Reform presupposes decline and endeavors to recover from it. It brings the old new again into a new age. The classic Protestant Reformers understood themselves to be wiping out a thousand years of canonized novelties in order to bring the older, purer gospel to new life. They knew that Renaissance scholars could not become simple fishermen, but they meant to express the same Galilean gospel under conditions of European life and culture.

The nub of the Protestant Reformation was the reform of doctrine, an issue that still divides Protestant from Eastern Orthodox and Roman Catholic churches. This does not mean that Rome stands still or that "Reformed" churches are models of continuing reformation. In principle, however, it is the dividing line between the church's claim to infallibility and its confession of sinfulness.

Reform cannot be predicted or programmed. It occurs **as new occasions, in God's providence, may demand.** Our own century has held incredible surprises and many encouraging reforms. The church must be ready to bring out of its treasure, when history demands, "what is new and what is old" (Matt. 13:52).

Both new and old are found in *The Book of Confessions,* which was created by ¶ 4 of the Preface to the Confession of 1967. A similar book called *The Harmony of Protestant Confessions* was put together in 1581 among the Reformed churches of Europe to sum up the Reformation. As a kind of answer to the *Canons and Decrees* of the Council of Trent and the Lutheran *Book of Concord,* the *Harmony* places side by side chapters from the confessions of various nations to display both their agreement and their individuality. Consensus and variety, or harmony with individuality, thus, were the hallmarks of Reformed ecumenicity from the start.

The old *Harmony* dared more than *The Book of Confessions* by including the Lutheran Augsburg Confession (revised form) and the Thirty-nine Articles of the Church of England. At the outset of the Westminster Assembly in 1643 a translation of the *Harmony* was republished with the permission of the Westminster divines. Although the collection did not become the official book of any one church, several Reformed churches adopted more than one document in their confessional standards. The Hungarian Reformed Church has had the same enviable combination since the year 1567: the Heidelberg Catechism and the Second Helvetic Confession. The latter Confession, by the way, accepts the four ancient creeds listed at the end of its Ch. XI.

In *The Book of Confessions* the church acknowledges itself **aided** and **is guided** by the witness of the church **from earlier ages and from many lands.** The present tense of the verbs is important. *The Book of Confessions* is not a monument to the past. It is a present aid in **understanding the gospel** today. Many things in history fall away and are no longer remembered. Others live in the present and help navigate the future. These great **subordinate standards** from earlier days and other lands are a living heritage.

The reasons for creating *The Book of Confessions* are these: First, it places our actual history and doctrinal patrimony before our eyes in a way that no single confession, old or new, can do. The church did not begin in 1643, nor at the Reformation. The Presbyterian Church never was limited to the Westminster Standards, as its teaching and preaching and the contents of the Westminster Confession itself easily demonstrate. Secondly, *The Book of Confessions* makes clear the actual nature of creeds and confessions. They have appeared irregularly at various times and places in response to various needs, and they bear marks both of transience and permanence. The study of these documents and their historical settings show how the Christian faith lives and moves in history, not on some romantically imagined plane. Thirdly, the older and newer creeds and confessions together give perspective on the thought, worship, and ethics of the church, which is just as important as a knowledge of the contemporary in our hurriedly changing world. Fourthly, the ecumenical age, still in its infancy, will come more quickly to maturity when each tradition knows its own unity and variety. This is especially true of the Reformed tradition where its true "distinctives" are its most Biblical and catholic elements. Fifthly, the freedom and courage to respond as new occasions, in God's providence, may demand will be strengthened by the examples of those who confessed in other times and places.

The Book of Confessions will hardly be read by every church member, desirable as that might be, but leaders have a duty to know it well. Elders on the committees that drew up the revised ordination questions (1967) insisted that they should have the same responsibility for studying *The Book of Confessions* as the ministers. Still, the suggestion might be useful that where the whole book appears to be too long, an elder can fulfill his responsibility for knowing the essentials by concentrating on one confession from each period. A combination such as the Apostles' Creed, the Heidelberg Catechism, and the Confession of 1967 would be splendid. All these together are only the size of the Westminster Confession by itself minus the Westminster Catechisms, and are easier to understand. In the long run, the total impact of *The Book of Confessions* will be strongest when channeled through seminary education and the training of teachers as was the influence of the Westminster literature. The study of theology must include Biblical beginnings and historical developments as well as contemporary constructions. The Confessions are valuable in each category.

The differing views among the Confessions, say, on Biblical authority, Biblical criticism, predestination, church and state, ethical problems, response to old and contemporary science—these and others make up a healthy richness within a single inheritance of evangelical Christianity. There is no ground for schism or separation to be derived from them. Because of this, no formula gives precedence to one document in *The Book of Confessions* above the others. There is an inherent logic in such a collection that gives the contemporary document more force and more immediate applicability than the others. New branches on a tree are higher and more prominent than older, lower ones. But this logic is not made into a legal formula as it was in the case of the Confessional Statement of 1925 in the United Presbyterian

Church of North America. If anyone holds to the "guidance and continual instruction" of even one of these confessions after the ancient period, he will be holding to the essentials of all of them. If on the grounds of variety or alleged contradiction within *The Book of Confessions* he separates from the fellowship of the church, it is likely a breach of charity, not a sufficient doctrinal issue, that brings him to it.

The Bible itself, which contains both Proverbs and Isaiah, and Matthew and James as well as Romans, should be sufficient warning against artificial formulas that oversimplify reality. The effort in the early church to reduce the troublesome variety of the four Gospels to a single narrative was wrecked by the same sense of truth. The Three and the One of the Trinity are ample caution against reducing the faith of Christians to something like $2 + 2 = 4$. The Reformers' preference for the letters of Paul, which has dominated the Reformed churches, should be frankly affirmed, and just as frankly submitted to the pressures of Wisdom Literature, or apocalyptic, or the Fourth Gospel. This is not a case for chaos or indifference, but for opening the eyes to the variety and the vitality that has gone with the speaking of the word and the incarnation of the Word in human history. The one word was spoken in many idioms yesterday, and will be spoken in new idioms today and tomorrow.

In the 1920's and 1930's, despite the "fundamentalist-modernist" tag that is hung on the controversies, the split in the Presbyterian Church in the United States of America did not come between fundamentalists and modernists. It happened when one group of fundamentalists refused to have fellowship even with other conservative people who were, in turn, willing to be in the same communion and church administration with those of a more liberal bent. A tiny few departed only to divide again, pathetically, when they were by themselves. The charitable truce among the great majority that developed in the first half of the century made the church happily broader than it had been. It may also have made it shallower. But a new and deeper oneness has emerged in the middle years, the 1930's through the 1950's, with the realization that Christ himself is the church's one foundation. Neither the Bible nor the Westminster Confession was crucified for us. Nor were we baptized in the name of Machen or Coffin or Speer or Brunner—names from those controversies may be news to many of our readers! The composing, revising, debating, and adopting of the Confession of 1967 have demonstrated that the broader church has also become more deeply united in relation to its Center. If the spring which invigorates this common Confession is truly the Spirit of Christ, the mission of the church in the late twentieth century will show it. If not, that too will become clear. The needs of men are ever more pressing, and the disaster of failing them is ever more obvious.

The final two paragraphs of the Preface tell the purpose of the Confession of 1967: to call the church to that unity in confession and mission which is required of disciples today. The Twelve were both called and sent by Jesus. So were the Seventy and so are all disciples, whatever their position in the church or society. The phrase confession and mission reminds us of the detachment of words and deeds in the recent past, discussed above. The unity called for is meant to express in action the fundamental unity to which we have just been pointing.

Anyone who reads the history of the Presbyterian family of churches in America will be aware that unity based on the Westminster Standards has not always prevailed. There have been heresy trials, party struggles, separations and reunions, in which the historical Standards have played a mixed role. Deviations from the inherited pattern have not all been in a so-called liberal direction. The Presbyterian Church in the United States (in the South) excluded fundamentalist dispensationalism only twenty years ago. Most present-day revivalism, widely supported among Presbyterians who recently defended the Westminster Confession against the new constitutional provisions, belongs to what the Westminster divines rejected as "Arminianism" or "free will" doctrine.

Behind the most important estrangement from the Westminster teachings were (1) the problem of Biblical authority in the light of advancing historical, social, and physical sciences; (2) the response of the church to rapid social change; and (3) the harshness of double predestination. The most common solution for those of varying opinions on these matters was finally to permit latitude within limits judged acceptable by the various presbyteries. In the case of ordination to the ministry this was quite legal and did not need to wound the conscience of any candidate who spoke his mind to presbytery and was accepted. Presbytery, not the candidate, was and is today the judge of subscription. Each individual submits to lengthy oral and written examinations and presents a confession of personal faith which he himself has composed. But the net result of such undirected procedures was gradual distancing from the Confession in most instances, and undue narrowness in others.

It must be admitted that the Westminster Standards have not distinctively informed the preaching, church school teaching, and theological education of either member church of the United Presbyterian church union of 1958 for many decades. Not only laymen or elders who have subscribed to the Westminster Confession, but ministers, by and large, have a hard time discussing and even identifying such Westminster teachings as double predestination or the double covenant, let alone "confessing" them. Under these conditions, the need for revision or for a new, contemporary statement has been widely recognized since the 1890's. The Confessional Statement of 1925, like the amendments of 1903, offered modifications and accommodations, but did not really respond to the major challenges of modern times: the challenge to Biblical authority and the challenge to Christian ethics. Against this background we read: **the purpose of the Confession of 1967 is to call the church to that unity in confession and mission which is required of disciples today.**

Whether the new Confession can contribute anything depends both upon its content and upon the seriousness with which it is received and made use of. The process of adoption, the excitement entailed, the dire warnings and high promises uttered about the Confession—all encouraged a period of thinking and self-examination that is without precedent in the Presbyterian churches in this century. Opponents met and talked things out. Study and frank debate generally took the place of mass meetings. Cheap publicity and expensive scare tactics were at a minimum, and were rejected by the common sense of the church. But if the document is now allowed to lie flat on the printed page and is not brought to three-dimensional life, the project for **unity in confession and mission** will be of interest to archivists only.

The phrase "**system of doctrine**" in the next sentence of ¶ 5 is placed in quotation marks because it is quoted from the Form of Government of the church. Until May, 1967, when a revision took place, these words were part of a question answered by ministers and others being ordained or commissioned in the church. The purpose was to make sure that the ordained accepted the Westminster Confession as containing "the system of doctrine taught in the Holy Scriptures." The meaning of "system of doctrine" was never defined constitutionally, but was left for each presbytery to decide as questions arose. The phrase had never meant accepting every detail of the Confession, and the effort to interpret it as a list of essential doctrines, while sometimes used, did not get into the Constitution. In one early usage, the three Westminster documents were referred to in the plural as good and sound "systems." The most natural and probably the most generally accepted meaning took the term to refer to the highly refined and consistently worked out structure of the whole. The chapter in this volume on the Westminster Confession deals with its systematic character, holding that the logic of certain doctrines was allowed to control that of others in a way that forced the Bible into an artificial mold.

The present remark, that **this Confession is not a "system of doctrine"** means to reject the position that either the Bible or the new Confession is a self-contained logical whole of this kind. The elaborate science and art of Biblical interpretation lies between the Bible and any "system." Further, it may be that theology should hold back where the Bible itself holds back, and not fill up all incomplete topics with systematic conclusions. The depth of the mystery of revelation and the limited capabilities of the mind of man will always leave a system incomplete. Also, the present day is not one in which massive systematic efforts are so likely to recommend themselves to the church as they did in the seventeenth century. Hence, the Confession of 1967 sets out to develop one major Biblical theme in its implications rather than all themes at once. The time may come again when the comprehensive type of confession will be needed. But the present day is not a systematic one in that sense, whether in theology or other areas of intellectual enterprise.

Closely bound to the former phrase is a second one: **nor does it include all the traditional topics of theology, for example, the Trinity and the Person of Christ.** These doctrines are **recognized and reaffirmed,** but they are not repeated or reconstructed. The chapters in this volume on the older confessions and especially the chapter on the Nicene and Apostles' Creeds contain some discussion of the doctrine of the Trinity and the doctrine of Christ. Rather than try to be either old-fashioned or new-fashioned in stating these teachings, however, the Confession of 1967 shows them functioning with relation to others. The doctrines are not only **recognized . . . as forming the basis and determining the structure of the Christian faith,** they are seen at work forming the basis and determining the structure of the Confession of 1967. Probably the easiest way to observe is to note that Part I of the Confession has a Trinitarian order and substance, and that Part II is a continued working out of the doctrine of the Holy Spirit. Also, the doctrine of Christ, especially in Part I, Section A, presupposes the balanced classical doctrine as a basis on which to make a particular special emphasis on Jesus' humanity.

The last paragraph of the Preface is transitional. It has no special content that is not discussed farther on as we proceed.

CHAPTER 2

MOTIF: RECONCILIATION
(¶ 7)

The nucleus of the Confession of 1967 is this small paragraph which states the theme "reconciliation." Everything that follows depends upon its content.

"Reconciliation" is a common, colorless word that everybody understands to mean "reunion," "agreement," or "harmony." It is almost as banal as the word "love," and almost as exalted. Do children, friends, lovers, families, or nations quarrel? They must seek reconciliation, but the reconciliation out of which the Confession of 1967 grows has a special character among all these good offices and pacific intents. It must be distinguished from the commonplace before we bring it again into relation to everyday affairs.

First, the reconciliation found in the Bible is one-sided. God alone reconciles the world to himself. The world has nothing to offer, no desire to be reconciled in this way, or even the capacity to imagine it. Secondly, reconciliation proceeds by conflict. It is not a straight line to peace, quiet, and harmony. At the center is Jesus on his cross, which the Bible presents as the zenith of human and cosmic enmity against God. Thirdly, the promise of reconciliation remains always a promise. It is an "end" event, a "last" thing, an ultimate truth that exerts its drawing power or pull upon the direction of human lives and history, but remains imperfect throughout our days. There is much more to say, but these three things will help set off the term for a while from its everyday use.

"Reconcile" is less common in the New Testament than are "redeem," "justify," "sanctify," "save," "covenant," and some other leading concepts. Further, "reconciliation" has not often been the catchword for a major topic or movement in theology. But it does appear at very important spots and has always had some place in theology, Bible commentary, and ethics. In addition, it is very close in meaning to all the ideas just mentioned and can replace or combine them in many cases without loss, and even with gain in meaning. It is one of the rare terms in the Bible that can epitomize the whole gospel in one word: **God's reconciling work in Jesus Christ and the mission of reconciliation to which he has called his church are the heart of the gospel in any age (¶ 6).**

The word "reconciliation," unlike "love," implies a previous violation of harmony and peace, a barrier erected, a battle going on. Persons or peoples who belong together are hostile, alien, estranged. It does not take a prophet to see estrangement from God and massive hatreds among men desecrating human society in the late twentieth century as never before. Supersonic travel, worldwide television, atomic weapons, satellites, exploding population, emerging nations—clichés all from the daily papers—these exacerbate conflict in a world at once too large and too small. The search for peace and plenty is itself a root of conflict. **Our generation stands in peculiar need of reconciliation in Christ. Accordingly this Confession of 1967 is built upon that theme (¶ 6).** The gospel and mission of reconciliation swing the sensitized church like a compass needle to the troubled places where its message and deeds are most needed.

There are two movements in reconciliation: God to man and man to man. It begins one-sided and becomes two-sided and many-sided. According to II Corinthians 5:19, "God was in Christ reconciling the world to himself." In the Sermon on the Mount, Jesus uses the same word to say "first be reconciled to your brother, and then come and offer your gift" (Matt. 5:24). The first shows God's forgiveness, and the second, peacemaking among men. Together these verses show the vertical and the horizontal, the unique and the common, meaning of reconciliation. They correspond approximately to Parts I and II of the Confession of 1967.

One of the most important passages in all of Scripture—which Calvin called "the best passage of all" on justification by faith—is II Corinthians 5:19, just quoted. It should be read and studied in context, beginning with ch. 5:14 and continuing through ch. 6:10. Also of prime value are Romans 5:10-11, Colossians 1:15-24, and Ephesians 2:11-22. Study groups would profit especially by thorough familiarity with these passages. It would be pedantic, however, to be limited to these passages which explicitly use the word. Many others strewn throughout this commentary should be useful for study, and they in turn are only a few suggestions.

On principle, the Confession of 1967 does not quote Biblical passages—except in ¶ 56, the concluding ascription of praise—and it does not mean to be an exegesis of any one passage or book. The use of the apostolic benediction in the subtitles of Part I does not mean that it contains a formal exposition of II Corinthians 13:14. Rather, after years of labor and much recasting, it was discovered that the order arrived at for the Confession coincided beautifully with the apostle's parting words.

The titles of the three main parts of the Confession are self-explanatory: Part I, "God's Work of Reconciliation"; Part II, "The Ministry of Reconciliation"; and Part III, "The Fulfillment of Reconciliation." That is to say, (1) the grace of God who called together a people to serve him, then (2) the service to which they are called, and (3) the promise which causes the people to hope and to strive, and not to despair. Without great effort one can see the Biblical covenant as the hidden agenda within this structure. The paraphrase sentence just given could serve quite well as a description of the covenant (see Harmony). Another program carried throughout is the exposition of the incarnation. The life of Jesus is the place where God's reconciliation takes place (¶s 8, 9) and the clue to the Creator's love (¶ 15). It also gives direction to contemporary lives (¶s 19, 24) and the pattern for the mission of the church (¶ 32).

This work of God . . . is the foundation of all confessional statements about God, man, and the world. There are, of course, hundreds of kinds of statements that can be made about God, man, and the world. For instance, there are metaphysical, physical, chemical, economic, psychological, arithmetic, and theological statements. Any given statement has to be judged within the rules of its own game. Here the game is a contemporary confession of the Christian faith. Hence everything that follows rests on the foundation that God was reconciling . . . and the confidence that he will continue and complete his mission.

CHAPTER 3

JESUS CHRIST
(¶s 8-11)

The Confession proper begins with a man's name and address, twice repeated, and his religious connection: **Jesus of Nazareth** and **Jesus, a Palestinian Jew.** Name, address, and nationality or religion are commonplace ways to identify a man.

But why should Jesus, who has already been called **Word of God, God with man,** and **eternal Son of the Father** now be so identified? And why the matter-of-fact biographical sketch that follows?

The subject at the outset is not deity, but a man **among his own people.** Accepting the ancient teaching that Christ is "truly God" and "truly man," this Confession begins and continues with a heavy stress on the manhood or **true humanity** of Jesus, who was "like his brethren in every respect. . . . For because he himself has suffered and been tempted, he is able to help those who are tempted" (Heb. 2:17-18).

Older creeds and confessions generally place God the Father before the teaching about Christ, and make no mention of his daily life and ministry. In the Apostles' Creed the ministry is represented only by the comma in the words "born of the Virgin Mary, suffered under Pontius Pilate." Both theology and practical piety, despite the balanced classical doctrine of the two natures, have historically emphasized the Deity more than the humanity of Christ. Today devotional literature, hymns, and sentimental pictures effectually, if unintentionally, rob his manhood. On the other hand, a skeptical view dispenses with the days of his flesh

43

in their New Testament setting and makes Jesus only a symbol of ethical or existential insights. In the face of such denial, traditionally called docetism, whether pious or skeptical, the Confession of 1967 starts with **true humanity.** Without this knot on the end of the thread the whole Christian faith slips away.

The New Testament itself begins with Jesus' life story, four times repeated. And this is right, also, for the pragmatic temper of our day. Everybody comes from Missouri. They need to be shown, like the Greeks who said to Philip, "Sir, we wish to see Jesus." Philip himself later asked Jesus to "show us the Father," only to be told, "He who has seen me has seen the Father."

Jesus was a unique man in whom **true humanity was realized once for all.** He was entirely what God meant him to be; thus he reflected God's "likeness" (II Cor. 4:4). He is called a "last Adam" in whom the creation of man, so to speak, started all over again (I Cor. 15:45; and ¶ 19). He is not here called "sinless." That negative is replaced by the positive **complete obedience** and **giving himself freely** (Heb. 10:7-10; cf. ¶ 19). These words in turn describe definite acts of Jesus, his way of living, his relations with people, and his death. Abstractness is avoided.

One fact, that Jesus was a **Palestinian Jew,** is placed where it cannot be missed. This is because "the Jews" appear so often as his enemies that Christians forget or suppress the more basic fact that they were **his own people.** The faith of the Jews, their zeal to obey and praise God, their hope of a Messiah, their Scriptures, were necessary for Jesus to be received at all. The greatest blot on Christian history, anti-Semitism, has its root and cure, respectively, in the wrong and the right understanding of what it means that the Jews were **his own people.** The root is the transfer, conscious or not, of the guilt of the crucifixion to others. The cure is to confess that **his own people, the people of God** (¶ 34), still shout, "Hosanna to the Son of David!" on some days and, "Crucify him!" on others. Did not we American Presbyterians just a few years back have our photograph published around the world when we were lined up in a cordon to keep black Christians out of an Easter service?

That Jesus, living among his own people, **shared their needs, temptations, joys, and sorrows** should be clear to any reader of the Gospels. Jesus' parables and the anecdotes concerning him disclose how close he was to common life. He knew the problems of planting crops, sheep-raising, and entertaining guests at a wedding. Jesus was personally acquainted with traitorous tax collectors and prostitutes as well as with prominent lawyers and other solid citizens. Deeply he felt the yoke of Rome, the hopelessness of the sick, the wounded, the prisoner, and the starving man. He appreciated common politeness, the play of children, and the joy of a woman who found a lost coin. He knew the sting of ingratitude as well as the excruciating pain of crucifixion.

In the New Testament, unlike in the creeds and theological books, we find ourselves among the flowers of the fields of Palestine, we meet the sudden terror of men in a small fishing boat during a storm, we are nagged by beggars and covered with the dust of the roads. We experience drawing water from a well, measuring grain, and sitting for a time in a friend's home. These experiences all are not backdrop or foreground for maxims and aphorisms. They are the stuff of the life in which **true humanity was realized once for all.**

Jesus did not float among the commonplaces of life inwardly untouched as one "unable to sympathize with our weaknesses, but [as] one who in every respect has been tempted as we are" (Heb. 4:15). The temptation stories at the beginning of his ministry are not to be understood as if he were otherwise free from such trial. In Luke we read that the tempting devil "departed from him until an opportune time" (ch. 4:13). He must repeatedly have been tempted to use his incomparable gifts and powers to do spectacular deeds (Matt. 4:1-11). Gethsemane and Calvary were the culmination of lifelong struggle and pain.

He did use his gifts and powers to cure those about him. The astonishing healings are recorded as "signs" of God's power and grace, given "that you may believe" (John 20:30-31). Those who looked only for miraculous physical food or who misconstrued the connection between healing and forgiveness were scolded by

Jesus (John 6:26; Luke 5:23). The differences in world view and the healing sciences between New Testament times and our own create many problems in appreciating the miracle accounts of Jesus' ministry. Each needs to be studied in its own setting. The Confession of 1967 does not attempt to do this. But it does rest everything on the resurrection of Jesus, the one sign from which the gospel itself flows. In the comments on ¶ 10, below, the whole subject is discussed further.

The stories of Jesus' life, many more than just now hinted at, lie behind the words of the Confession: **true humanity . . . lived among his own people and shared their needs, temptations, joys, and sorrows.** These make up the authentic secularity—to use a catchword current as this book is written—of the gospel. We refer, not to secularism, but to secularity, the turned-toward-the-worldness of the gospel. As the ministry of Jesus did not happen mainly "in church" but in the world, so the ministry of his contemporary disciples should be turned toward their fellowmen (see ¶s 24-25).

Jesus not only **lived among** and **shared** the life of his people, he fulfilled a function toward them. **He expressed the love of God in word and deed.** As God incarnate, as transparent to God, he showed God's love in every aspect of his life as well as in his death. "Come to me, all who labor and are heavy laden" (Matt. 11:28) and "Woe to you, scribes and Pharisees, hypocrites!" (Matt. 23:23) are both part of that love (¶ 14, below). Neighbor love (Matt. 19:19), brother love (Matt. 5:23-24), and love of enemies (Matt. 5:44) did not inhibit a harsh word in season (Luke 6:24-26) or a demonstration of violence (Mark 11:15-19). Jesus' **complete obedience** had a two-sided result. He **became a brother to all kinds of sinful men** and at the same time he was led **into conflict with his people.**

Jesus received the love and devotion of people in various walks of life. There were fishermen and tax collectors, Herod's steward, and a Roman military officer. There were women among his followers whom we know by the names of Mary Magdalene, Susanna, Joanna, and the sisters Mary and Martha of Bethany.

There must have been thousands all told in "the great throng" that heard him gladly in both the northern and southern parts of Palestine. But he was not always accepted. In Nazareth, his home, the people threatened his life (Luke 4:14-30), and similar things happened in Bethsaida and Capernaum. He was a disturbing influence to many because he consorted with social outcasts (Luke 15:2), attended too many parties (Matt. 11:19), and appeared to break the Sabbath (Mark 2:23-28). He said unconventional things at both synagogue (Mark 1:22) and Temple (John 2:19), and generally made controversial remarks that sounded irreligious (Luke 7:48-49), radical (Matt. 12:6), or unpatriotic (Matt. 22:17-21), if not merely cryptic (Matt., ch. 13 or 24, or again, John 2:19). It was probably the unexpected, unconventional part of his complete obedience that most irritated his own people, because they were a people of detailed, prescribed observance of law and religious tradition. Finally, and most important of all, were the claims he made or were made for him which, if untrue, were blasphemous (Mark 14:62; Luke 7:48-50).

Let it not be forgotten: the reconciling ministry of Jesus made him both a brother and an enemy (or so they thought) within his own people. Here and always the Biblical work of reconciliation both divides and unites. It is not a least common denominator formula for peace at any price. It may provisionally heighten animosities. The truth of ultimate reconciliation is not compromised to achieve cheap settlement and superficial harmony. One of the costs of discipleship is division (Luke 14:25-33).

His life and teaching judged their goodness, religious aspirations, and national hopes. Some eyes may take this for a misprint. Is it not sins that are judged? That God and his law judge men's sins is a commonplace of Biblical teaching and the teaching of the church generally, as well as the present Confession (¶s 12-14). But Jesus was heard more readily by "sinners" than by the "righteous."

The inhibiting goodness of the righteous was the legal obedience of the young lawyer who said of the Ten Commandments, probably truthfully, "All these I have observed from my youth."

But he turned away from Jesus' unexpected demand to give away his wealth. The devastating parable of the Pharisee and the tax collector was for the benefit of "some who trusted in themselves that they were righteous and despised others." It would have been hard to invent a less likely villain for the story than the man who could say, "I fast twice a week, I give tithes of all that I get." By contrast, the tax collector was, because of the Roman system of collection, usually a crook as well as a renegade. But he "went down to his house justified rather than the other." It is frightening to imagine where Jesus would find his examples if he were telling these stories today.

Law-abiding goodness was practiced in the service of **religious aspirations.** The Pharisees sought God's reward for virtuous living in the life after death. Closely interwoven, too, were **national hopes.** Many thought the Messiah to come would free the people from Roman domination. As a princely descendant of David he would fulfill both their political and religious destiny. **Goodness, religious aspirations, and national** hopes are among the chief points where Jesus' ways and words clashed with the Pharisees.

The same three words might be investigated by study groups as describing perils of American piety. Luther taught that the "white" devil clothed in virtue is more dangerous than the "black" one of obvious sins and crimes. Piety and patriotism, even Presbyterianism, may cloak a devil masquerading as an angel of light.

The conflict of Jesus with the "righteous" is not just one theme among many in the New Testament. It is a major motif of the Gospels, Paul's letters, subsequent church history, and individual Christian lives. Justification by faith taught by Paul. the ex-Pharisee, is the enduring doctrinal form of this motif. The New Testament role of Jewish Pharisees is nothing if not a mirror to modern Presbyterian Pharisees, as well as Catholic, Methodist, Lutheran, or Pentecostal Pharisees, whose zeal and righteous intent are still judged by **his life and teaching.**

The rebuffs Jesus experienced did not stop him. He gave himself freely for those who rejected him and demanded his death. Thus he took upon himself the judgment under which all men stand convicted. Here is one of the simplest yet hardest to grasp ideas in the New Testament. He who did not deserve death died on behalf of others, or in place of others. We shall discuss this more fully in the next paragraph. The purpose here is only to trace Jesus' obedience.

Many of his contemporaries rejected him and demanded his death. The conflict moved steadily toward an impasse. The same daily obedience that brought it about prescribed his role in it. "He humbled himself and became obedient unto death, even death on a cross." (Phil. 2:8.) The claims that he was Messiah (Mark 14:62), Son (Matt. 16:13-20), and the forgiver of sins (Luke 7:48) were the most significant reasons for putting him to death. Other charges, such as sedition, played their part, especially in Pilate's order for execution. He who obeyed the law in its full extent was put to death as a lawbreaker. The "true man" died a criminal's death. What was different from other deaths was the perfection of his obedience and the complete freedom of his self-giving, despite the total injustice of his suffering. In giving himself freely for them he took upon himself the judgment under which all men stand convicted.

The narrative here moves quickly along: God raised him from the dead, vindicating him as Messiah and Lord. These words echo Peter's sermon at Pentecost. "Let all the house of Israel therefore know assuredly that God has made him both Lord and Christ, this Jesus whom you crucified." (Acts 2:36.) The victim of sin became victor, and won the victory over sin and death for all men. But how?

The last paragraph (¶ 8) was in story form. Now comes a different kind of language made up of imagery taken from Old Testament worship, from Jesus' parables, and from Paul's and other epistles.

The first sentence calls God's reconciling act in Jesus Christ . . . a mystery. But it does not stop there. It is a mystery which the Scriptures describe in various ways. It is a described or revealed mystery. The New Testament word for mystery does not allude to puzzles, problems, or detective story secrets. It is more akin to the "mystery" plays of the Middle Ages which portrayed redemption through the life, death, and resurrection of Christ. We refer here to "mystery . . . revealed" (Eph. 3:4-5, and 9) and "the revelation of the mystery which was kept secret for long ages but is now disclosed" (Rom. 16:25-26). Again Paul says, "We speak the wisdom of God in a mystery" (I Cor. 2:7) and he extolls "the knowledge of God's mystery, of Christ, in whom are hid all the treasures of wisdom and knowledge" (Col. 2:2-3).

Throughout the Scriptures there is always a depth beyond knowing in the disclosure of mystery. In the act of revealing himself, God makes himself known as the one who is above man's knowledge. "For my thoughts are not your thoughts, neither are your ways my ways, says the LORD. For as the heavens are higher than the earth, so are my ways higher than your ways and my thoughts than your thoughts." (Isa. 55:8-9.) The source of the world and the fountain of grace is the infinite One who, as Calvin put it, "in some way descended" when making himself known to men, but who also remains beyond what man can grasp.

The best analogy for this mystery is a common experience of life. Each person we know is a mystery, more especially the person close to us. The passing stranger is not a mystery, for we do not know him. He might be a puzzle or a problem to solve if we try to guess from his manner what his occupation is. But only in meeting him, when he opens himself to us, freely, and lets us respond to his person, does he begin to reveal his mystery. It is chiefly in the closest relations of life—friendship, family, and marriage—that the mystery and the depth of another person is freely offered to us. In the freedom of the other to give or withhold, to receive or judge, to love or repulse love, we encounter him and also reach the threshold which no other can pass, the sanctuary of his inner life.

All this may be more than analogy, for the teaching that man is in God's image, a reflection of God, is related to the mystery-revelation character of ordinary personal encounter. The best-known passage on mystery in the New Testament makes marriage the symbol of Christ's love for the church. "'A man shall . . . be joined to his wife, and the two shall become one.' This is a great mystery, and I take it to mean Christ and the church." (Eph. 5:31-32.) "To know the love of Christ" is to know that which "surpasses knowledge" (Eph. 3:19).

The negative side of ¶ 9 is the warning that **theory** cannot reach **the depths of God's love for man.** The reminder concerns traditional theories about reconciliation, built on one or more of the images listed. Appropriate also is the comment of the Westminster Larger Catechism that the idolatry warned of in the First Commandment forbids "bold and curious searchings into his secrets" (Q. 105).

Scripture, however, offers many analogies, metaphors, images, and illustrations which "accommodate," as Calvin put it, divine mysteries to human understanding.

God's reconciling act is called the **sacrifice of a lamb** (I Peter 1:19; cf. Heb. 10:11-22), and Jesus was called the Lamb of God (John 1:29). Behind this imagery lies the history of Old Testament sacrifice in which the lamb was a common victim. At Passover a lamb was killed and eaten, and Christ was called "our paschal lamb" (I Cor. 5:7). On the Day of Atonement one goat was sacrificed and another allowed to go away (hence, a "scape-goat"), bearing on his head the sins of the people (Lev., ch. 16). The English word "atonement," meaning "at-one-ment," translates a Hebrew word that indicates the "covering" of sins so that they no longer stand between God and his people. The word itself, however, does not appear in the text of the New Testament, except in the King James Version at Romans 5:11, which has been corrected in the Revised Standard Version to "reconciliation."

Sacrifice in the Old Testament is essentially God's gift to his own people (Lev. 17:11) and is part of the salvation that comes wholly from him (Deut. 21:8). It is not man's act of appeasement or propitiation as in pagan sacrifice. The same accent is unmistakable in the New Testament where sacrificial imagery is referred to. "Since all have sinned and fall short of the glory of God, they are justified by his grace as a gift, through the redemption which is in Christ Jesus, whom God [!] put forward as an expiation by his blood, to be received by faith." (Rom. 3:23-25.)

The next figure, related to sheep in a pastoral setting, is one in which the good shepherd throws himself between his flock and a wolf. A hireling would have abandoned them. But Jesus said, "I am the good shepherd; I know my own and my own know me, as the Father knows me and I know the Father; and I lay down my life for the sheep" (John 10:14-18). Then we return to the sacrifice and atonement theme, this time looking at the priest who carries out the sacrifice as a representative of the people. The daily ceremony of intercession by a historical succession of many priests has been replaced by Christ, the one who "always lives to make intercession for them. . . . He has no need, like those high priests, to offer sacrifices daily, first for his own sins and then for those of the people; he did this once for all when he offered up himself" (Heb. 7:25-27).

Ransom of a slave indicates the purchase of freedom or giving sanctuary in a way that a slave could not accomplish for himself. Someone not a slave "redeems" the one in bondage. So Christ "gave himself as a ransom for all" (I Tim. 2:6). "For the Son of man also came not to be served but to serve and to give his life as a ransom for many." (Mark 10:45.) Again, sin is expressed as an amount of money, a debt (Matt. 6:12), or work for which a deadly wage is due (Rom. 6:23).

The vicarious satisfaction of a legal penalty shows the sinner as a lawbreaker and Christ as the one who gets him off by taking his place, "having canceled the bond which stood against us with its legal demands" (Col. 2:14). Again, "Christ redeemed us from the curse of the law, having become a curse for us" (Gal. 3:13). Finally, victory over the powers of evil refers to the triumph of Christ over all that opposes God in the world, and even the last enemy, death (Mark 1:27; I Cor. 15:54-57; Heb. 2:14).

Still more facets of reconciliation imagery could be exhibited among the figures and symbols, often overlapping, of the Old and New Testaments. Throughout the history of the church various emphases have been made which bring to the fore one or more of these expressions. They gather around two poles. Most frequently Christ's "work" in itself, as the objective fact of defeating the devil or paying the legal penalty, has been the emphasis. Substitutionary satisfaction and vicarious suffering have played especially large roles in Reformed theology. This always raises the problem of how one can bear the guilt of another or how the innocent can take the place of the guilty. At the other pole are efforts to see Christ's work as motivating the works of men, inspiring them to imitation. These views tend to make each man his own savior. Against these two tendencies, objective and subjective, the warning is offered that the truth of reconciliation remains **beyond the reach of all** such **theory.**

Three elements are essential. First, there is something "out there" and "back there" in the life, death, and resurrection of Jesus that is God's own work of reconciliation. Secondly, this work is for "us" and for "the world." Thirdly, "we" do not remain uninvolved but are caught up in it in a manner that is expressed as a "new life" or a life "in Christ." The theoretical split between the deeds of Christ "out there" and their subjective benefits within us is a false one from the beginning. Christ's work "in our place" and "on our behalf" functions to take away from us the self-centeredness of self-salvation. "It is no longer I who live, but Christ who lives in me; and the life I now live in the flesh I live by faith in the Son of God, who loved me and gave himself for me." (Gal. 2:20.) The "I" taken away is "crucified with Christ," and the life "in Christ" is the **new life** (¶s 21 ff.) of faithful obedience and trust. It is not that Christ suffered a definite amount and paid off a definite amount of guilt. Rather, his work for us and in our behalf removes exactly *us* from the scene, that is, the "I" or "we" of egotism and self-salvation. The slave of sin, the old "I," becomes the slave of God, the new "I" (Rom., ch. 6). The isolated one becomes a person among persons in a community that grows out of divine love.

The point of departure for the preaching of the apostles is the risen Christ. Unlike Jesus' birth stories which are told and not mentioned again in the New Testament, his death and resurrection are constantly retold. Both narratives and preaching focus on Christ risen and present.

Jesus' life before crucifixion was a public fact. Anybody could see him. But the risen Christ was known only to his followers. And he no longer lived and traveled with them. He did not preach to the general public or visit the synagogue. To quiet their doubts he spoke and ate with them and challenged them to touch him. But he appeared and disappeared unpredictably, once in a room "the doors being shut" (John 20:19) and another time, when recognized, "he vanished out of their sight" (Luke 24:31). At the last appearance in Matthew he commissioned the church to "go . . . and make disciples of all nations" (Matt. 28:19), promising to be with the church always. In The Acts, "a cloud took him out of their sight," and two men nearby in white robes promised that he would return (Acts 1:9-11).

The appearances of the risen Christ are very different from the life of Jesus, "while I was yet with you" (Luke 24:44), yet the whole point of the accounts is to prove his identity, vindicating him as Messiah and Lord. Another component, faith, must be present to make these happenings accessible.

Resurrection is an event that includes the faith of the church. This is clearly meant to be the case. Were the risen Christ a simple fact acceptable at face value to any who cared to look, Jesus might have made a new triumphal entry, showed himself to Pilate and the Pharisees, and disproved the rumor that his dead body had been stolen. But this external proof was not to be isolated from the gospel, from repentance, and forgiveness. If doubt could enter among the eleven disciples—"they saw him and they worshiped him; but some doubted" (Matt. 28:17)—certainly others would not be convinced. In one of Jesus' parables, as if to forestall objections, he had said, "If they do not hear Moses and the prophets, neither will they be convinced if some one should rise from the dead" (Luke 16:31). Clever arguments about the reliability of witnesses, the disposal of the body, or the honesty of the apostles never did and still do not produce a resurrection faith.

It is not sheer acceptance of miracle here or elsewhere in the Bible that is decisive for faith, but acceptance of that to which the miracle or sign is a witness, namely, God's grace. The New Testament itself warns that "false Christs and false prophets" will be equipped with "great signs and wonders, so as to lead astray, if possible, even the elect" (Matt. 24:24). Jesus refused to perform when requested (Matt. 12:38-39), he could not where there was no faith (Mark 6:5-6), and he deprecated miracles over against obedience (Matt. 7:21-23).

Accepting miracles or anything else merely factually is not faith (see below, Chapter 14), because it does not commit the accepter to the truth he holds. Calvin said that some people hold the Scriptures to be "an indisputable oracle," yet lack faith. Once in New York City about thirty people saw from their apartment windows a murder below on the street. There was no flaw in their factual knowledge, but no one tried to help or even call the police. Assent to facts, mere knowing, did not lead to personal response. In this sense, "even the demons believe—and shudder" (James 2:19). It was Jesus' followers, who believed and confessed him as Lord, who were convinced, some belatedly, that he was risen and among them.

Two attitudes must be guarded against: know-all and know-nothing. Such words as "physical" and "bodily" resurrection are sometimes thumped so hard as to commit the believer to a virtual chemistry of the event. But others so overplay subjective response at the expense of what once happend that the resurrection vanishes into symbolism. In the older Reformed confessions, such as the Second Helvetic (Ch. XI), the elaborate case for the identity of the "same flesh" also after the ascension was part of an attack on Lutheran and Roman Catholic views of the "real" presence of Christ's body in the Lord's Supper.

The Confession of 1967 uses the language that appears most frequently in the Bible, **raised him from the dead** (I Cor., ch. 15;

Rom., chs. 4 to 7; II Tim. 2:8), and does not add any adjectives. It asserts both the absolutely unique sign of the resurrection of Christ (raised him, . . . vindicating him) and the response of those joined to him by faith. "Have you believed because you have seen me? Blessed are those who have not seen and yet believe." (John 20:29.)

The revealed mystery of the **risen Christ** is closely related to the revealed mystery of creation (¶ 15). The two are connected by the apostle Paul when he shows a parallel between Adam and Christ precisely in relation to the resurrection (I Cor. 15:20-28; cf. Rom. 5:12-19). Christ is **the beginning of the new creation, and the pioneer of the new humanity** (¶ 19, emphasis mine), primarily as the victor over sin and death brought upon creation by the first Adam. Neither creation nor resurrection can be grasped by the mind of man. Neither is accessible to chemistry, physics, or mathematics. Both disclosure and response are gifts of the Spirit. The infinite God, Creator and Redeemer, speaks out of his inaccessible depths to man through faith by means of the life, death, and resurrection of Jesus. Thus we confess that the **Redeemer is the Lord and Creator who made all things to serve the purpose of his love** (¶ 15).

The risen Christ is the savior for all men. Here the significance of the resurrection of Christ is expressed in a triumphant, positive way. Christ's work **for all men** is summarized in the two terms **savior** (¶ 10) and **judge** (¶ 11). These express in another idiom the **gravity, cost, and sure achievement of God's reconciling work.**

The **savior** is the rescuer, deliverer, restorer of health, who **won the victory over sin and death for all men.** God is called **savior** and redeemer in the Old and New Testaments (Ps. 106:21; I Tim. 4:10; Ps. 19:14), and Christ is called "the Savior of the world" (John 4:42). Salvation, however, is not automatic. This accounts for a slight peculiarity of style in which the wording of the Confession of 1967 (in response to criticism) was changed from savior "of" all men, to **for all men.** The meaning, in either case, is that there is only one Savior, one grace, and one love of

God, and not a variety of them. The next sentence qualifies and completes the whole idea by adding those joined to him by faith are set right with God, etc. The negative side appears farther along: to refuse life . . . is to choose death, etc. Beyond this we should not go. Neither "universalism," which holds for the salvation of all, nor the Westminster Confession view of the predestined, that "their number is so certain and definite that it cannot be either increased or diminished" (Ch. III; cf. Ch. XXXV), have any place in this Confession. Such speculative constructions serve no good purpose. The church has a message, a task, and a hope, but the outcome is in the providence of God.

By faith. The word faith does not appear often in the Confession of 1967, and the fuller expressions "justification by faith" and "salvation by faith" do not appear at all. They are, however, assumed in the form taught in other parts of *The Book of Confessions*. At the same time, all essential elements of these Reformation teachings are here presented in the key or mode of reconciliation. The major treatment comes under the heading of "The New Life" (¶s 21-26), and the influence of these teachings permeates the entire Confession. For example, the thematic paragraph (¶ 7) shows that all salvation is from God alone, and "The Sin of Man" (¶s 12-14) presents the helplessness of man when dependent entirely upon himself. The Holy Spirit, who enables them to receive forgiveness, is the initiator of the new life. Acceptance is wholly gracious: God loves them and accepts them in spite of what they are, and no man has any ground on which to stand except God's grace (¶ 22). All these things, which will be more fully discussed below, are part of the faith by which men are set right with God and commissioned to serve, or "justified" and "sanctified," which are expounded throughout Part I and Part II of the Confession. The reconciling community, also, will be discussed below (under ¶ 31).

Judge of all men. The judge preeminent in the Scriptures is God, who passes sentence upon men, vindicating and saving those who trust him (Ps. 7:9-11), or condemning and punishing the wicked (Rom. 2:3; Acts 17:31). Christ is said to administer this judgment (Acts 10:42) as well as to intercede and ward off condemnation (Rom. 8:33-34). All the issues of life and death culminate in judgment and receive their denouement from the verdict. Hence the ultimate seriousness of life and the possibility of participating in God's final victory over the power of sin and death are held before men in judgment. Men face two alternatives: to receive life from the risen Lord or to refuse life from him. And these in turn issue in two alternate destinies: to have life eternal or to choose the death which is separation from God.

Life and death do not mean biological life and its end. The common meaning is, of course, present in the Bible (and see ¶ 26), and it is what gives point to all other uses of the words. But life and death here describe the relation of God and men more fully. They comprehend also other pairs of terms from the New Testament, such as flesh and spirit, letter and spirit, law and gospel, darkness and light, the old and the new man or creature, and even the old and new age or aeon. In each word pair the former term means enmity, opposition to God, disobedience, and separation from him. The latter means reconciliation, a relationship with God of love, obedience, and fulfillment. The special New Testament significance of these terms stands out so sharply from the common meaning that combinations, otherwise startling, appear frequently: "spiritual body," "fleshly mind," or "to set the mind on the flesh is death" (Rom. 8:6), or "I through the law died to the law, that I might live to God" (Gal. 2:19). These are not metaphors strained for literary effect, but words that point beyond observable facts to ultimate realities. To be "dead in sin" indicated for Paul a worse fate than physical death, and the "life with Christ" is so much greater than ordinary existence that "my desire is to depart and be with Christ, for that is far better" (Phil. 1:23).

Life is called eternal not only to indicate continued duration but to ally it with God. The term is no more limited to extending ordinary time than the term "Spirit" is limited to denoting something purely mental (¶ 20). So also for death, which does not mean extinction, but a wretched continuation of existence. The

Confession of 1967, to make the meaning clear, refers somewhat pedantically to the death which is separation from God. Separation is the opposite of love and reconciliation. It sums up all man's enmity, hostility, and rejection come to fruition. The cry of Jesus, "My God, my God, why hast thou forsaken me?" (Matt. 27:46, from Ps. 22:1) was the appropriate utterance for the one who was "made . . . sin" (II Cor. 5:21) and who "became a curse" (Gal. 3:13) on behalf of men. The horrendous "lake of fire" or "eternal fire" imagery of Revelation 20:15 or Matthew 25:41 really say no more than the opening words of the latter passage, "Depart from me" (also, Matt. 7:23), or "God gave them up" (Rom. 1:24).

The point, just now, is not to talk about the future but the decisive ultimate seriousness of the present. To receive life from the risen Lord is to have life eternal already within the daily round of activities. "This is eternal life, that they know thee the only true God, and Jesus Christ whom thou hast sent" (John 17:3). Note the verb to receive, for this life is not an achievement, but a gift. On the other hand, to refuse life from him is to choose . . . death. Such death is not a gift, but a "wage" earned by daily decision (Rom. 6:23). The final sentence is also in the present tense. All who put their trust in Christ face divine judgment without fear, for the judge is their redeemer. The confidence and the hope of the Christian life do not arise from a frivolous or contemptuous assumption that nothing finally matters, but from knowing that the ultimate judge is bent on forgiveness, and has himself won the victory over death.

CHAPTER 4

SIN
(¶s 12-14)

A piercing light exposes objects that are only vaguely seen at dusk. So the reconciling act of God in Jesus Christ exposes the evil in men.

Not that "evil" is otherwise unknown. All butchers, bakers, and candlestickmakers know evil, whether as pain or wickedness, from mosquito bites to world wars. There are countless views of the nature, causes, and kinds of evil to be found in legend, myth, common sense, and sophisticated theory.

The Confession of 1967, however, is not directly concerned with evil in general, but with moral evil, the evil in men. Even here it does not offer a theory among others. Moral evil may be partly this or partly that: a necessary spur to the good, a remnant of incomplete evolution, a universal Oedipus-Electra complex, a product of social organization, or what have you? The data can be gathered from many sources. The only evaluations that a confessional statement (¶ 7) rejects out of hand are those which would claim that evil is total, or evil is illusion, or evil is wholly meaningless or wholly separate from man's responsibility.

What God's work of reconciliation does for the understanding of evil is to expose or disclose that moral evil is not something in itself, but a quality of the relation between God and man. For this quality we use a special name "sin." The evil in men is hereby exposed as sin in the sight of God. Sin is the condition of man seen from a vantage point that man, because of sin, cannot achieve. It is not a question of partial love and obedience against perfect love and obedience, or comparing oneself to the man next door, or any other calculation. Rather, this is a total revelation of self, a look in an X-ray mirror, an immediate awareness of the human condition in dimensions that transcend all previous measurements. "You have no excuse, O man, whoever you are, when you judge another; for in passing judgment upon him you condemn yourself, because you, the judge, are doing the very same things." (Rom. 2:1.)

The encounter with God's holiness and love always brings about a reaction or reflex in men related to evil, profaneness, or uncleanness. Isaiah, an uncommonly virtuous man, saw himself in the Temple as a "man of unclean lips" dwelling among "a people of unclean lips" (Isa., ch. 6). Even pious and charitable —*more especially* the pious and charitable—acts of men appear unworthy or profane. When Jesus was in the home of Simon the Pharisee, a good citizen by most standards, and was presented with a gift by a prostitute, a bad woman, similarly judged, he treated both persons as sinners needing forgiveness (Luke 7:36-50). This does not equate good citizens with prostitutes, but shows how human scales of virtue shrink when set in the relation between God and man, where all appear as sinners.

Before proceeding, two asides: First, sin follows the teaching about reconciliation, because only in this setting is it fully appreciated. No one can confess his sin before God until he knows he is accepted by divine love. Repentance is a gift of grace, not an extension of remorse. In both the New and Old Testaments the condemning function of law takes place within a people already chosen, already recipients of the promise of divine favor. Secondly, there is no mention of Adam, Eve, and the serpent in the Confession of 1967. While the story of the Fall will not cease to reveal the nature of sin, it can no longer be taken as a literal account of sin's origin. It is set in views of life, history, and the cosmos (¶ 29) that in the providence of God have become antiquated by the advancement of human learning.

In sin men claim mastery of their own lives. An innocuous term was chosen as the first to describe sin, probably because apparent harmlessness and ambiguity lie close to the root of it. Like the rightful "dominion" that God gave Adam (Gen. 1:28), but which Adam extended into forbidden territory, we have here a concept that easily slips from measure to excess. The words bring to mind self-reliance (Emerson), self-direction (David Riesman), and self-mastery (shall we say, the Boy Scout Oath?), which are generally and rightly listed as virtuous. But there is more than an edge of pride, rebellion, distrust of God in the self-rule of Adam and his sons. They have a legitimate dominion, but they want autonomy.

A small boy once in a fit of anger cursed in the presence of his father, who happened to be a famous theologian. The father was also a good, no-nonsense Swiss parent, and he quickly slapped the child's mouth. The son replied, "Daddy, that was *my* mouth!" It was, said the father in telling the story, the first sign in this young life of full independence. His son now stood apart from him and claimed his own being and right, and that made the father proud. At the same time, he had asserted himself with a curse and had to be punished. *That* made the father, Emil Brunner, author of *Man in Revolt,* a famous classic on sin, sorrowful.

The meaning of **claim mastery of their own lives** is really in this story. A rightful self-assertion stands in compromising nearness to a curse. Every exertion of man's will includes an element of pride, autonomy, revolt. These are centripetal forces that pull everything toward the self in the center and make everything responsive to this one dominion. Self-love is an ingoing, not an outgoing, movement, and as such it produces alienation from others.

They **turn against God and their fellowmen.** This phrase expresses the violation of the "two tables" of the law, the two directions of love, the two aspects of faith, the two dimensions of human life, all of which have been before us already and are found throughout *The Book of Confessions.* To **turn against** is the opposite of, "You shall love the Lord your God with all your heart, and with all your soul, and with all your mind. . . . You shall love your neighbor as yourself" (Matt. 22:37-39).

Men are thus **exploiters and despoilers of the world.** A selfish
dominion will overpower and utilize others. This includes emotional exploitation as well as economic, sexual, political, or religious plundering of others. The poor man can exploit as well as
the rich, and the weak as well as the strong. Pity, affection, and
mother love can evolve into destructive domination, conscious or
unconscious. Every relation of life, from the car pool to the
United Nations, from marriage to the communion of the saints,
can be, and has been, the instrument of **exploiters and despoilers
of the world.**

The destroyed relation to God, other men, and the world's
goods, called sin, is like a fate bringing on general destruction.
It is not partitioned into sectors of life, leaving others untouched,
but is comprehensive in its effects. It is a colored glass through
which the whole world takes on a single tint, or a gravitational
pull in which every object is affected. Man as sinner is a badly
tuned instrument that ruins whatever is played on it. This was
the meaning of "total depravity" in the theological wordbook of
our forefathers. It was not that no goodness remains at all in
men (although the Westminster Confession, Ch. VI, fails to
mention this proviso), but that the total life of man is so affected
that no part is pure. The language of the Confession of 1967 for
this same teaching is that they **lose their humanity.** If by humanity we mean only homo sapiens, a biological description, the
term is inaccurate, for sin does not disqualify the sinner as a
member of the human race. Redemption is for sinful *men,* not
alligators or apes. But over against the **true humanity** of Jesus
and the unrefracted image of God that shows in him (¶ 8), this
intentional hyperbole is not too strong. The dramatists, novelists,
poets, and painters, Christian and otherwise, can help us here
probably more than philosophers or theologians. Their subject is
almost always humanity. Conrad or Dostoevsky, Sartre or Eliot,
hold up the mirror to humanity lost.

Good, too, is related to sin. **Wise and virtuous men through the
ages have sought the highest good in devotion to freedom, justice,
peace, truth, and beauty.** This short statement recognizes human
wisdom, idealism, the search for the just, the good, the true, the

beautiful, whenever and wherever they occur, without a trace of irony or deprecation. Anything less is priggish and an insult to the providence of God. Virtue, even saintliness, is not absent from the world, nor are they Christian monopolies. Who is in a position to be contemptuous of Plato's vision of justice, Zola's holy zeal for the truth about Dreyfus, Gandhi's way of peace, or Marx's call to the disinherited?

Yet all human virtue, when seen in the light of God's love in Jesus Christ, is found to be infected by self-interest and hostility. Evil is evil and good is good, yet both cast a shadow **when seen in the light of God's love in Jesus Christ.** This statement and the general verdict following are not scientific judgments. That would require universal questionnaires and interviews. This judgment is part of the seriousness **(the gravity, cost, and sure achievement, ¶ 9)** of the incarnation and the experience of those who respond to the gospel. Its chief function is to explain further what it means that the gospel is to be preached to all men. Jesus approached everyone, whether "righteous" or a "sinner," as needing forgiveness, and so did all those who first announced the gospel. This is the tenor of the entire Biblical message and such specific passages as, "All have sinned and fall short of the glory of God" (Rom. 3:23).

The Confession next presents in common speech the traditional view of the universality of sin: **all men, good and bad alike, are in the wrong before God and helpless without his forgiveness.** The phrase **good and bad alike** recalls the wide spectrum of virtue and vice already discussed. **In the wrong** is easy to grasp. It makes one think of the traffic violator trying to "talk his way out of it" or the aggressor nation bullying a victim while protesting self-defense. From common courtesies offended to the profaning of love and contempt for God, we have all been and seen others "in the wrong" enough for the common phrase to serve as a fresh synonym for sin. Also, these words and the former **set right with God** (¶ 10) are contrived to remain very close to the language of justice, righteousness, justification, and the like.

Thus all men fall under God's judgment. Who is exempt? Let him step forward and claim his right, or let him go his own way, satisfied with himself. No one is more subject to that judgment than the man who assumes that he is guiltless before God or morally superior to others. Again and again, the peril of the "guiltless" and the "morally superior," as of the "righteous" in Jesus' ministry and the "proud" and "mighty" throughout the Old and New Testaments, is held up to the one who would make confession of his faith through this document.

God's love never changes. There is much throughout the Bible on the anger or wrath of God, his vengeance or retribution, sometimes expressed in a very primitive way. Generally, the disobedience of men brings on the divine response. But we never read that God *is* wrath, anger, or the like. We do, however, read, "God is love" (I John 4:8). Accordingly, the works that are proper and appropriate to his being are all works of love, mercy, justice, and righteousness. When men rebel and reject God, he responds in a way alien (Luther's term) to a direct working of love, and this is wrath or vengeance (Rom. 1:18), but it is not without love and not in contradiction to it. Opposite dangers are to attribute emotional reactions to God, or to conceive him as wholly transcendent, in no way registering or reacting to the quality of human life. God expresses means by an active verb to show God as a subject responding to man. What he expresses is love in wrath, which shows the ultimate seriousness (¶ 11) of life, the gravity and the cost (¶ 9) of reconciliation.

The concluding sentence of ¶ 14 brings us back to where we began—God took on himself judgment and shameful death in Jesus Christ—and looks ahead to what this reconciling work is intended to accomplish among men, to bring men to repentance and new life.

CHAPTER 5

THE LOVE OF THE CREATOR
(¶s 15-19)

We have progressed from cure to disease. Now we return to learn the full identity of the physician. The grace of reconciliation and the love which never changes are finally and fully identified as the grace and love of God. From Jesus to God.

"No one has ever seen God; the only Son, who is in the bosom of the Father, he has made him known." (John 1:18; cf. Eph. 1: 15-23 and Col. 1:15-20.) Christ gives access to the Father. Not natural science or metaphysics, nor history or psychology, but the witness of the Spirit to the message of reconciliation in Jesus Christ is the ground of confessing, "I believe in God the Father Almighty, Maker of heaven and earth."

God's sovereign love, the love that never changes, is again called a mystery beyond the reach of man's mind. What was said above (¶ 9) about the meaning of mystery applies here also. And the warning, beyond the reach of all theory, is even more needed. To grasp God in a theory, fix him in a formula, or to be his intimate confidant are all forms of idolatry. "He walks with me and he talks with me" are perilous words. To comprehend the "breadth and length and height and depth, and to know the love of Christ which surpasses knowledge," and to be "filled with all the fulness of God" (Eph. 3:18-19), never means to have divine truth in a package or private knowledge of the divine will. It means to be brought to the One who is mysteriously near and transcendent, known and unknowable. Whether in worship, teaching, or helping a neighbor, whether in stenography, steelwork, or executive decisions, the life of a faithful man is suffused with a knowledge of the depth of the mystery revealed.

The next sentence indicates that man cannot climb up to God, even in thought. The natural impulse is to conceive the infinite as a very, very big finite, God as the superlative of a good man, and the "beyond" as something far away from what is present. But it is not from just beyond the heights of human power or culture, from philosophy, artistic imagination, or scientific analysis of the world that Christian teaching and language about God take their starting point. The Christian knowledge of God the Creator begins with the cross of Jesus.

Here the stargazer stubs his toe. The cross is a stone in the path of those who worship ultimate beauty or goodness and a scandal to philosophers (I Cor. 1:18-31). Paul knew personally why the Pharisees boggled at a king riding a pack animal. He himself had done the work of the Omnipotent One by stoning followers of the Weak One who had died a criminal's death. Educated in pagan Tarsus, Paul also knew the folly of claiming that a cross held the truth not to be found in Plato, Aristotle, Zeno, or Epicurus, or the mysteries of Demeter or Dionysus. "For Jews demand signs and Greeks seek wisdom, but we preach Christ crucified, a stumbling block to Jews and folly to Gentiles, but to those who are called, both Jews and Greeks, Christ the power of God and the wisdom of God." (I Cor. 1:22-24.)

The shock is no less today than when the promise was first given in tiny Israel or first preached by the motley crew of apostles. We still expect power in the form of a king, wisdom from a sage, and goodness from a saint. But here **power** took **the form of a servant,** who was put to death. And **wisdom,** strange to say, emanates from this **folly.** And where do we find the holy blistering **goodness** before which Moses veiled his face (Ex. 34:33; II Cor. 3:13), and which paganism identified with the searing Mediterranean sun? The answer is **in receiving sinful men.** The **superlatives of power, wisdom, and goodness** are reduced and transformed into their opposites—servitude, folly, and sinfulness.

Having been introduced to God's sovereign love, the love which never changes, we are now led to see that this love has its own kind of power . . . to transform the world. It is nothing more than we have already observed in Section A, "The Grace of Our Lord Jesus Christ." In the life, death, and resurrection of Jesus Christ, his complete obedience, his giving himself freely, his existence as the perfect child of God, and God's having raised him from the dead, his removal of the judgment under which all men stand convicted, the new life provided by which men can face divine judgment without fear and are sent into the world, the promise of the consummation in the final triumph of God: all these things and many more constitute the power . . . to transform the world, which is the source of the Christian's confidence that the Redeemer is the Creator, that salvation is the gift of the Triune God.

The adjective sovereign is used once only in the Confession of 1967. Is this, then, meant to be the "sovereignty of God," the traditional hallmark of Calvinism? Although the writers of the Confession did not concern themselves with reputed hallmarks and the like, the immediate answer to the question is yes. There is no discussing a "sovereignty of God" that is not gracious and righteous. Calvin, by the way, did not use the term "sovereignty of God," although translators have occasionally managed to slip it into his works. What we do find in Calvin is the "free" grace or the "gratuitous" love of God. At the center of his teaching is not the divine decree of the Omnipotent One, but the gracious Redeemer-Creator. The sovereignty and omnipotence of God are not known from the naked power of him who moves the stars or hardens the heart of Pharaoh, but by way of his free condescension in receiving sinful men. The reader may wish to refer here to divine sovereignty as presented below in comments on the Westminster Confession. The Confession of 1967 means to avoid the scholastic puzzles into which Reformed orthodoxy fell in its classical period. The root of the teaching is, however, the same: God's initiative in providing salvation to the undeserving, his condescension in the incarnation, with the result that no man has any ground on which to stand except God's grace (¶ 22).

The power of God's love (or, sovereign love) in Christ to transform the world discloses that the Redeemer is the Lord and Creator who made all things to serve the purpose of his love. We began this commentary by saying that the first confession of the Christian church was "Jesus Christ is Lord" and that "Lord" is one of the divine names or titles. Now again the servant people of the servant Lord recognize God the Redeemer as **Lord and Creator.** The title **Lord** comes first because it is the immediate, present form of sovereign love. **Creator** alone might be taken as referring to a remote event. Both creation and providence are included when God is called Lord. In the history of Israel, the oneness of God was first and primarily expressed in the exclusiveness or "jealousy" of Yahweh's relation to his people, rather than in the numerical idea that God is One and not many.

The phrase **who made all things to serve the purpose of his love** deserves some careful attention, as does the sentence that follows: **God has created the world of space and time to be the sphere of his dealings with men.** It might seem to modern men with vastly increased knowledge of the intricacy of the universe, and with the stupifying amount of information that science conveys to him in billions of light-years about millions of celestial galaxies—together with the equally impressive vastness of the infinitely small—it might seem worse than "folly" to identify salvation with God who **made all things.**

It would of course be folly of another variety not to learn from the newer knowledge given us by science. To continue affirming the solid bowl of sky overturned on a plate of earth, with primeval water above and below (Gen., ch. 1, and following), would be sheer nonsense. Transforming old accounts into poetic imagery, as if they had not once been meant as a literal world view, is a tricky device of those who are often quite literalistic about the rest of the Bible. The church once tried to defend against Galileo a picture of the universe that itself had been smuggled into the Bible a thousand years before. When the church fights on these fronts, Galileo or Darwin or someone else will always win his point, and so he should. The path of harmonizing, taking Genesis "days" for geological ages and Adam for the primitive ancestor of man, is dilettantish. Some take comfort in the uncertainties of scientific study, as if these were a loophole through which Biblical data could return to its former role of describing how the earth came to be. Others truculently demand to be presented with "proved errors" of Scripture, standing ready with irrelevant counterarguments. This is an endless, fruitless, and wasteful game, a misunderstanding of the meaning of **Creator,** and a search for a wrong kind of security.

The Confession of 1967 repeats the age-old faith of the church that **God has created the world of space and time,** but it does so aware that this teaching in Genesis is spoken in **language** and **thought forms** (¶ 29) no longer usable. How, then, do we both say what Genesis says and also say it differently? For one thing, Genesis, ch. 1, is summarized in the first verses of John's Gospel without the outmoded scientific detail. The same teaching appears in Colossians 1:15-17 and implicitly in each of the hundreds of places in the Bible where God is called Lord. Once the scientific lines are clear, there is no need to sacrifice the wonder and praise of Genesis, ch. 1, Job, chs. 38 to 41, or Psalm 104 to Ptolemy, Galileo, or Einstein. "O Lord my God, thou art very great! . . . Who hast stretched out the heavens like a tent, who hast laid the beams of thy chambers on the waters, who makest the clouds thy chariot, who ridest on the wings of the wind, who makest the winds thy messengers, fire and flame thy ministers." (Ps. 104:1-4.)

In theological reflection, the Christian church has always understood that there lies behind the cosmology and the poetry of the Bible the truth that God has created all "out of nothing." This is a symbolic rather than a literal statement, because it is inconceivable as fact. Man, the creature, can think transformations and changes but not absolute beginning out of nothing. It is the humble confessing posture of trust and thankfulness, the obedience and praise of the servant before his **Lord,** the receptiveness and responsibility of the steward to his master, that has always been the deepest import of the doctrine of creation. We shall not find from the Bible how big the universe is, nor how intricate, nor the mechanics of its evolution or operation. Nor

will the astrophysicist, biologist, or psychologist discover the God
of Abraham, Isaac, and Jacob, the God and Father of our Lord
Jesus Christ. "By faith we understand that the world was created
by the word of God." (Heb. 11:3.)

God in the Scriptures says, "I." "I am the Lord your God, who
brought you out of the land of Egypt." And he also says "you" or
"thou." "You shall have no other gods before me." Jesus taught
men to pray saying, "Our Father," and the Spirit witnesses that
men are children of God when they pray saying, "Abba! Father!"
(Rom. 8:15). Throughout Scripture, from the first Paradise to
the New Jerusalem, the mode of intercourse between God and
men is a **personal relation.** Whatever else the history of mankind may be, it is according to the Scriptures, a story of divine-
human encounter and the rejection, destruction, and recovery of
that encounter. This is the kernel of the teaching about man
created in the "image" of God.

Just above we warned against the imaginary intimacy of con-
versations with God. That was a warning against denying the
divine person by use of sentimental imagination. The encounter
with God through his Word incarnate takes place by means of
the word written, spoken, and partaken of at the Lord's Supper
(¶ 52, etc.).

The word of God is a call out of isolation and selfishness into
community. Nowhere is this more fully presented than in The
First Letter of John. The words of the Confession of 1967, **that
man may respond to the love of the Creator,** could serve as a
statement of the theme of this beautiful little book. "Beloved, let
us love one another; for love is of God, and he who loves is born
of God and knows God. He who does not love does not know
God; for God is love. . . . God is love, and he who abides in love
abides in God, and God abides in him." (I John 4:7-8, 16, and
throughout.) Love of God and love of men are inseparable. "If
any one says, 'I love God,' and hates his brother, he is a liar; for
he who does not love his brother whom he has seen, cannot love
God whom he has not seen." (V. 20.)

The Confession now turns to certain facts of life which are

recognized as gifts of the Creator. Male and female are a work of the love of the Creator. Sexuality is not a disaster, although it suffers probably more than most other aspects of man's life from the condition of rebellion, despair, and isolation (¶s 12 and 47). Sexual life is for the fulfillment and realization of the purpose of creation. The two-ness of man and woman, the three- and four- and more-ness of the family group, which leads into a wide complex of social relations, has the blessing and promise of the Creator (Gen. 1:27-28).

Life has natural starting and end points. It proceeds from birth to death in a succession of generations, and this, too, is the gift and blessing of the Creator. Death is as regular and natural a fact of life as birth. Its "sting" comes from sin, and the "power" of sin to bring this about comes from love unfulfilled (I Cor. 15:56). Note well! Law unfulfilled and love unfulfilled are the same thing (Matt. 22:37-40). Love frustrated brings such a sting and a curse that sin and death mean the same thing sometimes to the apostle Paul. The terror-stricken and hopeless rejection of death, the sorrow of utter despair, are products of our condition (¶ 11).

The Confession of 1967 aims to avoid docetism related not only to the life of Jesus (¶ 8) but to every life. The term "flesh" (like "death" and "world") acquires through sin the connotation of evil and depravity. This meaning applies only within the parentheses of sin. A faith that feeds on love and hope, that expects blessedness despite perplexity and perversity, that knows the Redeemer is the Creator, affirms at the same time the goodness of creation and of the bodily, daily life of men. A contempt for the world may be not only a flight from reality but ingratitude toward the Creator. Vows of celibacy and poverty, so highly touted as to mark the "religious" life in much of the history of Christendom, may be wise at times to achieve special ends. But as a norm of life they deprive men and women of both pleasure and responsibility that belong to the goodness of creation.

Man is expected to move, to think, to develop. God has endowed man with capacities to make the world serve his needs and to enjoy its good things. Granting that man has become the exploiter and despoiler of the world (¶ 12), his destined purpose is not suspended. Nor is the use of the world to supply the **needs** of men and to enable them to **enjoy its good things** a minor element of the Christian faith. It is part of the praise of the **Creator.** Economic life, agricultural achievements, industrial development, and scientific advance have their firm foundation in the Christian faith as part of the teaching about creation. Contempt for the world of things or people, withdrawal from it, is no more acceptable than complete attachment and submersion within the world. A wholesome imaginative delight in nature, a hearty yes to man in his natural and technical environment, belong as much to a life of praise as does the confession of sin. These things all, however, are said within the overarching **purpose of God** for the building of a human fellowship which is a token of Christ's Kingdom (¶s 53-56).

Life is a gift . . . and a task. This familiar pair of words expresses the dual aspect of life: the given, the there, the already, the unalterable of human existence; and the not yet, the to-be-won, that which responds to our wills and is shaped by our efforts.

No one brings about his own life or has more than a minor part in shaping and maintaining it. A cheap rifle in the hands of a crank can suddenly end the life of the most powerful man on earth. And the meanest life is nonetheless **life . . . to be received with gratitude.** Ruminations about life without the story of the cross would leave this last statement an open question. Gratitude for some lives, yes; but for others—pain-ridden, guilt-ridden, nasty, brutish, short—of course not. Even the happiest man might have been better off if he had never been born. But the cross, which is at the same time the darkest and the brightest spot in the history of man, where **true humanity** was at once shattered and made to shine in splendid hues, where God was silent only to bring about reconciliation and hope—this cross is the introduction to and the reconfirmation of the goodness of creation (Col. 1:15-19). Life, then, is not a "tale told by an idiot," but a painful, glorious saga illuminated by the wise folly and the strong weakness of the defeated **victor,** and drawn along by hope of Christ's Kingdom.

Life is also **a task to be pursued with courage.** Certainly it is a **task.** Even those who would drop out of the competition, who would take the gift and skip the task, find it is a task to accomplish even that—a task within and without. The life force that pushes on restlessly within each man, the desires that disturb his quiet and draw him willing or unwilling toward things and toward other people, do not function automatically. They engage his energy, effort, and determination, willy-nilly. Some tasks are welcome and exhilarating and others a drag and a drudge. Hence **courage** stands alongside **gratitude.** The virtues of athletes and soldiers were frequently on the mind of Paul, who saw the faithful, hopeful life as a race (I Cor. 9:24), a boxing match (v. 26), and warfare (I Thess. 5:8). **Courage** implies not only a **task** or contest but a threat against which one must be bold and well armed. More will be said on these subjects in the section on the **new life** (¶ 23, and thereabouts).

Man is free. He is, of course, in bonds of many kinds. But as a creature of God he is not wholly deprived of the life of will, decision, and self-direction. He is **free to seek his life within the purpose of God,** that is, according to what he *is,* a man. He is not free to be a pig, a god, another person, or a nothing. Freedom is not and cannot be utter, disconnected, haphazard, helter-skelter. Freedom, too, has the character of fate and determination by virtue of who it is that is more or less free. The freedom of man is to be man, **to seek his life.** And since man is one who stands in a **personal relation** with God and others, who is **male and female,** who **proceeds from birth to death,** through the **generations,** etc., his essential freedom is directed toward the exercise and achievement of the **true humanity** (¶ 8!) for which the purpose of God brought him into being, maintains his life, and promises him fulfillment (¶s 53-56).

After the colon in this sentence in ¶ 17, there follow a few phrases which, like so many in this or any confession, could be expanded into volumes. These are samples specifying the meaning of within the purpose of God. The first phrase, to develop and protect the resources of nature for the common welfare, could be the base for discourse again on economic life as already suggested in the lines above. Two pregnant words of everyday endeavor start off the phrase, develop and protect. Or, we might say, "exploitation" in its good sense of using to the full. The second word is, frankly, a conservationist term. Both are to be undertaken for the common welfare. They are really no different from "need" and "enjoyment" several sentences back, but the word welfare, more especially common welfare, reminds us that most of mankind is deprived. The common welfare or well-being overrides private and individual fulfillment when it takes place at the expense of others. There is a universal stewardship as well as a dominion which marks the life of man in the natural order. Here is the context in the teaching about creation for the later paragraph on enslaving poverty (¶ 46). The single, universal gift of life by the love of God binds all men who apprehend that love through Jesus Christ to the universal task of the stewardship of creation for the common welfare.

Now the purpose of God is specified again with reference to the wide complex of social relations in terms of justice and peace in society. Justice means the distributive justice or fair play whereby each receives his rightful due and share before the law. The state with its devices of order and control, development and defense, is included in this simple sentence. The state is further in view in ¶ 25 and various parts of ¶s 43-47. Whether in teeming cities or in the sparsely settled deserts of the world, there are men whose rightful destiny is to make the world serve [their] needs and to enjoy its good things, and there is a common stewardship of social justice and peace in which they are included. Even if they do not know in what they share, it is part of this stewardship to raise men's hopes (¶ 46) that they may share more fully in the use and the enjoyment of the goods of the earth and of society.

And in other ways to use his creative powers for the fulfillment of human life. This sentence is an open end to the short series that follows the colon. Probably the most important expression is creative powers. The phrase is rightly chosen. Whether in art, science, or society, there are ever-new "creations" that bewilder even specialists in various fields of study and action. From the dawn of history until quite recently, despite discoveries, inventions, and revolutions, man moved at about the same speeds, organized life approximately as taught by his elders, and changed his ways of thought very slowly. Now he moves faster than sound, occasionally escapes from gravity, and creates electronic brains that think faster, and in some respects better, than he can. It is only recently that contraceptives entered the relation of male and female on a large scale and gravely altered what it means to marry and have a family. World population control is probably not far away. And what of recent antibeautiful painting, antiharmonious music, and the theater of the absurd? One soon shows himself a confused amateur if he even tries to list what the creative powers of men have been doing to change his life within the watch tick of the last few decades. Even to distinguish between creative and destructive powers is often foolhardy. The Confession of 1967 only observes that these powers and capacities, too, are gifts of the Creator, and that they are to be affirmed. It holds above all such achievements the criterion of the purpose of God, the common welfare, and the fulfillment of human life.

We must stop a moment for orientation. The subject matter of Section B progresses as follows: ¶ 15 presented the sovereign love of the Creator and how this love is known; ¶ 16 affirmed God's creation and his image reflected in creation to the eye of faith; ¶ 17 focused upon the life of man as God's creature made to respond to his love. Now ¶ 18 turns to one particular stream in the life of man, the covenant people, Israel. And ¶ 19 fixes specifically on one man, Jesus, as the goal of that history and also as the beginning of the new creation, and the pioneer of the new humanity. We move thus from creation, to man, to Israel, to Jesus, who is the new man and the new creation: from Adam to the Last Adam, and from Israel to the New Israel.

The love of the Creator for all mankind is expressed through Israel, whom he chose to be his covenant people. The message and purpose of creation being lost on self-centered, sinful men, it is communicated anew in a special way. It is a special "way," not a special content, since the covenant told again the will of the Creator, and it gave Israel a mission to all mankind. Creation and covenant, thus, have a single focus, the personal relation in love and obedience of the creature to the Creator. Appropriate here is the statement of Karl Barth that creation is the outer ground of the covenant and the covenant is the inner ground of creation. What in creation is meant for all mankind and is obscure through sin, is promised especially to a chosen people and fully communicated again in their Messiah (the true image of God), by whom their mission was directed again outward to all the world. This in a nutshell is the covenant scheme, described more in detail below in connection with the Westminster and Scots Confessions. A covenant is a pact or an agreement. But in this case it was composed wholly from one side, its text was divine love (or law, when expressed in sharp negatives), and its demands were only the rights of the infinite love of the Creator, namely, that his people serve him in love and faithfulness.

When Israel was unfaithful, God did not abandon her. Instead, he disciplined the nation with his judgments and maintained his cause through prophets, priests, teachers, and true believers. That sentence of the Confession is a twenty-two-word summary of what holds the Old Testament together. It is the continuity of the people through a history of incredible vagaries and misfortunes, marked by faith and unfaith, through which God remained in all fidelity their God. The sagas, histories, laws, and prophetic writings, the incomparable psalms, the cult and liturgy of the Ark and the Tabernacle and the Temple, held before the people Yahweh's faithfulness and punishments. He disciplined and chastened his people as a wandering tribe in the days of the exodus and the Judges, through the monarchy and its division, through exile, dispersion, and partial return from exile. Both his mighty deeds for their rescue and their chastisement, both his law and his promises were announced and called to mind by prophets, priests, teachers, and true believers.

These witnesses called all Israelites to a destiny in which they would serve God faithfully and become a light to the nations. Here is the background for all that the New Testament teaches—and not only background but present exposition for the Christian church—about the Redeemer as Creator, the electing grace of God, his steadfast love, his holiness, his justice, his wrath, and his power. In this gritty, earthy history, which rises to hymns of praise to the one God over against the multiple deities of the nations, in which the sins of patriarchs, kings, and sundry heroes are recounted along with the fickleness of the faithless children, the word of God still speaks to the church. Every temptation of the Christian church to gauzy, fragile "spiritualization" is combated by the flesh-and-blood history of the often fleshly and bloody members of the "old" covenant.

The Hebrew Scriptures looked forward. The same witnesses proclaimed the coming of a new age, and a true servant of God in whom God's purpose for Israel and for mankind would be realized. The promises are varied; sometimes they point to inhabiting a new land, again to rescue from slavery or victory over various enemies. Some promises tell of future justice and peace in an age when swords shall be beaten into plowshares and of a future judgment when God shall vindicate his ways with his people and destroy all adversaries. Many promises relate to a coming Prince, or Messiah, and to a mission for Israel of universal importance. The Hebrew Scriptures become Old Testament for the Christian church when these particular elements are singled out and when the new age and the true servant of God are identified with Jesus.

Probably our ¶ 18 would be accepted as a passable statement about the covenant in the Hebrew Scriptures by most readers, regardless of religious affiliation. But when these elements are seen as preliminary to the New Testament and fulfilled by events of Jesus' life (¶ 19), we are speaking exclusively within the area of Christian confession. Christian reading of events and the meaning of events in the "old" covenant derives from theological hindsight, by which Christ the fulfillment is taken to be the chief clue to understanding. The pattern for such understanding is found throughout the Christian books which, for this reason, are called "new" testament or covenant.

Out of Israel God in due time raised up Jesus. His faith and obedience were the response of the perfect child of God. This much simply recalls what has already been said of Jesus in the opening paragraphs of Part I (¶s 8-10). There the immediate purpose was to describe the encounter of Jesus with men of his own day and to confess and encourage that encounter today. Now the life of Jesus and the response to him is placed more fully in its Biblical setting. As the fulfillment of God's promise to Israel, he is significant in the three arenas of the preceding paragraphs, respectively: creation, the beginning of the new creation; man, the pioneer of the new humanity; and history, he gave history its meaning and direction. Then the last words of the paragraph introduce the New Israel, the new servant people, he . . . called the church to be his servant for the reconciliation of the world.

Somewhat more fully, God's promise to Israel, that for which he chose and called them, was a destiny in which they would serve God faithfully and become a light to the nations (¶ 18). The universal mission appears in such passages as Isaiah 42:6 and 49:6, and is claimed by verbatim quotation in Luke 2:32 and Acts 13:47 (and ch. 26:23) for the work of Christ and the mission of the church. Jesus is designated the authentic son of Abraham (Matt. 1:1, and the genealogy); the bringer of forgiveness and salvation after the domination of Moses and the law (Luke 1:77; Rom. 5:12-14); the Messiah or Prince inheriting the throne of David (Luke 1:32; Matt., ch. 2).

In Jesus of Nazareth, God the Redeemer and Creator has done a new thing. As another "Adam" (I Cor. 15:45), one who bears the true "image" or "stamp" of God (Rom. 8:29; Heb. 1:3), he overcame the "trespass" and "death" that reigned from Adam to Moses and through the time of the law after Moses (Rom. 5:12-16). In Him a contemporary man becomes "a new creation" (II Cor. 5:17).

He in whom true humanity was realized once for all (¶ 8) is

the pioneer of the new humanity. In various respects he is the first, the one who goes before, or even the path by which others go (John 14:5-6), the "first fruits" of the resurrection (I Cor. 15:20), the "first-born" among the brethren (Rom. 8:29), the "Leader and Savior," the "Author" of life (Acts 5:31; 3:15), the "pioneer" of salvation and of faith (Heb. 2:10; 12:2). Already in these references we are edging over into the subject of the new life (¶s 21-26) which finds its direction in the life of Jesus (¶ 24), and the mission of the church which derives from him its pattern (¶ 32). Rightly, reconciliation and redemption lead on into creation and the new life. "He [the Son] is the head of the body, . . . that in everything he might be pre-eminent. For in him all the fulness of God was pleased to dwell, and through him to reconcile to himself all things, whether on earth or in heaven, making peace by the blood of his cross." (Col. 1:18-20, and the whole passage.)

From this center, where the Reconciler reveals the purpose of the Creator, the goal of human life, and the forward movement of history, this same history receives its meaning and direction, and the church receives its call to be his servant for the reconciliation of the world. It would be grandiose of a working scholar in this or that academic field of history to chart the future from the past, or to elaborate the purpose of things. He may write "The Rise of the West," but if he wishes to retain his professional standing, he had better not write a "Meaning of History." And this is correct. The direction and meaning found in a confessional statement are of a different quality. Based on the confession that God has carried out his word, fulfilled his promise, and vindicated his people, and that he will yet consummate his purpose, the church expects and trusts in the "coming" of the Kingdom (¶s 53-56). This is history's direction and meaning, by which the church and its members are called together and set on a mission.

CHAPTER 6

HOLY SPIRIT AND NEW LIFE
(¶s 20-26)

"The Communion of the Holy Spirit" answers questions about how "The Grace of Our Lord Jesus Christ" (Section A) and "The Love of God" (Section B) reach us and affect us today.

"Spirit," however, is more question than answer to most of us. We waver between "it" and "he" when speaking of the Holy Spirit. The name "Holy Ghost" sounds occult or wispy. The descent of the Spirit at Pentecost produced strange behavior. Ecstatic speaking, quakings, healings, and emotional excesses have often been attributed to the Spirit, especially by sectarian movements, throughout Christian history. The more staid, formal churches appear strangely uncomfortable about the one whom the Fourth Gospel calls the Comforter.

The many uses of the word "spirit" in the Bible can be unsettling. The word itself means "breath" or "wind" in both Hebrew and Greek, and is applied to God, to man, to man's condition, as well as to angels and demonic spirits. God's Spirit is "poured out," "searches," "dwells in," and gives "life" and "liberty." The Spirit "witnesses," "intercedes," and is variously related to wind, fire, water, a dove, and a sword. And what are we to make of the statement that "every sin and blasphemy will be forgiven men, but the blasphemy against the Spirit will not be forgiven" (Matt. 12:31)?

The freedom of expression within Scripture indicates that the Spirit is not to be caught in a formula. Vitality, movement, and secret operation imply that the Spirit is likely to upset the rigid,

81

programmed institution. But it is wrong to link the Spirit only with enthusiasm, eccentricity, or (a last resort of the middle-class church) silent meditation. The Spirit speaks through the words of men wherever the grace of God is communicated, and is so identified with the Word himself that deviations of the message must be attributed to another spirit (I John 4:1-3). It is not alien to the Spirit that the whole Christian faith derives from a Word through a book, and is passed along by word of mouth (¶s 20-27). Words are the chief avenues of communion and community, and the highest form of personal intercourse. The sign of the Spirit at Pentecost was, after all, a tongue.

The root of the New Testament word for personal **communion** or fellowship, "koinonia" (koi-no-NEE-ya), means "common" or "shared." It is the exact opposite of isolated, alone, or separate. Outside the New Testament it sometimes means marriage. Thus, like reconciliation, it is by definition a society idea, not a private, individualistic one. There are things that individuals do alone, but they are not reconciled alone and they do not have communion alone, any more than they can be married alone. They are always reconciled "to" or "with" God and others, and thereby are brought into **communion** with them. Quite understandably, the sending of the Spirit in tongues at Pentecost issued in the fellowship which is the Christian church.

Communion in the subtitle becomes **community** in the first paragraph's most important sentence: **The Holy Spirit creates and renews the church as the community in which men are reconciled to God and to one another** (I John 1:3-7). These words are almost a definition of the church. The key terms in what follows—**forgiveness** . . . **peace** . . . **power**—describe the daily basis of the church's existence, the quality of life in it, and the impetus for its mission. All these are the work of the Holy Spirit, confused and disturbed, of course, by the frailties of men.

All the verbs in the lead paragraph are in the present tense: **God the Holy Spirit fulfills** . . . **creates and renews** . . . **enables** . . . **gives them power**, etc. God is now acting and working. Communion must be happening now, otherwise it is not communion at all, but a memory or hope or theory of communion. The Holy Spirit might be described, thus, as more a verb than a noun. While it is customary to speak of the "presence" of the Spirit, it is much more fitting to speak of the Spirit's action or movement. The Spirit is *God* active, not part of God or a phase of God, as if there were a reservoir of inactivity behind what the Spirit does. The Holy Spirit, Third Person of the Trinity (see Chapter 14, "The Nicene and Apostles' Creeds"), is the one by whom the new life is begun and continued.

One criticism. It is unfortunate that the relation of the Holy Spirit to creation was omitted in the final version of the Confession. The first published form had said, "God the Holy Spirit is active in the creation working to achieve the purposes of his love." The writer does not recall anything in discussions that would repudiate the statement, nor the process by which it was lost. Its absence prompts a reminder of the universality of God's power through the Holy Spirit.

We turn now to "The New Life," one of the two main topics in the Confession of 1967 that appear under the heading "The Communion of the Holy Spirit."

In ¶ 19, Jesus is called the beginning of the new creation, and the pioneer of the new humanity, who gave history its meaning and direction. We have just observed that the Spirit is the action of God through the Word, the binder between God, the world, and the human community. We turn now toward the other pole in this field of force: man. The Holy Spirit fulfills the work of reconciliation in man.

At once we see that in man includes both human history, the life of mankind, and the individual, personal crisis and present hope. Both person and community, history and the future, are always in play. To isolate one element is as impossible as dividing convex from concave. But we cannot say everything at once, and the place has come to speak more especially of the present and the personal, the new life. Part II of the Confession will emphasize the community aspect. Part III will draw together the numerous threads of Christian hope that are woven throughout.

Each paragraph on the new life contains a key word which was chosen to sharpen the focus of a Biblical or traditional term, as follows. Crisis in ¶ 21 is used for judgment; acceptance in ¶ 22, for justification or forgiveness; conflict and struggle in ¶ 23 refer to temptation and to the warfare between flesh and spirit; direction in ¶s 24-25 is a stand-in for sanctification; and fulfillment, ¶ 26, indicates eternal ife.

The word crisis ordinarily means a decisive moment or turning point. New Testament Greek carries a stronger sense of final determination and ultimate division through divine judgment (John 12:31). The reconciling work, thus, is called the crisis on which the entire life of mankind hinges in the sight of God. Then the same term is applied to the life of each man when the cross and resurrection, respectively, become personal crisis and present hope.

In what way does it make sense to say that the reconciling work of Jesus was the supreme crisis in the life of mankind? In one sense only: as a confession of the uniqueness and seriousness of reconciliation in Christ, which took place "once for all" (I Peter 3:18; Heb. 9:26). It is beside the point to speculate just how Neanderthal man might be saved from his sin through Christ. Also, it would be grandiose to offer this as an opinion based on shrewd observation and comparison of other crises of history. This is a confessional statement (¶ 7) deriving from the divine-human encounter in faith. Like the assertion of the universality of sin (¶ 13), it is a confession about the condition of man rather than a theory about this one or that one. As such, it is no more and no less fantastic to proclaim God's grace and God's judgment to any group than to include all history in it. A Neanderthal man, if one can be found, is as much a subject of reconciliation in Christ as any customer of Sears Roebuck. No one is exempt or excluded. This is said because of the gravity, the cost, and the ultimate seriousness that attach to Jesus.

That which was, past tense, the supreme crisis in the life of mankind becomes present and active personal crisis and present hope for men under certain conditions. That which was, becomes personal and present. "Then and there" becomes "here and now." As John Calvin put it, "We must understand that as long as Christ remains outside of us, and we are separated from him, all that he has suffered and done for the salvation of the human race remains useless and of no value for us. Therefore, to share with us what he has received from the Father, he has to become ours and to dwell within us. . . . We obtain this by faith" (*Institutes,* III.i.1).

The conditions under which "then" becomes "now" are **when the gospel is proclaimed and believed.** The single word **gospel** is a shorthand way of referring to all the foregoing, namely, that **in Jesus Christ God was reconciling the world to himself.** The Biblical words **proclaimed** and **believed** are used to signify all ways of announcing and receiving effectively the **gospel.** Announcing or proclaiming is discussed several times farther along in the chapters on ¶s 30, 36, 42, and 49. Believing, or faith, appears in the discussion on ¶s 10, 27, and "I believe" in the chapters on the Apostles' Creed and the other Confessions (see Harmony). The double action, **proclaim and believe,** is explained (¶ 21) in an additional sentence freighted with traditional terms that have their origin in the New Testament: **forgiveness, faith, repentance, obedience,** and the **new life.**

It should not be missed that the entire process is called **experience: in this experience,** namely, **when the gospel is proclaimed and believed.** Perhaps the more exact word would have been "event." "In this *event* the Spirit brings God's forgiveness, "that is, the two-sided event made up of proclaiming and believing. But it is important that the language used shows connection with those who make much of "religious experience," although often experience used in this way makes too much of private emotions and personal life stories. **Forgiveness, faith, repentance,** etc., are more than emotional states. They express a relation to God initiated by God. The active agent is the Spirit, which **brings God's forgiveness, . . . moves them to respond,** and **initiates the new life. Repentance** is not heightened remorse, **faith** is not extreme credulity, nor is **obedience** the summit of self-discipline.

All three are gifts received daily rather than cultivated habits, as the remainder of *The Book of Confessions* shows well enough.

The new life takes shape in a community. Why takes shape? And why community? At the risk of a silly truism, let it be said that life is not dead. Life, especially new life, is moving, vigorous, active, assertive. Also, it develops in definite ways. Little turtles become big ones, acorns become oaks. Men have a richer potential. "Man's chief end is to glorify God, and to enjoy him forever," says the Shorter Catechism. God has created man in a personal relation with himself that man may respond to the love of the Creator, and use his creative powers for the fulfillment of human life (¶ 17). The Biblical symbols for glorification, enjoyment, and fulfillment are social or community symbols, whether the Old Testament people, the New Testament church, or the heavenly city, the father's house, and the marriage feast (¶ 54) of reconciliation fulfilled.

Every community, whether a family, a card club, or a revolutionary movement, shapes its members' lives. A community based on forgiveness should do the same. If God loves and accepts, thereby drawing men into fellowship, the members might be expected to accept themselves and love others, taking this shape from the image of him by whom they are assembled.

Most communities are based on a value wanted or a desire fulfilled. This community is the other way around. The Source and Founder has no desire and lacks no value. God's love, for which the Bible uses the special Greek word *agapē* (ah-GAH-pay), is not a desire or want for the valuable. It is a love that freely, graciously, without apparent reason, goes out to the unlovely, the unvaluable, the disobedient, and invests them with love, value, and free obedience.

God loves and accepts men who are in the wrong and helpless without his forgiveness (¶ 13). He does so in spite of what they are. The most important word in this paragraph is the word accepts. Luther and Calvin both used "free acceptance" as synonyms for forgiveness and also for justification by faith, as does the Westminster Confession: "accepting their persons as righteous" (Ch. XI, Sec. 1). Modern popular psychology uses similar language. Hostility and self-loathing mark the person who cannot accept or even face himself as he is. But in the presence of a therapist who will not reject him, to whom his security is transferred, he begins to see and accept his own condition. Self-hatred and hostility diminish together. Analogies with psychotherapy, like the traditional analogies of theology with the practice of medicine, should not be surprising, since all deal with the healing of men.

Free and undeserved acceptance is in some measure an everyday experience and in pure form the rarest occurrence in life. The same can be said of love. Love and acceptance are essential in all human communion, especially the closer relationships. Hearty acceptance, warts and all, is entailed in happy marriage. The pledge does not read, "I, John, take thee Mary, provided that you stay cheerful, thrifty, brave, clean, and reverent." Nor is love for a child suspended until the parents see how he turns out. Home is where you have a *birth* right, and the church is the same. Love is the reason for birth in both instances. The same phrase for acceptance is used in the Heidelberg Catechism: "*In spite of* the fact that my conscience accuses me, . . . and that I am still ever prone to all that is evil, nevertheless, God, without any merit of my own, out of pure grace, grants me the benefits . . . of Christ, . . . as if I had never committed a single sin" (Q. 60).

Parenthetically, because of the frailty of love, at the high point of human acceptance, when a man and a woman want to marry, live together, and raise a family, the state steps in and requires a contract. Free, loving acceptance is underwritten by a legal vow. This proves to be no hindrance, but when marriage declines to contract alone, it is no longer marriage. So gospel, if the spirit lapses, reverts to law, and the end is separation (¶ 11).

God's acceptance, then, is the basis for a loving community among men. They therefore accept themselves and love others, knowing that no man has any ground on which to stand except God's grace (Eph. 2:8; I Cor. 4:7).

The new life is not brand-new in every respect. It does not

alter personalities beyond recognition, end cares and worries, or pop the believer into Utopia. The new life does not release a man from conflict with unbelief, pride, lust, fear. And the list is not final or complete.

Some of Luther's most famous words describe this condition. "The Christian man is at the same time righteous and a sinner, an enemy of God and a child of God." Calvin, too, after defining "faith" with no mention of doubt, writes: "Surely, while we teach that faith ought to be certain and assured, we cannot imagine any certainty that is not tinged with doubt, or any assurance that is not assailed by some anxiety. On the other hand, we say that believers are in perpetual conflict with their own unbelief. Far, indeed, are we from putting their consciences in any peaceful repose, undisturbed by any tumult at all" (*Institutes,* III.ii.17).

God's promise is not the sudden end of all troubles, according to the stories of the Old Testament. In the New, struggles of all kinds persist along with the hope of victory over them. "We are afflicted in every way, but not crushed; perplexed, but not driven to despair; persecuted, but not forsaken; struck down, but not destroyed." (II Cor. 4:8-9.) Sin continues, "I see in my members another law at war with the law of my mind" (Rom. 7:23); doubt persists, "I believe; help my unbelief!" (Mark 9:24); God is obscured, "My God, my God, why hast thou forsaken me?" (Ps. 22:1; Matt. 27:46); and profligacy can be found, "There is immorality among you, and of a kind that is not found even among pagans" (I Cor. 5:1).

The language of this paragraph is brief and general, but easily filled with detail by the candid reader from his own experience. It is a small inoculation against the popular literature that equates faith with pep, success, and sound sleep. The cult of the waxy smile, sex denied, and doubt glossed over has no place in the Christian faith—although at times it enjoys great vogue. The new life would be a pipe dream if it blocked genuine awareness of the way things are, good and bad alike, within and without.

Nevertheless, despite the conflict and struggle just described, the Christian is not defeated. The disheartening in life does not

kill off freedom and good cheer, nor does it destroy his confidence
that the new life is pleasing to God and helpful to others. The
words that follow nevertheless are an answering chorus that
carries over the motifs of persisting struggle and conflict. It is
the stronger chorus because it is sung in anticipation of the fulfillment of reconciliation, the triumph of God over all that resists
his will and disrupts his creation (¶ 54). Although fulfillment is
reserved for the end of this section (¶ 26) and the end of the
Confession (Part III), it exerts influence throughout. Without
steadfast hope (¶ 55) the new life would lose its identity and
would not survive, except possibly as crusading idealism.

The Confession now describes the new life in terms of organic
growth. As he matures reminds the reader of Biblical imagery
related to birth, growth, nurture, education, and the full development of the believing person. Maturity does not result from an
act of will or a task accomplished. It is a natural, expected process, but one that can be hindered or helped.

Life with Christ may be a minor slip in the style of the Confession. The preposition "in" is more appropriate to the New
Testament, and appears also in ¶s 21 and 26. "With," as in Philip-
pians 1:23, refers chiefly to life beyond death. This is not a major
point, but worth mentioning, to guard against understanding the
phrase mawkishly, as if Christ were a divine companion or pal.

Good cheer comes from John 16:33, "In the world you have
tribulations; but be of good cheer, I have overcome the world."
The Greek is also translated "take heart" or "have courage"
(Matt. 14:27). But these phrases imply grimness rather than gay,
exuberant courage. It is a familiar theme that there is no bona
fide tragedy in Christian life because no impersonal fate relent-
lessly crushes human courage. Despite pain and suffering, Jesus
is not a tragic hero, nor is Jeremiah, nor Paul. Where the grace
and righteousness of God are ultimate, where the judge is the
redeemer (¶ 11), and the outcome is described as a new heaven
and a new earth, the drama of history is rather a "Divine Com-
edy." There is exultation in a Christian writer such as Paul (Phil.
4:4-13) that is lacking in the noble, crabbed courage of the Stoic.

The Christian will laugh and cry, for he is not stonehearted (Rom. 12:15), and he will live in good cheer. We speak not of personality traits, for some people are naturally more cheerful than others. A life of trust and hope, however, cannot fail in the process of maturing to reflect the good news on good days and evil days, confident that the new life is pleasing to God and helpful to others.

The apocalyptic image of choirs of angels around the throne of the "Lamb" singing "blessing and honor and glory and might" (Rev., ch. 5) is a world away from a tragic Greek chorus. Yet it is a Lamb "slain," and the prevalent harmony rings with that dissonance. In one case as in the other, the chorus echoes a conception of the life of man and its outcome. Here it is neither Stoic apathy nor simple optimism, but a life of conflict, struggle, freedom, good cheer, confidence, and steadfast hope.

Direction is a word newly chosen for the Confession of 1967. It is meant to help clarify sanctification, which is hopelessly outmoded and overloaded with conceptions of sanctimoniousness. "Sanctified," in the Bible, means "set apart for a divine purpose," or commissioned to serve (¶ 10). What made the people of Israel holy (Latin, sanctus, the root of "sanctify") was not their moral condition but the fact that they were chosen and set apart for a special mission in the world. The same is true of the church and each of its members. When a person or a group moves toward a purpose or end in life, their life is given a direction. "Conversion" in both New and Old Testaments means "turning around." It agrees nicely with this figure of a new direction. Christian obedience, also, is the result of being called and forming life according to the will and purpose of God.

Similar imagery for the Christian life as a path or journey was common from the beginning. Jesus called himself the "way" and summoned men quite literally to follow him. When early Christianity was called the Way (Acts 9:2; 19:9), it was with twofold reference to a road or journey, and to a custom or pattern of conduct. Direction and pattern (¶s 31-32) are closely related concepts in the life of the individual and the whole church.

There are three elements in ¶ 24 that give the direction in which the Christian way goes: (1) the life of Jesus, (2) the teaching of apostles and prophets, which is a way of referring to the whole of Scripture, and (3) the Christian community.

The "imitation" of Christ is clearly taught in Scripture. "Be imitators of me, as I am of Christ," wrote the apostle Paul (I Cor. 11:1). The best-known text is probably the one in I Peter: "For to this you have been called, because Christ also suffered for you, leaving you an example, that you should follow in his steps" (ch. 2:21). Again, after washing the disciples' feet, Jesus said: "I have given you an example, that you also . . . ought to wash one another's feet. . . . Love one another; even as I have loved you. . . . By this all men will know that you are my disciples, if you have love for one another" (John 13:15, 14, 34-35).

An imitation may be a rather superficial copy. Certainly, to repeat foot washing today, when it no longer belongs to ordinary hospitality, would be caricature. This kind of thing has tended to put the theme of the imitation of Christ out of favor. The Protestant Reformers did not like it very well because it encouraged shallowness; it had long been interpreted as requiring monastic celibacy and poverty, and it served too well the doctrine of salvation by works. More recently in America the popular program of asking oneself, "What would Jesus do?" when trying to follow "in his steps" was a well-intentioned recipe for emptiness.

Despite these objections, the Confession of 1967 brings a reminder that the new life means a life "conformed to the image of his Son" (Rom. 8:29). The life of Jesus is a picture of a man turned toward his fellows, a man for other men. Every aspect of his life and teaching can be so understood. The account at the beginning of the Confession (¶ 8) stressed Jesus' public ministry, during which he constantly spoke with people, healed and forgave them their sins, announced that a new era was beginning, and invited them to prepare for it. His death, even more, was for other men (¶ 9). The direction, then, of the Christian life is outward, toward and on behalf of other human beings.

Had Jesus not preached forgiveness and reconciliation, his life and teaching would impose an impossible law on his followers. But the same voice announced forgiveness, commanded love, and promised that the Kingdom already begun "among you" would be consummated at the proper time by God.

The indicative of "your sins are forgiven," and the imperative of "thou shalt love," have been bridged by many theologies and ethical theories through the ages. Some have proposed to withdraw Christian ethics from all but the most intimate personal relationships, where love is presumably easier and more natural. Others would try to formulate a law or principle of love and calculate with a moral slide rule the relative justice of this or that act. Still others, especially today, try to derive from each new situation a way of acting out love, unencumbered by law or principle.

This Confession is hardly going to produce an answer to the dilemmas posed by centuries of experience and ethical theory, but it does urge with confidence that knowing the life of Jesus and the lives and writings of those closest to him will cause a person to become incurably sensitive to his neighbors' and his enemies' needs. Following Christ will not allow us to let up, to give up, and to mind our own selfish business. Like the parents of a malformed child, or friends of a disintegrating person, the follower of Jesus will do and do, try and try, pay and pay, explore every avenue for help and cure—but for people he has never seen. Among the corruptions and dizzying complications of modern life, following Jesus may take only a moment for a kind word, or it may take an IBM computer and an act of Congress. To express this love may require an unostentatious pledge to the church budget, a couple of hours of free baby-sitting, or a jail sentence for civil disobedience, or all three. One or more of these schemes may fail. We read in I Corinthians, ch. 13, that spectacular sacrifices, miracles, prophecies, and wisdom may all fail, but love never ends. "Make love your aim" (ch. 14:1), or let love give you a direction, is the teaching of the Confession.

Then, lest love be taken as a disembodied ideal, we are pointed again to the life of Jesus, his deeds and words, his struggles against temptation, his compassion, his anger, and his willingness to suffer death. Possibly these should have come first, for they are not to be seen as illustrating a principle called "for others." The setting in life of this or that saying will often guard it against becoming a bloodless maxim or a cliché of proverbial wisdom.

The Ten Commandments loomed large in Jesus' teachings, as seen most clearly in the Sermon on the Mount. The inner meaning of law and the motives of the individual are prominently to the fore. Jesus observed and taught the law, but despised exaggerated and superficial obedience. He denounced fussy tithers of mint leaves and caraway seeds who "neglected the weightier matters of the law, justice and mercy and faith . . . , straining out a gnat and swallowing a camel!" (Matt. 23:23-24). His anger was generally reserved for the hypocrisy of the self-righteous and the superrighteous. His compassion was drawn most quickly to great offenders, to the poor, and the sick. The picture is of virile, gentle, personal, sensitive, compassionate, rarely rude, and rarely violent encounters with the people he knew and met. Even his rudeness and denunciation were unfailingly aimed to heal and save. The personal idiom of Jesus is highly individual. It can be "imitated" only in the personal idiom that is genuine for each disciple in the encounters of his own life.

The direction which the new life takes from the life of Jesus is not abstracted or isolated from either its Biblical setting or its present setting in the church. The teaching of apostles and prophets, which is a way of referring to the whole of Scripture, guides men in living this life. The Christian community nurtures and equips them. Here the reader and other commentators will wish to elaborate on ways of Bible study and all aspects of Christian nurture carried out in church, family, and community (cf. ¶s 27-30, 36-38, 48-52).

In the course of their daily work, members of the church are naturally engaged in all kinds of human endeavor. The direction derived from the life of Jesus points them toward peace and the good of man (¶ 17) in and through their employment and leisure activities. Readily, therefore, they are to cooperate with powers and authorities in politics, culture, and economics. As the apostle

Paul enjoyed the protection of Roman law and Roman citizenship and took advantage of Roman roads and trade routes in his mission travels, presumably the present-day believer will do the same in the land where he lives. Governments, political parties, businesses, unions, police departments, welfare agencies, schools, and museums are all among the common institutions in which faithful men will do their part (¶s 38-39).

But they have to fight against pretensions and injustices when these same powers endanger human welfare. The direction of their lives will not allow them to participate and cooperate in everything or under all conditions. Criticism, reform, and revolution are Christian options as alive and ready as cooperation, when conditions require it. The time, place, and form of opposition cannot be prescribed or proscribed in advance. Ends do not justify all means, but in revolutionary situations, as in time of war, higher priorities often make startling demands upon tender consciences.

The history of Christian men in peace and war, persecuted and persecuting, conservative and revolutionary, makes confusing reading and even more confused Biblical exegesis. Do the "governing authorities . . . instituted by God" (Rom. 13:1) include a Hitler or a Stalin with their systematic mass murder? What of a Cuban Presbyterian under the successive dictatorships of Batista and Castro? What does a black Christian or a white Christian do about Black Power and black powerlessness? Does each do the same thing regardless of whether he lives in South Africa, the Congo, Mississippi, or New Jersey? Can a Christian be a pacifist, and another a soldier, and another an enemy soldier? May he fight one war and refuse the next? Should he withhold tax payment or registration for military draft because of government policies? Does "Render therefore to Caesar the things that are Caesar's, and to God the things that are God's" (Matt. 22:21) solve these problems? Or, "We must obey God rather than men" (Acts 5:29)?

The Confession of 1967 does not offer solutions, individual or mass, for these specific problems. It accepts such problems, however, within the bosom of the church when it affirms that the

direction pointed may at one time mean **cooperation with** and at another time it may mean **fight against** the otherwise legitimate **powers and authorities in politics, culture, and economics.** The Confession also deals with the tension created (¶ 38). These are extremely dangerous issues, not to be decided by abstract judgments in advance, nor by convulsive emotional reactions. Both the individual and the Christian fellowship need one another in deciding courses of action. There is a vast area for common informed judgment and there are issues that will divide brother from brother.

The strength of the church and its members, even when torn by conflicts arising from political and social life **is in their confidence that God's purpose rather than man's schemes will finally prevail.** These **schemes** include those devised by churches and churchmen as well as others. All men sin in all they do, and the church is highly fallible. This should not cut the nerve of action. "Sin boldly," said Luther, "and more boldly still believe!"

Life in Christ is life eternal. This paragraph is to be understood in closest relation to Part III of the Confession, "The Fulfillment of Reconciliation." Here the chief content is from the writings of Paul and John, which present the fulfillment of reconciliation in terms of life eternal. There, imagery of the **kingdom** from the teaching of Jesus in Matthew, Mark, and Luke moves to the center of the stage. The two are practical equivalents. While each expression includes a personal and a social dimension, **life eternal** is more personal and **kingdom** is more communal. Of both it is said that they are already present and are yet to be completed.

Life eternal is the present reality of the eternal. It is not to be thought of first as a future extension of life, but a different quality of life in which, present and future, God's love is the dominant and victorious feature. "God is love, and he who abides in love abides in God, and God abides in him. . . . This is eternal life, that they know thee the only true God, and Jesus Christ whom thou hast sent." (I John 4:16 and John 17:3.)

The words **beyond death** do point to an unending future, but not to a simple extension of life. It is a popular Christian superstition as well as an old theological idea (Westminster Confession, Chs. IV; XXXII) that the soul of man is immortal. This comes from Plato, not from the Bible. Although some passages seem to refer to man's soul or spirit apart from bodily existence, they do not teach the soul's "immortality," or inability to die. Where immortality is taught, it is not as a quality with which the soul is endowed, like the hardness of granite. Rather, it is a gift of God, **beyond death.** It is difficult to get clarity from the Scriptures about soul, spirit, and mind, especially since the Old and New Testaments vary somewhat and the New Testament writings are not harmonious with one another, but clear it is that no part of man is, as such, immortal. The New Testament teaches **life eternal** and **resurrection,** not the deathlessness of the soul.

What distinguishes Christian hope from a mere desire to live forever is the willingness to die and to trust everything to God as known in Christ. Desire for immortality can be the worst form of lust, and belief in it can be a tragic delusion supported by wishful thinking. One way of rooting out such religious egotism and preventing such delusion was the question asked long ago in Calvinist New England of candidates for church membership: Are you willing to be damned for the glory of God? This brutal demand is happily abolished, but it serves to remind us sharply that resurrection takes place not by man's wish but by God's grace **beyond death.**

Speculations about the nature of resurrection and the sounds and colors of eternal life are rejected by the apostle Paul (I Cor. 15:35 ff.) and the writer of I John (ch. 3:2). Paul wrote the strongest and purest affirmation of trust to be found anywhere in the Scriptures. "If God is for us, who is against us? . . . Neither death, nor life, . . . nor things present, nor things to come, . . . nor anything else in all creation, will be able to separate us from the love of God in Christ Jesus our Lord." (Rom. 8:31, 38.) Such faith is neither otherworldly nor futuristic. It rests on the Eternal made known in time and exists in a history to be fulfilled in the reconciliation by God of the world with himself.

THE BIBLE
(¶s 27-30)

The Bible is one of the glories of the human race. The poetry, history, and oratory of the Hebrew Scriptures have flowed into the culture of Judaism, Christianity, and Islam. The imagery of the New Testament Gospels, letters, and apocalyptic run through the language and literature of Western man like the veins in marble. Mosaic and painting, music and architecture, sculpture and drama, theology, philosophy, and the ethos of daily life reveal that thinkers, artists, and Everyman have lived under the tutelage of Scripture, even when rejecting faith.

But it is faith that concerns us here. Unless the Scriptures lie, it is better to know the grace of God than to have built the Cathedral of Chartres—or a moon rocket. What about faith, when the Bible's picture of the universe and the history of man have been losing ground for three centuries? Can the Bible still communicate the grace of God? Our answer will not surprise those who have read thus far. It can and does, when the word of God is distinguished from the words of men through which God speaks. We worship and praise God, not a book or Christian culture, yet not without the book or separate from cultural expression.

The reader, especially if he is peeking at this chapter first, is sharply reminded to note where we are in the Confession of 1967. The Bible is discussed under the heading "The Communion of the Holy Spirit," that is to say, as part of the present, live action of the Spirit which today fulfills the work of reconciliation in man. This is the proper place to discuss the Bible, as a brief recap will show:

The story of Jesus in ¶s 8-11 is an answer to the question, Where do we find salvation? and the description of sin in ¶s 12-14 answers, From what are we saved? Sin comes second because men have no height from which to appreciate the seriousness of sin until they are in the process of rescue. Then, Why are we saved? is answered by an account of the sovereign love of God shown in creation, history, and the old covenant, ¶s 15-19. How does God's love reach and affect us today? brings us to the communion of the Holy Spirit and the new life, with other aspects of the new life to follow in Part II. The present section, ¶s 27-30, is a partial answer to, How do you know all this?

The Bible is the second of the "how" questions because it is an explanation after the fact, a review of a process that has already begun. It cannot be answered in advance, for then there is no process to review. The first step in the Christian faith is to believe in Christ and receive new life. Reflection on how this has come about necessarily leads to discussion of the Bible.

In the Confession of 1967 the discussion rightly begins not with the book but with Christ: **The one sufficient revelation of God is Jesus Christ, the Word of God incarnate.** A capital *W* alerts the reader to the fact that he is being introduced to a special meaning for "word."

There is nothing special about most of the tens of thousands of Hebrew and Greek words that make up the Bible. They can be read in the Bible and written in other forms of literature by clods, geniuses, or ordinary people. They can be looked up in dictionaries, traced down to their roots. They were generally spoken before they were written down at all, and subsequently are known more through speaking than writing. Like all words, these words are *about* something. Every child knows there is a difference between word sounds and what they signify. Saying "horse" does not produce a horse, or we'd all be riders.

But there is a **Word of God** within the words of Scripture that is not *about* something else, but *is* what it *does* or says. It is God's will in action. The statement itself *is* what it signifies, or accomplishes its end merely by being said. For example, "By the word of the LORD the heavens were made" (Ps. 33:6); "And God said, 'Let there be light'; and there was light" (Gen. 1:3). God's word in these cases is the same as God's deed.

Another example brings us closer to the point at issue. In the first verses of John's Gospel, patterned after Genesis, ch. 1, we read: "In the beginning was the Word, and the Word was with God, and the Word was God. . . . And the Word became flesh and dwelt among us." The speaking or word of God at this point took an unprecedented kind of action, it *became* flesh. The divine word at this point *is* a human person, inhabiting ordinary history. The Word is the same power and will that made all things, as Paul wrote, "For it is the God who said, 'Let light shine out of darkness,' who has shone in our hearts to give the light of the knowledge of the glory of God in the face of Christ" (II Cor. 4:6).

Jesus Christ, then, is God's talking deed or acting word. He is God approaching mankind who are self-wrapped in "darkness" (John 3:19), in a "lie" (Rom. 1:25), and who live alien and estranged "without God in the world" (Eph. 2:12), although God is very much in the world and does disclose his "righteousness" and "wrath" (Rom. 1:17,18). For this he is called **the one sufficient revelation of God.** Jesus Christ is himself **revelation** because in him God discloses himself, piercing the world's hostile "darkness" (Col. 1:13) with the Word of reconciliation. He is the **one sufficient revelation** because he is not something *about* God but God himself in the act of revealing. All other disclosures in creation, in the promise to Abraham and the prophets, fall short of this full personal disclosure.

The word of the Lord that came to patriarch and prophet in "various ways," says The Letter to the Hebrews, is now "spoken to us by a Son . . . [who] reflects the glory of God and bears the very stamp of his nature, upholding the universe by his word of power" (ch. 1:1-3). As prophets were precursor witnesses, apostles were eyewitnesses after the fact of this last event.

The word of the Lord to prophets and apostles is a witness directly or indirectly to the Word himself. As a result, the **prophetic and apostolic testimony,** gradually collected together in the Scriptures or spoken aloud today is also called the **word of God written,** or **God's word . . . spoken** (¶s 27,30). In these cases the capital *W* is dropped for a small one, because they are **witness** rather than identical with the **Word.** It is **through** the Scriptures, rather than **to** them (as the Westminster Confession teaches) that the Spirit bears witness.

The awkward device of the capital *W* for Christ and the small *w* for other expressions of God's word is taken from the King James and Revised Standard Bibles (cf. John 1:1; Jer. 29:20; Acts 4:31). It is the best we can do in English without trying to revamp our entire older vocabulary, which seems both hopeless and unwise. Calvin, Erasmus, and others showed the difference between Word and word more easily in Latin by using *sermo* for Christ and *verbum* for the Bible (see Calvin's commentary on John, ch. 1). A century after the Reformation, unhappily, the Westminster Confession called the Bible the Word of God about thirty times but did not use the expression even once for Christ. This probably contributed to the common error of thinking that faith means to believe the Bible. It does not. Faith means to believe and trust in Christ. The Bible is an instrument through which faith's encounter with Christ takes place.

In the first sentence of ¶ 27 we come across the key terms of **revelation** which we have just been discussing. The order of appearance represents the order of their primacy: (1) **Word,** (2) **witness,** and (3) **word.** First, Christ is the **Word** in the preeminent sense. Secondly, the Spirit **bears . . . witness** to him, creating **faith, repentance, obedience,** and initiating **the new life** in men (¶ 21). Thirdly, we have the instrument of the Spirit's witness, the **word** which is either **written** (¶ 27) or **spoken** (¶ 30).

The **witness** that the Spirit bears to Christ **through** the Scriptures is called **unique and authoritative.** The Confession carefully avoids saying either that Scripture "is" God's word or that Scripture "is" unique and authoritative as such or in its own right.

It is in the function of living witness to Christ the Word that it has its unique place, without parallel, and on this basis the Scriptures are received and obeyed as the word of God written. The case does not rest on a view of inspiration as in the Westminster Confession (see below, Chapter 18) but on revelation, not on how the books were written but how they continue to communicate the message of salvation. The French Confession of Faith (1599), stemming from Calvin, did not hesitate to rest its case on the contemporary work of the Spirit: "We know these books to be canonical, and the sure rule of our faith, . . . by the testimony and inward illumination of the Holy Spirit, which enables us to distinguish them from other ecclesiastical books" (Art. IV). The other chief instrument of the Spirit is God's word . . . spoken (¶s 30, 49). This was stated in the days of the Reformation in the most famous words of the Second Helvetic Confession: "The preaching of the Word of God is the Word of God" (Ch. I).

The uniqueness and the authoritative quality of the Scriptures come from the fact that they contain prophetic and apostolic testimony, that is, the witness of those specially commissioned to speak on behalf of God to his people under the old and the new covenants. Both terms are used here in a broad sense. Prophetic testimony refers to the Old Testament and apostolic testimony to the New. Together they are a common traditional way of designating the entire Biblical canon. The word of God spoken in a living voice is generally superior to and more common than the written form as a way of communicating the gospel, not only for those who cannot read, but for those who profit especially by explanation, illustration, and application in sermons and various forms of personal and common witness. Nonetheless, the prophetic and apostolic testimony remains the prime source, criterion, and corrective of what is said in current idiom and with attention to contemporary hearers (¶ 49).

The phrase received . . . as, twice repeated in the first paragraph on the Bible, is a short one that covers a long process. Not only were the books of the Bible written over a very long period of time, but the process of being taken into the official canon, while other books were being excluded, sometimes lasted for centuries after writing. The Old Testament canon was taken over from Judaism, practically complete by the time of Christ. But the first official list of books corresponding to the twenty-seven books of the New Testament as we know it today appeared in the year A.D. 367. Recognition in this form was not general until a century and a half after that date.

"Scripture" in the New Testament refers to the Old Testament except for one reference in II Peter 3:16 (itself a second-century writing), which compares Paul's letters to "other scriptures." The Gospels and a group of Paul's epistles were in use quite early as a nucleus of authoritative, apostolic teaching that was read and expounded in the manner of Old Testament Scripture. But the first clear reference to a "New Testament" was by Irenaeus. This foremost orthodox father of the second century, however, though he quoted the writings of the apostle Paul more than two hundred times, never used the common formula for Scripture, "it is written," in doing so. Some books that were listed early in the canon later dropped out of sight and some, such as Hebrews, James, and Revelation, were long winning their way into the official lists. James is not even mentioned in the Western Church until the fourth century. The growth, sifting, and completing of the canon, thus, was a gradual process.

How is this gradual process best described? One thing is clear, the church meant to recognize apostolic authority. It hesitated long over Hebrews and James because they did not themselves claim to be by apostles. It finally excluded as spurious the so-called Apocalypse of Peter. It accepted II Peter on its own claim and for its content although, as Calvin recognized, its style shows it to be by a writer different from that of I Peter. The word received is used because it describes this posture of the church, recognizing apostolic authority rather than claiming for itself authority over the writings. Thus, **The church has received the books of the Old and New Testaments as prophetic and apostolic testimony.** The Scriptures are not given by the church, nor are they subordinate to church authority, but they are received in the church as a gift of God's providential care and are responded to in obedience to the word they communicate.

The words **obeyed** and **obedience** are each used also in this paragraph with reference to the witness or testimony borne. The latter use is a particularly happy one: **in which it hears the word of God and by which its faith and obedience are nourished and regulated.** Throughout the Confession of 1967 (especially in ¶s 3, 21, 24, 30, and 49) obedience is faithful obedience, or that which results from faith in the gospel. It is the total response in service and love which receives its **direction** from the deeds and words of Jesus, found in Scripture, and in the total setting of Scripture and the Christian community: **The teaching of apostles and prophets guides men in living this life, and the Christian community nurtures and equips them for their ministries** (¶ 24).

There is some repetition in ¶ 27 which remains as a scar of debate, discussion, and revision from the process of adopting the Confession. For instance, the whole second sentence (taken from a report composed by the present writer) seems to add only a rhetorical flourish to what has gone before. The last clause of the first sentence says rather awkwardly what the final sentence says with fine precision and clarity. The clause was designed apparently in order to have somewhere in the document the phrase **word of God written.** This is a perfectly legitimate expression, although it cannot be construed in this context after the manner of the same phrase as it appears in the Westminster Confession. Here, Scripture derives the name from its role as witness to Christ; there it "is" the word written by virtue of its author, God. To avoid misunderstanding, the phrase was originally not included in the draft of the Confession of 1967. Probably it is wise to have included it after all, although some will no doubt misunderstand and use the phrase in the older sense.

We halt a moment for orientation. The paragraph just discussed, the first of four under the heading "The Bible," presents the Word and the witness to him; the next presents the earlier and later witness in the form of the Old and New Testaments.

The third paragraph of this section discusses the interpretation of Scripture; and the fourth, the word spoken aloud. The reader will also have noticed important related discussions throughout the Confession and commentary, for instance, at ¶s 3, 10, 16, 18, 19, and especially 49.

The New Testament comes before the Old in ¶ 28. This arrangement is not often found, but the reason for it is obvious. To call the Hebrew Scriptures an "Old" Testament is to speak from the point of view of a "New" one. It is an implicit Christian confession which the present arrangement expresses frankly and clearly (see also ¶s 18-19). Delicate questions of objectivity in interpretation arising from this distinction are well known to those who study these materials.

The New Testament or new-era books are called the **recorded testimony of apostles,** not to solve questions of authorship, but by contrast between **prophetic** and **apostolic, old and new,** to show that times have changed, a promise has been fulfilled, and the turning point of history has been reached with the **coming of the Messiah, . . . and the sending of the Holy Spirit.** The books are apostolic either by authorship or by content as well as by their missionary message and their zeal to convert. "These are written that you may believe that Jesus is the Christ, the Son of God, and that believing you may have life in his name" (John 20:31) might be said of the whole New Testament.

The testimony of apostles is **recorded.** This simple descriptive word presents a fact, minus theories about the origin or state of the text. The Scriptures **in** which the church hears the word of God and **through** which the Spirit bears witness to the Word incarnate do not need to be bolstered artificially. They carry their message well enough under the live aegis of the Spirit.

Although there are more old manuscripts of the Bible than other ancient writings, there are no originals anywhere to venerate. Tens of thousands of minor textual variations are observed in the New Testament alone when the oldest manuscripts are compared. These have been reduced to about fifteen hundred of the most important for the sake of translators in the latest American Bible Society edition of the Greek text. The usual theological students' edition contains about fourteen thousand alternate readings of one kind or another. These things should not be denied or locked up in theological seminaries as if God's own method of revealing himself were too faulty for laymen to bear. They damage no faith except that which is directed to a theory about the Bible rather than to Christ. The wonder of the New Testament is that through four different lives of Jesus, an almost casual collection of apostolic letters, and a sometimes faulty text, the message of reconciliation, eternal life, and the Kingdom of God shines through like the sun on a bright day. Those who see and respond will gladly confess that this has taken place under the guidance of the Holy Spirit (¶ 29), and will humbly receive it in the terms on which it is proffered.

The inseparability of the Old and the New Testament is one of the chief burdens of ¶ 28. Old Testament history, prophecy, law, poetry, sacrificial imagery, and more are absolutely indispensable for understanding the New Testament. The briefest look at Matthew, Romans, Hebrews, or any of the primitive Christian writings will show that they speak of the present and future only in terms of what has already gone before in the Old Testament. Occasional efforts through the history of the church to discard the Old Testament or cut off the New and transplant it in some other soil have always resulted in a destruction of the gospel. At the same time, the Old Testament is not simply to be mined for types and prophecies of Christ. It is a total disservice even to the New Testament to detach the Old from its own environment and natural history. It is the Old Testament in its own literary and historical integrity that contributes to understanding the New, and thereby to nearly all phases of preaching, teaching, and daily living in the Christian church.

That the Old Testament is not itself fully understood without the New was practically the axiom of apostolic preaching. For years the Old Testament was the only Christian Scripture. Writings of the early church, canonical and uncanonical, are heavily preoccupied with showing that Judaism had missed the main

point of its own sacred writings. All who make a Christian confession must inevitably hold that Jesus was the looked-for
Messiah, hence the fulfillment of and the clue to full understanding of the Old Testament. This does not mean that Christian
theology can easily solve all problems or may blithely import
meanings at will. It does mean that by looking through the lens
of Christ into the Israelite past the Christian reader of the Old
Testament finds the central events and the chief teachings focused
on a promise of salvation that was fulfilled in Jesus and the
Kingdom he inaugurated.

Interpretation of the Scriptures has always been necessary.
When one no longer lives in the same setting as Jeremiah or the
apostle Paul, or does not speak Hebrew or Greek, he needs help
to understand their discourses. In any case, "all things in Scripture are not alike plain in themselves, nor alike clear unto all"
(Westminster Confession, Ch. I, Sec. 7). Paragraph 29 offers two
types of principle for interpretation. The first focuses on Christ
and reconciliation, and the second shows sensitivity to the historical and cultural forms in which the message of reconciliation
is communicated.

The Confession of 1967 makes the focus on Christ into a
method of studying the Bible. **The Bible is to be interpreted in
the light of its witness to God's work of reconciliation in Christ.**
Seeing, as we did above (¶s 8-19), the scope of the theme of reconciliation, we appreciate that this is not a restrictive principle.
Rather, it is the theme of the Scriptures themselves and ramifies
in curious and marvelous ways throughout the sixty-six books.

Not all parts of the Bible have the same significance for faith.
"The serpent said to the woman" or "Samuel went to Ramah"
hardly rank with "The whole earth is full of his glory" (Isa. 6:3)
or "God so loved the world that he gave his only Son" (John
3:16). If one were studying the geography of Palestine or the
history of snake symbols, the order might be reversed. Christian
belief has always recognized that some elements of Scripture are
more central and others more peripheral. Even the Westminster
Confession taught that "the principal acts of saving faith are

accepting, receiving, and resting upon Christ alone" (Ch. XIV, Sec. 2). Calvin said that "since man's heart is not aroused to faith at every word of God, we must find out at this point what, strictly speaking, faith looks to in the word" (*Institutes,* III.ii.7), and he goes on to single out "the freely given promise in Christ." More than one of the older confessions centered in Christ, as does the Barmen Declaration. The Confession of 1967 thus is not doing something new when it gives this principle of interpretation. It advances over the older statements, however, in responding to changes in history and culture and letting drop antiquated and secondary elements within the Bible that modern men cannot honestly accept as true or good. It is necessary to do this so that the divine folly and scandal of grace and forgiveness can be preached directly to the hearts of those who need it, unencumbered by the human folly of erroneous statements about the Bible.

This principle, like all interpretative principles, has its dangers, right and left. The reader of the Old Testament should not create a restricted canon of Christ-related passages and ignore the remainder of the Old Testament, nor should he try to fix on every passage or book a typology related to salvation. Sobriety, modesty, integrity, and close attention to the New Testament's own use of the Old should prevent excesses of either kind.

The second principle offered in ¶ 29, corollary to the first, shows quite a different kind of interest. It obligates the church to investigate literary and cultural diversity within the Scriptures in order to free the word of God from nonessential elements that are bound to the setting in which it was first uttered. The idea is not to hold on to everything, but to move on with the things that really matter. Before entering this subject, we must note an infelicity of expression. The adversative **nevertheless** seems to set the remainder of the second sentence in opposition to the clause **given under the guidance of the Holy Spirit.** Both were inserted in this sentence during the revision process. Taken at face value, the surprising implication would be that the Spirit normally would communicate in some other language than the **words of men.** This is wholly gratuitous. The phrase in question was, as I remember, taken from another source where the adversative made sense and was inserted here without proper care. What it serves to do in this paragraph on Biblical interpretation is again to remind the reader that the books he is dealing with are gifts of the Spirit.

The bulk of ¶ 29 dwells on the literary, historical, and cultural variety of Scripture. Sensitivity to this variety has been greatly increased in the past century and a half, during which an enormous amount of scholarship has made Biblical literature and history probably the most passionately studied and best-known area of our ancient past. The church not only welcomes these studies but itself has carried out most of them, even those which have proved to be extreme and irresponsible. Some quarters have rebelled, fearing a loss of the gospel or of faith, as if anything true could be a threat to him who is Truth itself. Quite the contrary attitude prevails in the Confession of 1967 as the last part of this paragraph affirms: **As God has spoken his word in diverse cultural situations, the church is confident that he will continue to speak through the Scriptures in a changing world and in every form of human culture.**

Probably the best way to appreciate fully the six categories that follow—**language, thought forms, and literary fashions, . . . views of life, history, and the cosmos**—would be for study groups to select a series of passages from the Old and New Testaments and analyze them, checking constantly for the presence of these elements. Then, most importantly, these elements should be discussed in relation to the Bible's **witness to God's work of reconciliation in Christ.** A selection of the first chapters of a number of Biblical books would be very rewarding for this purpose. Our procedure in what follows will be to make comment and give some random examples under each heading.

First, the phrase **the words of men.** There are hundreds of instances in the Old Testament, especially in the Pentateuch and the books of the prophets, of such phrases as "the Lord said," "and God spoke all these words saying," "thus says the Lord God," "the word of the Lord came to Ezekiel," and so on. There are also such variations as, "the word of the Lord that came to

Micah, . . . which he saw," and "the vision of Obadiah. . . ." In
other parts of the Old Testament this mode is completely lacking.
Such formulas disappear also in the New Testament except generally where the Old is quoted, for example, in the letter to the
Romans. In any case, whether attributed directly to God or to the
prophet, the words used exhibit the same vocabulary, the varieties
of style, the appropriateness to particular conditions and thought
forms and literary conventions—sometimes God speaks in poetry
and sometimes in prose—that are found elsewhere in the Bible
and other literature.

Language. The Old Testament is in Hebrew, a Semitic language from the ancient Near East, which reached its peak of
beauty and power in the psalms and prophecies of Israel. Jesus
spoke a kind of later Hebrew called Aramaic, although his
sayings and all accounts of him have come to us in a language he
did not speak, Greek. Papyrus finds in the last century showed
that it was the popular Greek of the time, although differences
from the classics encouraged the idea for generations that the
New Testament speech was a special vehicle for revelation. Since
all but an infinitesimal number of Bible readers are dependent on
translations, technical language skills are absolutely necessary in
order to make even the most elementary firsthand knowledge
available. Since every translation is inevitably part interpretation
and commentary, not least the one that aims to be literal, these
scholarly matters are a serious concern of the church.

The **thought forms** of various writings, related closely to the
languages, have fascinating histories. For instance, the term
"word," already discussed, has one history in Hebrew and another
in Greek. The creating and prophetic word of the Lord in
Genesis or Isaiah is very different from the word or logos of Stoic
or Platonic philosophy. The Greek translation of the Old Testament had mingled these two long before the time of Christ, and
the great Jewish theologian Philo created important devices for
linking Judaism to classical culture through the logos. These
were taken over by Christian thinkers. Controversies of immense
significance took place in which the teachings about Christ, creation, sin, and the trustworthiness of human reason were the

issues at stake. The same problems are still with us, and others of the same type. The Confession of 1967, for instance, depends heavily on an understanding of "word" that magnifies the uniqueness of revelation rather than the abilities of ordinary men to know the word of God through the use of unaided human reason.

A concept such as "people of God" has to be understood in terms of the peculiar history of Israel and the later status of Christians in Jerusalem and in the cities of the ancient world. There are other problems created when this phrase is translated into the situation of the state churches of Europe or the American denominations. Apocalyptic passages of Scripture exhibit **thought forms** puzzling to both learned and unlearned. Finally, what **thought forms** are we dealing with when we read that God "smelled the pleasing odor" of Noah's sacrifice, or conversed with Satan about Job, or that "unclean spirits" drove two thousand pigs to drown themselves in the sea, or that "it is shameful for a woman to speak in church," or that a man "was caught up to the third heaven"? These last are a miscellany that have in common only their presence within the canon and their strangeness to modern experience and **thought forms.** They further illustrate how the Scriptures reflect in more peripheral matters the places **and times at which they were written.** Either to ignore these varieties or to exaggerate them is to caricature the Bible which has as its main burden the **witness to God's work of reconciliation in Christ.**

Literary fashions, styles, and forms are very important in understanding the Scriptures. Poetry, history, letters, parallel accounts of the same event, strata showing various authors' contributions interwoven, or which show one book such as Isaiah to have three authors—all these matters which have long been commonplaces of Biblical study must be taken into account for responsible interpretation. Fine study Bibles make all these important matters available to any interested reader.

Much the same as above is to be said for the **views of life, history, and the cosmos** found in various parts of the Bible that have been long ago left behind. The view, for instance, that **life** is in the blood lies behind the sacrificial system (Lev. 17:11) as well as some of the dietary laws (Deut. 12:23) of the ancient Hebrews. History was a period of time, rather short, that began with Adam, the animals, then Eve, living in a garden of perfection and plenty. In some parts of the New Testament, history was expected to end rather soon with catastrophic events, and in other portions plans are being made for a longer future. The cosmos or picture of the physical universe that is either described or taken for granted in the Bible is, of course, antiquated by modern astronomy. It still holds, however, that these old forms continue to function as vehicles of revelation, once they are freed from crippling literalism (¶s 16-17).

Given this variety, **the church . . . has an obligation to approach the Scriptures with literary and historical understanding.** Anything else is a disservice to the way God chose to make himself known. His wisdom and providence have hid from the church what it has so often wanted—and so often pretended to have!— original manuscripts or their attested copies. The Bible has come to us through processes that we have an **obligation** to respect by appropriate, responsible study. The gospel is accessible to all, learned and unlearned, and all are to use what learning they have as an aid in hearing and obeying it.

The final paragraph, beginning **God's word is spoken to his church today,** will be discussed in connection with **preaching and teaching,** ¶ 49. Only one aspect cannot be allowed to wait until that point: **in dependence on the illumination of the Holy Spirit and with readiness to receive their [the Scriptures'] truth and direction.** It is hardly possible to remind the reader too often that the entire section on "The Bible" falls under the general heading, "The Communion of the Holy Spirit." Whether we use Calvin's favorite word **illumination,** or **guidance** and **direction** that are more common in this Confession, or various prayers from the New Testament, the intent is the same. Word and Spirit belong together and the hearing of the word is a gift of the Spirit, regardless of the amount of intelligence or learning that are brought to the hearing and reading.

CHAPTER 8

AIM OF THE CHURCH'S MISSION
(¶s 31-33)

To be reconciled to God is to be sent into the world. The force of the entire Confession is in this short expression. The first phrase, **to be reconciled to God,** is a concentrated summary of Part I. The last part of the sentence, **to be sent into the world as his reconciling community,** epitomizes Part II. The verb **is** holds them together like the pin in a hinge.

"Calling" and "sending," as they appear in the Bible, are as important to one another as two parts of a hinge. Patriarchs, prophets, and apostles were chosen only to be given a mission. Israel was called that through her all nations might benefit. Jesus sent off on a mission those he had called together (Matt. 28:19). The church maintains continuity with the apostles and with Israel by faithful obedience to his [God's] call. The church is a mission.

But the church is not a crusade. There is a thin line between the very different qualities of a mission and a crusade. Like the difference between a wage and a bonus, it can be carelessly crossed with prodigious results. A crusade sets out to change the world into what it is not. The church is a mission to invite the world to be what it already is: reconciled to God. God is not waiting for the church to succeed or for men to resolve their differences, but, so to speak, God is waiting for men to receive the fact of their oneness and to realize their true humanity. The oneness of humanity is his gift in "Adam" and in the "last Adam." The role of the church is to announce and demonstrate what this means. It may join hands with this or that crusade for special ends, but its own mission neither succeeds nor fails with a particular campaign. The church is entrusted with God's message of reconciliation (II Cor. 5:19) and it also shares his labor of healing the enmities which separate men from God and from each other (II Cor. 6:1). In this sense the church is his reconciling community, and for this reason Christ has called the church and given it the gift of the Holy Spirit.

The role of the church and its members is ministerial. A minister is a servant or agent who carries out missions for someone else. As Christ came to minister or serve (Matt. 20:28), his disciples are sent to do the same. This applies to both offices within the church and the whole people, indicated by titles such as "witness," "ambassador," "steward," and "servant."

"The Ministry of Reconciliation" which is "The Mission of the Church" gets its direction from the ministry of Jesus, as in ¶ 24. To say the same thing differently, the pattern for the church's mission is found in the life, death, resurrection, and promised coming of Jesus Christ.

"Body" of Christ is the most prominent metaphor for the church in the New Testament. This is not best understood as a "continuation" of the incarnation, but a relation to the risen Christ like that of a body to its head (Eph. 5:23). Each part of the body has a function to perform in carrying out the purpose or mission that the head determines (I Cor., ch. 12).

What Christ did in his own body is repeated for the third time in the Confession with slightly different selection and emphasis. We comment only on the chief theme. By his life as man and service to men he both involves the church in the common life of men and commits it to its mission. Every form of human well-being reminds us of the true humanity (¶ 8) and the new humanity (¶s 19, 32), as well as the power . . . to transform the world (¶ 15) that relate Christ to redemption and creation.

Jesus' suffering as well as his compassion and anger (¶ 24) makes the church sensitive to all the sufferings of mankind so that it sees the face of Christ in the faces of men in every kind of need (Matt. 25:35, 40). His crucifixion shows man's inhu-

manity to man, a naturalized phrase from the poet Robert Burns. Not only the fickle populace, the leaders of the people, the Roman officials and soldiers that directly brought about his death, but the closest and boldest followers of Jesus that "forsook him and fled" or denied him with curses were sharers of the work of Judas.

It is perfectly correct to identify the sufferings of other men with those of Jesus, as he himself did: "I was hungry and you gave me no food, I was thirsty and you gave me no drink, I was a stranger and you did not welcome me." Then the question, "Lord, when did we see thee hungry or thirsty or a stranger?" He replies, "As you did it not to one of the least of these, you did it not to me." There is profound irony in the incognito of God as man. Who would not have been hospitable to Him or even an angel undisguised (Heb. 13:2)? The instinct in legends and stories such as Saint Christopher or *The Story of the Other Wise Man* is sound. Any service or ministry to others, any cup of cold water, is for Christ, and any denial is complicity in the crucifixion.

The risen Christ and the hope of his coming again, promise fulfilled and yet to be fulfilled, first brought the church into being. **Victory** over everyday enmity, hatred, and misdirected zeal, reflected larger than in common life by the **complete obedience of** the victim, give **promise of God's renewal of man's life in society and of God's victory over all wrong.** It is not the success of this or that campaign or program on which the church pins its hope, but on the confidence that **God's purpose rather than man's schemes will finally prevail** (¶ 25).

All this is by way of saying in principle what Part II will now proceed to spell out more concretely, namely, what it means for the church to **confess Christ as Lord.** To call him Lord, to own up to him among men, to speak the gospel, and act toward others in this manner is to **live and serve** as a confessing Christian. "Not every one who says to me, 'Lord, Lord,' shall enter the kingdom of heaven, but he who does the will of my Father who is in heaven." (Matt. 7:21.) Hence, **the church follows this pattern in the form of its life and in the method of its action.**

CHAPTER 9

CHURCH FORMS AND ORDER
(¶s 34-40)

Institutions are ways in which societies do things together. Those who call themselves the people of God, or reconciling community, or church, like other societies, require institutional forms in order to do things in common. The church "invisible," when conceived as the church noninstitutional, is imaginary.

The institutions of the people of God, however, are meant to change and vary as their mission requires in different times and places. Growing tasks create new offices (Acts 6:1-7). Whenever institutional elements become ends in themselves, controlling the mission they were meant to serve, and when they are grounds of separation and rivalry, they defeat the ministry of reconciliation. Creeds and confessions, forms of common worship, administrative procedures, and mission strategies themselves have often been the ground of sectarian divisions, exclusive denominations, and rival factions which hide and distort the gospel. This melancholy story is too well known to need repeating here.

All institutions, like the habits of societies, tend to become fixed and intractable with age. Groups studying the Confession can produce for themselves examples of the lag of the church in the face of change. Hopefully, they will know also of aggressive change where the church is meeting new situations with new patterns and methods of action. In our ecumenical age, the churches are drawing together for common action at the same time history requires that their mission be more diversified and complicated. The two tendencies do not clash because the unity of the church is compatible with a wide variety of forms. Indeed, compatible may be too weak a term here, as if in some ideal state one form would or should prevail everywhere. Unity and fullness together expressed in ways appropriate to the varieties in human history would seem naturally to issue in many different forms (I Cor., ch. 9).

The Confession of 1967 stretches the forms and order of the church in tension between the two poles of its life, the personal and the communal. For the sake of mission in the world the members of the church are both gathered in corporate life and dispersed in society.

Few phrases in the Confession of 1967 were written and erased so often by the drafting committee as gathered . . . and dispersed. Their use in recent sociological and ecumenical discussion, it was feared, would cause the reader to import meanings rather than see them within the context of this document. Further, they are at best a bit too formal, and have the disadvantage of making the church appear like droplets of oil floating on water rather than in true identity with the world. Nevertheless, no words could be found that better express the twofold state and two-way movement of the church's life. The two terms remind us only that some things are done in concert and others solo, without either wholly losing the quality of the other. It would be pedantic to try to distinguish with complete precision which are the gathered and which the dispersed functions of the church, and which belong to both. The two movements are like the expansion and contraction of one beating heart.

Two misconceptions should be avoided. The gathered working of the church should not crush individuality. A clergy-ridden church, or one in which highly objective forms of worship prevail, tends to omit the personal from its common life. Dispersed, on the other hand, should not be thought of as isolated, individual existence where the Christian, like a fish out of water, is cut off from all sustenance. The mentality of diaspora, alien among enemies and longing for home, is not appropriate here. The Christian is in a certain sense not "of" the world, but he is truly and rightly "in" it. The two forms of the church's life are equally natural and necessary and neither has priority over the other.

Common actions of the church **gathered** are listed in ¶ 36. This may be the most concentrated paragraph in the entire Confession and one of the most comprehensive. It shows the rootage in the common life of the church of various inward and outward movements, all of which are discussed separately in other parts of the Confession. Because of the other discussions, we forgo individual treatment here. We suggest, however, that a rewarding study would be to trace each phrase to where it is treated more fully, and relate that place to the present theme.

The church disperses to serve God wherever its members are. It is not individuals who disperse, but the **church.** The **gathered,** concerted activities are no more "church" than what goes on when its members are **at work or play, in private or in the life of society.** The church is not limited to sacred precincts outside of which each member is on his own. The **prayer and Bible study, the witness, the daily action,** the **relation with other persons** of individual members are not carried on outside the church, but are a form of life in the church. This was stated above in different words in ¶s 20-25: **the new life takes shape in a community,** the **members of the church are representatives of Jesus Christ,** and they are **emissaries of peace.** The purpose of this conception is not to put a special stamp on Christians so that others may see the church in action—that occurs easily enough, for better or for worse—but to show the confessor that his confession is not pigeonholed in special words, times, and places. It comprehends the whole **new life** which he lives throughout his days.

More strongly, in ¶ 38: **Each member is the church in the world.** If the church can be called a body with parts or members, then each part is actually identified with the whole and each is the body in the special function he fulfills. "Now you are the body of Christ and individually members of it." (I Cor. 12:27.) Paul states it more bluntly when combating immorality in the church at Corinth. "Do you not know that your bodies are members of Christ? Shall I therefore take the members of Christ and make them members of a prostitute? Never!" (I Cor. 6:15.)

Each member is endowed by the Spirit with some gift of ministry and is responsible for the integrity of his witness in his own

particular situation. Each member acts and reacts in his own way
and place. Here tension may build up to the breaking point. It
did so in the primitive church when pious Jewish Christians were
shocked by the secular ways of converted Gentiles. The leaders
battled over this issue, and Paul accused Peter to his face of in-
sincerity (Acts, ch. 15; Gal. 2:11-16). Unconventional behavior
by those moving with change threatens old ways and fixed institutions, actually or apparently. The old description of a Christian
(as in Col. 3:18-25 and other tables of duties) begins to look stale
and hypocritical to some members, while it remains the bulwark
of church and family in the minds of others. Experimental new
forms shock those still happy with old forms. Neither all new
ways nor all old ways are vehicles of grace. The next two sentences deal with these tensions which are particularly strained in
American churches today.

On one hand, the man in a unique or changing situation is
entitled to the guidance and support of the Christian community.
He should not be cut off from the instruction, strength, and comfort (¶ 36) of the church because he is far out in new problems
of human relations or social order or theological thought that
conventional churchgoers fail to recognize. On the other hand,
the fellowship member remains subject to its advice and correction. Faulty as it may be, the community is or has the potential
to be the church, which no isolated person can be by himself.
Readiness to share the fellowship of hearing the word, of praise
and prayer, of the Lord's Supper, of common endeavor and
mutual criticism may mark the difference between a prophet-
reformer and a mere *enfant terrible*.

He in turn, in his own competence, helps to guide the church.
The interaction goes both ways. The church needs to know what
is going on, whether the problems are of youth or old age, thugs
or drugs, developing nations or the success of Jehovah's Witnesses. Those of experience and competence must be asked to
bring the best technical judgments to bear on issues and forces
that run through the life of the church, gathered . . . and dispersed. At the same time the purposes and goals, sensitivity to

both means and ends, the consciousness of sin, and the confidence of hope that reside in the Christian fellowship cannot be surrendered to technicians and specialists. Objectivity and commitment together will contribute better than either alone to the plans and programs of the church's mission.

. Those qualified are **set apart by ordination or other appropriate act and thus made responsible for their special ministries.** Ordination is by the church for a special function within or on behalf of the church. Those ordained are **set apart** and **made responsible** by the solemn promises found in *The Book of Order*. There are no sacerdotal differences between the ordained and unordained, but there are differences of function, responsibility, gifts, and training that are to be respected. Inflated clericalism and anticlerical laymen's movements are equally disruptive and foreign to proper **leadership** and **oversight.** The method of ordaining and installing leaders has varied in the history of the church. "Laying on of hands" was sometimes practiced in the New Testament church and is wisely continued if not treated as a piece of magic or the sole method of establishing legitimate offices.

Now follows a more general treatment of institutional forms. The church **orders its life as an institution with a constitution, government, officers, finances, and administrative rules.** These are not calamitous. They are to the church what tools are to a carpenter or instruments to a musician. The unhappy illusion that prayer and anthems are spiritual while finances are fleshly and commercial will not be fostered by the study of this Confession. Prayer can be very fleshly and budgets can be quite spiritual— depending on which is self-centered and which is in the service of the mission of reconciliation. Of course, budgets can become **ends in themselves** and thus subvert all other aspects of the church's life. The same goes for the **constitution, government, officers . . . and administrative rules.** Leaders and officers must beware especially of making the **instruments of mission** into bureaucratic **ends in themselves.** The church that has the right **to order and organize its own corporate life** is subject at all times to being **tested, renewed, and reformed** (¶ 36).

Just as in the case of creeds and confessions, **no one type of confession is exclusively valid, no one statement is irreformable** (¶ 3), so in the case of church order, different orders have served the gospel, and none can claim exclusive validity. Should the church be presbyterian in polity, or congregational, or episcopal, or a combination of the three, or something quite new and yet to be evolved? The Confession answers only that no given order or element in it **can claim exclusive validity.** This leaves the church of the Confession of 1967 open to new possibilities and free to change. But it forbids adopting or being taken into some non-reformable order. The bishop is a case in point. A bishop as a way or ordering the church is a live option. A bishop as a way of defining the church through a special right of ordination and control of the Sacraments is a very, very different matter. Merely to name an office "bishop" is neither here nor there. The issues at stake should be thoroughly canvassed whenever discussions of church union take place.

Why, then, a presbyterian polity? Because, says this short account, it is a good one. The claim is not made that graduated, Presbyterian judicatories are the only, best, or exclusively Biblical way to order the church. What is here written is a moderate justification that agrees generally with the "Preliminary Principles" in Ch. I of the Form of Government: "Every Christian Church, or union or association of particular churches, is entitled to declare the terms of admission into its communion, and the qualifications of its ministers and members, as well as the whole system of its internal government which Christ hath appointed."

Taking ¶s 38, 39, and 40 together, four principles seem to be at work: (1) **the responsibility of all members for ministry,** (2) **the organic relation of all congregations,** (3) **responsibility . . . for . . . special ministries, . . . for leadership and oversight,** and (4) **such reformation as may be required to make it [the church] a more effective instrument of the mission of reconciliation.**

It is fair to call the conception of the church put forward in this section functional, since everything is subject to the service assigned the church in the ministry of reconciliation.

CHAPTER 10

REVELATION AND RELIGION
(¶s 41-42)

The next two sections of the Confession, "Revelation and Religion" and "Reconciliation in Society," show two aspects of one mission as it confronts, first, world religions and, secondly, crises in society. Concerning **revelation and religion** we must begin with a caution.

The caution is that these paragraphs are not essays in comparative religion or philosophy of religion. They are hints for evangelism in today's world, meant to help the church confess its faith. If some of the distinctions imply a general theory of religion, this is incidental to the main purpose which is practical. A case in point appears already in the title of the section, "Revelation and Religion."

The term **revelation,** as we have already seen, points to God's disclosure of himself, to what comes to man from beyond himself. The terms **religion, religions of men,** and (note well!) **the Christian religion** point to things that come from man in response to revelation and reaction to the wonders and miseries of his existence. The distinction is primarily a way of conceding that not everything that goes under the name of the Christian religion belongs to the gospel, although the line between God's revelation and man's response can hardly be drawn with precision even in the Bible. Symbols, words, ideas, and practices derived from the gospel are embedded in all aspects of Western culture. Similar elements, not essential to the gospel, are taken for granted in church life and thought.

121

It is crucial in a world where Africa, Asia, America, and Europe are at one another's bedside and breakfast table to be able to confess a difference between **revelation** and **religion.** It is crucial because it is the gospel and not European-American Christianity that the church is commissioned to carry to all men. Much practical progress has already been made in expressing what this means. The days when missionaries made converts from other continents into tacit Englishmen, Americans, and Germans have largely passed. Churches in all parts of the world are received as full and equal members of the Christian ecumenical family. The United Presbyterian Church sends fraternal workers to far parts of the earth under the auspices of Ecumenical Mission rather than "foreign" mission with its stigma of the white man's burden. Still, it would be fatuous to claim that the gospel is often preached with the sensitivity, purity, and tact by which its own power is distinguishable from accompanying forces of Western culture. Really indigenous Christian thought, worship, and ethic are a thing of the future in most of the former foreign mission fields. Since the meeting of East and West is only beginning, the new synthesis of culture in which the gospel must make its way is still in its early stages of development. The problem of distinguishing between the cross we carry and the extra baggage we must discard, also within the West, is not going to be solved in a few words or a few years. The best minds and the wisest spirits will have to labor with these issues throughout the forseeable future. The task may play as large a role in the next century as foreign missions and the ecumenical movement, which have made the problem acute, have played in the last two.

Personal contact with men and institutions of other faiths and cultures makes more pressing a problem that always accompanies the preaching of the gospel: distinguishing between the word of God and the words and deeds of men. **The church in its mission encounters the religions of men and in that encounter becomes conscious of its own human character as a religion.**

The phrase **human character as a religion** and the **parallels** mentioned in the next paragraph refer to elements that superficially or profoundly resemble one another among the religions of mankind. Sacred assemblies, prayers, ceremonial songs and meals, ritual sacrifices, ethical concern, belief in a god or gods, alleged revelations, and so on, are widespread religious phenomena. The compromising nearness of some aspects of the Christian religion to similar features of sectarian Buddhism, or Islam, or secular humanism drives the Christian to ask what is the distinguishing quality of his own faith, both present and in history, that he brings to others.

We have already taken note that within the Christian Scriptures there are views of life, history, and the cosmos, as well as language, thought forms, and literary fashions that are vehicles of God's word rather than the word itself (¶ 29). Here again we read that God's revelation to Israel, expressed within Semitic culture, gave rise to the religion of the Hebrew people, and approximately the same comments apply.

Also, God's revelation in Jesus Christ was, as we have observed, the work of a time, a place, and a man among his own people. There were problems from the first arising from cultural differences among Jewish Christians and those of Gentile background, and between Greek-speaking and Palestinian Jews. Subsequently, both worship and doctrine reflected Greek and Roman culture, and as Europe became more civilized West and East meant different types of worship, doctrine, and Christian ethos. One could hardly hold that revelation was different in Europe from what it was in Constantinople, or that one was simply true and the other simply false. Rather, the Christian religion, as distinct from God's revelation of himself, has been shaped throughout its history by the cultural forms of its environment.

There is something artificial and abstract about the phrase as distinct from God's revelation of himself. It might, wrongly understood, lead to a theory of a wordless, actless, unhistorical gospel that becomes partially and distortedly shaped . . . by the cultural forms of its environment. As a theory in the history of religions or a Christian theological statement, this would be faulty. The only gospel we know is the one spoken to us. But the purpose of this paragraph is practical rather than theoretical, confessional rather than philosophical, and the statement is, as such, defensible. The purpose is to quicken in the average person the awareness that the gospel is not simply the First Presbyterian Church and its program, or even Protestant, or American, or Western Christianity—although hopefully none of these are bereft of the gospel. Rather, the gospel of grace and reconciliation is rightly both embodied in and critical of many religions and cultural forms. It should not be shocking to him that **the Christian finds parallels between other religions and his own and must approach all religions with openness and respect.**

The Bible's approach to other religions runs all the way from the mocking and murdering of the prophets of Baal (I Kings, ch. 18) to Paul's irenic effort to discover a point of contact with the philosophers at Athens: "What therefore you worship as unknown, this I proclaim to you" (Acts 17:23). Jesus seems to offer a wide range of strategies in telling his disciples to "be wise as serpents and innocent as doves" (Matt. 10:16).

The goal is not indifference. The Confession of 1967 is a 100 percent missionary document, which approaches every man as someone who needs God's grace and forgiveness. The **openness and respect** prescribed in approaching other religions is that with which a Christian should approach all things human. Much can be learned by the humble questioner, nothing by the zealous fanatic. The Christian should put his own faith on the line and test it in any competition if he wishes others to risk their faith in encounter with his. At the same time not every cult or faith deserves continued or equal respect. To contemplate sweetly and emptily without discrimination Zen, Christian Science, Islam, the Latter-Day Saints, voodoo, and dialectical materialism would be a form of stupor, not **openness and respect.**

Repeatedly God has used the insight of non-Christians to challenge the church to renewal. Who might they be? Marx? Freud? Gandhi? Bertrand Russell? Malcolm X? It may be the village atheist who is sick of religious sham but is sacrificially devoted to his fellowman, or a humanist killed on a march for racial equality. Any reader can ponder this statement with profit. It is the one who has never been so challenged who should probably not bother his head about it.

All forms of religion, including the Christian, are judged and found wanting by the reconciling word of the gospel. Religious institutions and practices, Christian laymen and leaders, the programs, causes, and campaigns that are launched in the name of Christ all fall short of their goals. "We have this treasure in earthen vessels, to show that the transcendent power belongs to God and not to us." (II Cor. 4:7.) These forms are not thereby to be abandoned, but tested, reformed, and renewed, and put to work again.

The gift of God in Christ is for all men. This is an evangelical statement, of a piece with the whole of Biblical and historical Christianity. The Confession, here and throughout, speaks wholly from within a Christian setting, not with bland neutrality. The uniqueness of the Christian message and the universal field of the Christian mission come from the "once for all" character of God's reconciliation in Jesus Christ. By contrast the "religious" and response elements are neither "once" nor "for all," but subject to change and variation. It is the gift of God and not every aspect of Christian religiousness that is for all men. The church, therefore, is commissioned to carry the gospel to all men whatever their religion may be and even when they profess none.

The last phrase requires one remark. Without entering the theoretical question of whether this or that practice or idea is hiddenly or openly "religious," the Confession adds this last phrase simply to be inclusive. No one is excluded because he professes no religion at all.

CHAPTER 11

RECONCILIATION IN SOCIETY
(¶s 43-47)

The prophets of Israel spelled out the meaning of covenant and law in foreign affairs, justice for the poor, public morality, and the fidelity or apostasy of rulers and people.

Jesus, similarly, expounded the law and illuminated the significance of his own ministry in contemporary terms of Jew and Samaritan, Pharisee and publican, rich and poor. One of his tasks, different from those of the prophets, was to separate his own role from the political fantasies of a people who no longer had a national future.

The personal and social ethics of the primitive Christian church are found in tables of duties from the letters (Col. 3:18 to 4:1; Eph. 5:22 to 6:9, or I Peter 2:13 to 3:7). In Romans, similar material particularly reminiscent of Jesus' teaching is combined with a discourse on obedience to governing authorities (chs. 12 to 14). The tables of obligations, styled after those of Stoic philosophers, show the working out of Christian love and the meaning of Christ as Lord in the family, the state, and daily labor. The positive view of government in the letters changes to antipathy in Revelation after Rome had become a sinister power threatening the church.

Change in these matters goes without saying. Old Testament judgments on nomadic hospitality, farm boundaries, or the right way to choose a king are not very helpful in Yonkers or Portland today. If love and justice are to be exercised in daily life, and if Christ is Lord of both church and world, then the church had better bestir itself and meet the world where it is today. Directly and indirectly, the church is active on many fronts at all times through its corporate life and the lives of its members. It may be active on too many fronts or on too few. It may dissipate its mission or shrink it to insignificance unless it pays attention to the world which is its mission field. **In each time and place there are particular problems and crises through which God calls the church to act.**

Crises **in society** are particularly pressing in the late twentieth century, and to some of these the next paragraphs are directed. The corporate church, determining the direction of its action, seeks first to be **guided by the Spirit.** This means hearing the Scriptures expounded and applied to present problems. It means prayer for illumination, and for the ability to hear and to respond. The church does not look down on the world from above, exempt from the problems with which it must deal. **Humbled by its own complicity** or complicity in injustice (¶ 32), it sees itself in solidarity with the confusion and wickedness that it also means to deal with. **All attainable knowledge** is called upon. High intent and eagerness do not cover for ignorance or vagueness; **guided, . . . humbled, . . . instructed,** the church seeks to **discern the will of God and learn how to obey in these concrete situations.**

To learn how to obey is a daily riddle of the sensitive Christian life. Some men respond once, in one way, and are stereotyped by that response. Both when and how to act must be studied thoroughly. Whether to address its own members (the most frequent action taken in the Presbyterian communions); or to address the government (as the Westminster Confession, Ch. XXXI, advocates "in cases extraordinary"); or to speak to the general public; or whether to urge action at the polls, or police action, or war, or civil obedience or disobedience, or public demonstrations; or whether to go underground, or keep hands off; or whatever—the action must arise from and must serve the reconciliation of men to God and to one another. Although it may be shrewd and wily action, it must also be "innocent"

(Matt. 10:16). If such a mission divides the fellowship, it may do so only when the gospel is at stake and then it does not so much divide as reveal the fellowship.

The church's confession of faith is not a policy or position paper, nor a specific program of action. At least this one is not. The Barmen Declaration was itself action against a law and it did divide the church, or, should we say, it called together the church from among those who were compromising with Hitler and inhumanity (below, Chapter 20). In the Confession of 1967 the specific kind of action is left to appropriate, timely, and orderly church decisions.

This section of the Confession of 1967 is a finger pointing at some of the most destructive enmities of modern man. It exposes their relation to God's reconciliation so that the church on its missionary journey cannot avoid them. The personal reconciliation of men to God and one another is obstructed in four ways: racial discrimination, international conflict, enslaving poverty, and sexual anarchy. Race, war, poverty, and sex do not exhaust the list. But they commit the church to these problems and to these kinds of problems.

At the end of each of the following paragraphs is a self-condemnation of the church by the church. It resembles in some ways the anathema lists of heretics in older creeds and confessions, or the negative theses of the Barmen Declaration. They are a magnifying mirror for individual and group self-examination.

RACIAL DISCRIMINATION

All peoples of the earth are included in the purposes and goals of human life described in ¶ 17, and none are excluded from the mission of the church. The metaphor, family and brothers, pictures the relation of all men viewed in Christ. There are not several saviors, several salvations, or several churches offered to men according to their color, culture, or customs. There is only one: "one body and one Spirit, . . . one Lord, one faith, one baptism, one God and Father of us all" (Eph. 4:4-6).

No provision is made anywhere in Scripture for the church to exclude anyone or to discriminate among men in any degree whatever, on racial, national, or cultural grounds. It is bluntly forbidden. "Here there cannot be Greek and Jew, circumcised and uncircumcised, barbarian, Scythian, slave, free man, but Christ is all, and in all." (Col. 3:11.) God's reconciling love thus **breaks down every form of discrimination based on racial or ethnic difference.**

Racial or ethnic difference refers in a common or colloquial way to varieties of features, skin color, and cultural patterns among large groups of mankind. Wisely, the words **real or imaginary** are added, for differences are easily blown up into exotic or threatening qualities and scaled as inferior or superior. Some groups in any race are more and some less educated, physically sound, or emotionally compatible with others, and the grounds for this may be quite complex. No matter. **The church is called to bring all men to receive and uphold one another as persons in all relationships of life.**

Mutual acceptance **as persons** is more than legal or institutional recognition. Civil rights is not enough. Formal integration does not bridge personal apartheid. One thing is needful: that **all men . . . receive and uphold one another as persons in all relationships of life.** Civil and economic freedom, integrated institutions, and so on, are necessary steps, advocated or hindered for a great variety of motives. The church will cooperate here and fight there, with or against specific tactics of nonviolent or violent, open or clandestine, attack on racial discrimination, depending always on how the goal of the full mutual acceptance of **one another as persons** is served.

These things are easily put on paper. But the writer, like many others, harbors special conditions for acceptance of people. Congenial, intelligent persons turn out to be very like oneself. This is predictable, given our recent history. It is also demonic and a blasphemy when it controls the life of the church. It is this that makes the **reconciling community** into its opposite, an exclusive club. The general remark about acceptance is followed by a list of selected particulars, familiar enough. We shall comment only on one, marriage and family.

The Confession of 1967 was being written, debated, and adopted through the years of Martin Luther King's nonviolent demonstrations, the march on Washington, and on into the time of rioting in black ghettos and the emergence of Black Power and black segregation movements. New civil rights legislation, which was once a distant goal, soon appeared to be the first mile in a long trip. In the first years of drafting the Confession, mention of marriage and family revealed inhibitions about going "too far." But the drafters were forced by the meaning of the gospel and the presence of haunting negations among both whites and blacks to write this subject into the list of particulars. In the Columbus, Ohio, United Presbyterian General Assembly (1965) it caused passionate debates, public and private, far into the night. But during the two years following, in the Boston and Portland assemblies, little or no opposition arose. This reflects in part rapid changes going on in the nation. More to the point, it was observable in the church that Christian people, when forced to think through the subject, discovered that no veto of marriages on the grounds of race could be derived from the gospel.

The paragraph does not prescribe marriage among couples of different races, or give pastoral advice for particular cases. There is never such a prescription for any marriage. Each couple must be counseled personally. However, the Confession does root out and absolutely prohibit the automatic, silent veto that is waiting in the backs of the minds of many people and many pastors when couples of mixed races plan to marry.

The all-American list of particulars should not stop the reader from seeing that this paragraph is not limited to the white-black race problem in America. It applies to the hundreds of millions of the peoples of the earth who are participating for the first time in the goods and services, enjoyments and perils, of higher economic, political, and cultural life. Peoples are arising to national life with mixed admiration and hatred for what has been an international white man's show since the rise of world travel four centuries ago. Every level of international and intercultural relations, as well as all levels of life in American farms, cities, and towns will be haunted by the specter of race hatred and fear for generations ahead. **Therefore the church labors for the abolition of all racial discrimination and ministers to those injured by it.**

Condemnation at the end of the paragraph falls on those who **exclude, dominate, or patronize their fellowmen, however subtly.** The three blows are of increasing deftness. In the United Presbyterian Church, which has done some splendid things to improve human relations, exclusion on racial grounds begins to be on the run. Domination, so far as conscious purposes are concerned, is probably diminishing. The patronizing attitude will be the slowest of all to die, not least within the doer of good who is often more anxious to give suggestions than to receive the true needs of his neighbor.

INTERNATIONAL CONFLICT

Peace, justice, and freedom among nations belong to the prime purposes of government. In the church, this conception is recognized as grounded on God's reconciliation in Jesus Christ, which gives a clue to the purpose of all human life in the created order (¶ 17). **All powers of government are called to serve and defend** these ends. The Christian individual and community are expected to cooperate with and support the rightful powers of government as explained in ¶ 25. Here as there, the positive relation is stated first.

Turning then to ruptures of peace, justice, and freedom, the Confession calls first upon the church **to practice the forgiveness of enemies** in its own life. Like charity, forgiveness begins at home. A church or individual embroiled in aggressive, vindictive measures against enemies is in no position to commend forgiveness to the state. But the church that recognizes its own call and mission shall rightly **commend to the nations as practical politics the search for cooperation and peace.** The Confession does not say how the church **commend[s],** but presumably direct address, formal or informal overture, and ways appropriate to the various talents of its members would be put in play. The church is not a state or government and does not generally have impressive economic or political power. While its pulpits and publications are free, it should be able to be heard. If it meets repression or imperviousness, it must find ways to be heard. The search for cooperation and peace is that part of the government's function in which the church, because of its mission, renders special help.

This requires, . . . that is to say, the search for cooperation and peace . . . requires the pursuit of fresh and responsible relations across every line of conflict. The upward spiral of pride, hate, and vilification that rises in time of conflict, particularly in time of war, is a field for the church's mission. More than once the Christian church has been drawn into the vortex where war fevers were inflamed, enemies cursed, and national policies blessed without examination or reservation. The reconciling community, servant of a Lord who reigns and reconciles on both sides of every battle line, by so doing betrays its calling. "We have no king but Caesar," were the last self-condemning words from the priests of God's people before the crucifixion of Jesus Christ.

National security is the solemn obligation of statesmen and governments. Calculated risk of national security is regularly forced upon national leaders. From Chamberlain at Munich to Johnson and the Vietnam war the security of many nations has been in constant delicate balance. The voiced will of the people, including the church, enters that balance. In the Confession of 1967 the phrase even at risk to national security places the pursuit of fresh and responsible relations across every line of conflict on the statesman's agenda, even in time of highest risk. The church does not manage the national safety, obviously, but it rightly commend[s] to the nations what their wounded and often demonic pride might cause them to ignore. Even when men are dying and vast areas lie in ruins, the church ought to "obey God rather than men" (Acts 5:29).

Modern instruments of war, nuclear, chemical, and biological weapons, in a world of increasing rivalry, make more pressing the need for reconciliation. Even when the threat of annihilation is an effective deterrent, maintenance of a war machine is destructive of itself. The awesome diversion of **manpower and resources from constructive uses** is a distortion of the national economy and credit structure. The building of private fortunes and impressive careers on weapons of annihilation is a grotesque scandal and a folly. A military establishment is necessary, but the church may not lose the perspective of the folly and weakness of the cross upon man's efforts at nuclear military strength.

The final warning, like what goes before, states first the positive: **nations may serve God's purposes in history.** But nations also by their cumulative pride and easily wounded honor may usurp the prerogatives of God. If the nation's sovereignty is taken to be absolute, and **one way of life,** say "the American way of life," is identified **with the cause of God,** then the freedoms and rights of others go to the devil. "Like the nations that the LORD makes to perish before you, so shall you perish, because you would not obey the voice of the LORD your God." (Deut. 8:20, and throughout.) When the church is party to narrow nationalism and overblown patriotism, it **denies the Lordship of Christ and betrays its calling.**

ENSLAVING POVERTY

One verse from the Bible might stand alone as the commentary on this paragraph. "But if any one has the world's goods and sees his brother in need, yet closes his heart against him, how does God's love abide in him? Little children, let us not love in word or speech but in deed and in truth." (I John 3:17-18.) The verse, however, needs translating.

Utter deprivation of the goods of the world is a form of slavery, and more than half the world's population is its victim. Clustered with such poverty are disease, ignorance, emotional incapacities, the cheapening and brutalizing of life. By poverty, the Confession does not mean the chosen poverty of monks, or even those merely less well off by the generous standards of Europe and North America, although there, too, an ample number of people live on bare subsistence.

Two grounds are given for the church's concern, over and above the general humanitarian instincts that are felt both within and outside the church. The first is the meaning and purpose of the world's goods to the lives of men. If the grace of God known in Christ is that of the Creator, and the creation is meant to be good and to serve men's needs (¶s 15-17), then **enslaving poverty in a world of abundance is an intolerable violation of God's good creation.** This is so regardless of the specific causes for poverty in one area or another. Secondly, **Jesus identified himself with the needy and exploited.** "The poor," in Luke's Gospel especially, and throughout the New and the Old Testament, are the special care of those who would obey the will of God. They are to receive from those better off, with no caveat about whether they are lazy, smell bad, or enjoy being poor. "Give to every one who begs from you." (Luke 6:30).

Alms for the poor, charity to beggars, and food for the hungry have been a self-evident part of the gospel throughout its history. Today, however, we do not give so directly. We refer the beggar to a city agency, and we assume that the blind man with a cup is trying to supplement his pension without doing the work of which the blind are capable. This does not mean that Jesus' teaching is irrelevant, but only that times have changed in some parts of the world. Long gone are the days when private, hit-or-miss charity or church budgets can adequately fulfill the command to give. These ways are inefficient at home and inadequate abroad, although they will always fulfill some functions better than any other means.

One index to the increasingly staggering problem of poverty in a world of astronomically increasing abundance is the rate of population growth. *Life* magazine reports that "in 1970 there will be more people living on earth than have died in all its history." This population will probably double within thirty years despite heroic efforts in some quarters to keep it under control. Not only gifts but plans must be made. The loathsome phrase "money down a rathole," which men in American public life have used for aid to depressed peoples, has a tinge of truth unless inclusive plans, including self-help, are developed. Population size is only one element in the list given in the Confession of causes of contemporary poverty: **The church cannot condone poverty, whether it is the product of unjust social structures, exploitation of the defenseless, lack of national resources, absence of technological understanding, or rapid expansion of populations.**

Tithing, informal charity, and philanthropy will continue, of course. The Christian is not relieved of his responsibility to men's needs by the existence of established agencies for meeting them. But beyond this, the tax-paying, voting Christian producer and consumer of goods and services is a part of the economics of wealth and poverty, freedom and slavery, from Vietnam to Tanzania. He is a disciple of Christ and a steward of creation also when he votes, buys, sells, and pays his taxes. The church is not a political party or an economic power bloc, but unless it wishes to speak in unknown tongues, it had better help its people to translate the command to give and to meet other needs of their neighbors in contemporary terms. This is what we mean by the "translation" of the Bible verse given above. On these grounds **the church calls every man to use his abilities, his possessions, and the fruits of technology as gifts entrusted to him by God.**

Probably the most pregnant sentence in this paragraph is that which says that the church **encourages those forces in human society that raise men's hopes for better conditions and provide them with opportunity for a decent living.** The blight by which the despairing cannot even raise their eyes is spread across the world mission field. To raise the hopes of the hopeless and hold out possibilities toward which they may strive is a contribution the church is peculiarly equipped for. The church lives from hope of a Kingdom already begun and yet to be realized. It is motivated by a faith that acts in love. It prays without ceasing, "Thy will be done on earth."

There are surely much higher hopes than those held out in this paragraph. However, **hopes for better conditions** and **the opportunity for a decent living** cannot be held back, if the church is to escape the curse: "Depart from me. . . . Truly, I say to you, as you did it not to one of the least of these, you did it not to me (Matt. 25:41, and following). Sometimes a hope held out in the name of Karl Marx appears more convincing to those in need than the Christian gospel. Marx at least taught men to look ahead. But if the church truly believes that reconciliation is accomplished, and will be consummated, and so lives, it need not fear the competition of Marx.

The negatives at the end of the paragraph hold up the mirror to American Christianity. It is the easiest thing in the world to be **indifferent to poverty** when one is not poor himself, and few Presbyterians are really poor. Squalor in India or Brazil, despair in South Africa or at the other end of Park Avenue, are too often borne with only momentary pangs, assuaged with a street gift on tag day. Not only in sentiment, and in sermon, but in the **economic affairs** of systems that create or continue the enslavement of millions, the church has a responsibility to fulfill. The church that is **open to one social class only** is familiar on the American scene. It is a natural development of congregations located in residential areas where the price of a house largely determines who lives near this or that church. Also, for related reasons, denominations tend to be typed economically. Probably few would admit to closing out those who do not speak, dress, or generally comport themselves like old-timers, but a look around next Sunday or next General Assembly may show that the one-class church still predominates even when neighborhoods have changed and the nation's population is highly mobile.

The harsh phrase about expecting **gratitude for its beneficence** is one from which few people and few churches can escape. It is a pleasure second to none to be applauded for generosity, but the pleasure of being thanked may destroy the subtle chemistry of giving. Most important, giving itself is an act of thanksgiving to God for which no thanks is due in return.

SEXUAL ANARCHY

The life together of man and woman is the world in miniature, an epitome of the love, mutual dependence, freedom, and fruitfulness **for which he [God] created mankind.** The range of human experience embraced when a man and a woman, different and complementary in every sensitivity, share existence, delight in physical union, make a living, a home, and raise a family, does **exemplify in a basic way God's ordering of interpersonal life.** By the same token, discord and destruction here mirror the universal miseries of the race. **Anarchy in sexual relationships is a symptom of man's alienation from God, his neighbor, and himself.** Anarchy means confusion, disorder, lack of principle for understanding and acting.

The Confession refers as well to **man's perennial confusion about the meaning of sex.** The history of Christianity is shot through with this anarchy and confusion. The Old Testament wholly affirms married life and the raising of children, although the role of a woman is culturally inferior to that of her husband. The New Testament is the same, with some added inclination toward celibacy, thanks to the squeamishness of the apostle Paul.

Always in the wings, and later in center stage, was total sexual abstinence as a religious ideal. Possibly the life of Jesus, his severe condemnation of lust, the later linking of his sinlessness with virgin birth and immaculate conception, and veneration of the perpetually Virgin Mother contributed to the celibate ideal. Both sexual excesses and ascetic strains in the surrounding ancient world encouraged withdrawal from family life among those most highly devoted to the gospel and the church. Augustine taught that inordinate desire was the root of sin, and sex its chief locus. Sin was thought to be passed along from parents to children in sexual intercourse. The ascetic ideal for men and women reached its zenith, and the celibacy of the clergy became church law during the European Middle Ages, when the cult of the Virgin Mother was most popular.

The Protestant Reformers swept all this away on Biblical

grounds in favor of married love and families for clergy and lay-men. Calvin more than others saw God's order and blessing in the family, although Luther was more hearty and candid about the physical facts of life. Some sectarian groups revived Old Testament polygamy, and were savagely crushed by both Rome and the Protestants. But while the Reformation elevated the family ideal, it still generally saw marriage mainly as useful for procreation and the control of lust. The finest statement from Reformation times is found in the Second Helvetic Confession (below, Chapter 17).

Great changes have come in our century both in the under-standing of sex and in the relations of men and women. The psychological force of sexuality is appreciated to be powerful in sectors of life once thought to be neuter. The many-sided eman-cipation of women—still far from complete—and the accompany-ing possibilities for enrichment and also for impoverishment of family life may be the most fundamental changes taking place in our society. Probably the most important omission in this para-graph (written by men) is attention to the inner conflicts caused by the steadily and inevitably changing role of women. The Con-fession of 1967 manages to cite some of the most critical problems in the relations of the sexes and shows readiness to face them. If it does not move far toward their answer, at least it commits the church to work on them.

Confusion about the meaning of sex, which has just been acknowledged for the church, **has been aggravated in our day by . . . new means for birth control.** Family planning has been widely practiced for decades as a benefit to both mothers and children. The statement here seems, however, to refer to **new means,** which have a much wider implication than family plan-ning. Contraceptive pills and small mechanical devices are used by millions of women in all parts of the world to control repro-duction. Granting first the values of easy contraception, especially for large-scale population control, problems of meaning arise. At hand is the wholesale enjoyment of casual sex apart from life together in marriage and family. Removal of restraint does not produce freedom or meaning. In this case it threatens to issue in barrenness, triviality, isolation, and emptiness, all of which are forms of bondage to self.

Suffering among children and adults has been immensely lessened by means for the **treatment of infection** connected with intercourse and reproduction. The more or less natural deterrents of syphilis and gonorrhea, understood commonly as punishment for illicit sex adventures, still ravage victims by the millions. Constantly more effective and convenient methods for prevention and treatment are saving lives and lessening misery, and at the same time they make impersonal sex episodes easier.

The massing of people in cities and the staggering problems of **world overpopulation** are questions in themselves. Here the issue is the effect of increased numbers and crowding on the quality of human life and the meaning of reproduction. Should hordes of persons be born only to die in infancy or to live meanly for no reason but the undirected sex drives of their progenitors?

A problem of another variety is **the exploitation of sexual symbols in mass communication.** This nicely resounding phrase refers to cheap sex in advertising, a subject on which material is common enough not to need elaboration here. Study groups will find themselves soon embroiled in questions of social responsibility for mass media for which satisfactory answers appear to be a long way off.

The church, as the household of God, is called to lead men out of this alienation into the responsible freedom of the new life in Christ. According to the letter to the Ephesians, the **household of God** is made up of those who were formerly "separated, . . . alienated, . . . strangers, . . . having no hope" and are now reconciled (ch. 2:11-21). In another place the relation of husband and wife symbolizes the "great mystery [of] . . . Christ and the church" (ch. 5:32). It is not too much, then, to expect that the church should contribute by every means it can devise to reconcile the alienated sexes and to enrich the enjoyment by men and women of life together in their homes.

The church does not have a special supply of technical information. Here as elsewhere there is a duty to be instructed by all attainable knowledge. The physiology, psychology, and sociology of sex, and the pathology of all these, are to be learned from those who know most responsibly and thoroughly. The church must be informed, and it must allow the light of the gospel of reconciliation to expose what newer and better knowledge means for the relation of persons to each other and to God.

The beautiful love lyrics of The Song of Solomon apparently entered the canon of Scripture as allegories of God and his people and stayed on as allegories of Christ and the church. They may yet come into their own as joyous celebrations of the delights of physical beauty and sexual union.

The latter part of ¶ 47 reads something like the "duty tables" of some of Paul's letters, although it does not so much exhort as describe what reconciliation produces: **joy** and **respect** for the humanity of oneself and others, **mutually shared life, sensitive and lifelong** concern, and the **grace to care for children in love.** This is a good if partial list of expressions showing some of the qualities of existence in the Christian home and more generally the direction in which the gospel points the church.

The negative judgments at the end of the paragraph fall on the church under two conditions: when it fails to help and when it withholds compassion. Probably the two could be brought together as compassionate help. Throwing stones at offenders, as Jesus seemed to know, distracts attention from the similar guilt of the accuser (John 8:7). Casting platitudes has approximately the same effect on both parties as throwing stones. The **compassion of Christ** should flow from the church toward **those caught in the moral confusion of our time.**

CHAPTER 12

EQUIPMENT OF THE CHURCH
(¶s 48-52)

The writer of the letter to the Ephesians, after an eloquent passage on the oneness of the church—"one Lord, one faith, one baptism, one God and Father of us all"—moves on to the varieties of gifts that the church receives. Then he returns to the oneness of the church under the figure of a body of which Christ is the head. The varieties of gifts are for the growth and strength of the one body. "But grace was given to each of us according to the measure of Christ's gift. . . . And his gifts were that some should be apostles, some prophets, some evangelists, some pastors and teachers, for the equipment of the saints, for the work of ministry, for building up the body of Christ." (Eph. 4:7, 11; also, ch. 6:10-20.) This theme of a variety of gifts for the equipment and upbuilding of the one body is extended here in Section B of the Confession of 1967. The opening paragraph (¶ 48) lists in advance the various elements that follow.

More interesting, probably, than any specific subject in what follows is the conception that these gifts are the equipment of the church for its mission. In a way that we are now well aware of, this Confession stresses function and movement, which is, after all, quite appropriate to a body. A body that is groomed and cared for to no end but its own health and comfort might have Narcissus for its head, but not the Christ of the Great Commission.

The gifts are permanent in the church, they remain. But they are not to be held in some fixed, unalterable form while the rest of the world goes by. The possibilities for new development are limitless. The church is obliged to change the forms of its service in ways appropriate to different generations and cultures. Probably the prime example in most minds of an unchanging form of service is the Latin Mass of the Roman Catholic Church, now at last put into the language of the people. However, the lag and fixity of forms of worship extends across all lines of division. The free worship and free prayer so prized by some Protestant groups turns out often to be more repetitious and predictable than the regular cycles of more formal worship—and less rich. There is no more virtue in change for its own sake than resistance to change for its own sake. Worship has a purpose and an end. Its forms should be directed toward that end among those who participate.

Much of what appears in the next paragraphs, especially ¶s 49 and 50, has been said already in earlier parts of the Confession. This is perfectly normal, since the church and its mission cannot be abstractly separated from the means by which the mission is carried out. Also, quite clearly, ¶ 36 on the church gathered (and also ¶s 29 and 30) is the immediate ground for much that is written here. What follows is directed specifically to the literal gathering of the members of the church in public assembly for common worship. The church's Directory for Worship (which was rewritten and adopted into the Constitution of the church before the Confession of 1967 was completed) contains more explicit directives by which the actual form and content of public worship in the congregation are arrived at.

Preaching and Teaching

The opening words of the next two paragraphs point to two movements or actions in public worship as in all aspects of receiving the gospel. God instructs (¶ 49) and the church responds (¶ 50).

Preaching is primarily announcement, and teaching is the educational strategy through which the announcement is made understandable. Preaching is not identical with the Sunday sermon, nor is teaching identical with a classroom, for either situation is appropriate for either activity, depending upon special conditions. Innumerable other situations are appropriate to both. By "preaching" we mean primarily what is preached. Calling it an announcement or proclamation indicates that what is preached is not to be derived from the hearer or catechized out of him as Socrates drew geometry from a slave. Rather, it is always fundamentally the underivable, unexpected, sheerly gracious gift of the message of salvation. When put into words or pictures or any other medium that will carry it, the message is passed along and the church is built up by it. Teaching has more to do with preparing both the recipient and the "preacher," with elaborating the message, and with tracing out its significance. Where the two activities converge, there is no clear dividing line, but where they diverge these descriptions are apt. Calvin was able to use the same word, *doctrina,* for both preaching and teaching, allowing the context to make the distinction.

Preaching differs from other discourse by its content. It is to be carried on in fidelity to the Scriptures and dependence upon the Holy Spirit. Both these elements, particularly when expressed in the sermon before the assembled community, impose a discipline and a limit on the preacher. He is not to substitute his own message for the Biblical one, nor is he to preempt the occasion for sundry private errands and causes, however beneficent. If the sermon does not have reconciling grace as its leitmotiv, it probably does not deserve the name "preaching." This is not a constricting feature, for grace ramifies into every subject imaginable, but it is a directing feature, for grace gives a direction and a tack by which to move toward a goal. It is conceivable that a sermon could be quite "secular" in vocabulary and subject matter and yet be unambiguously the communication of the grace of God. It is conceivable also that a sermon could be quite Biblical in vocabulary and "religious" in subject matter, and yet be utterly graceless. Who has not in fact experienced both?

Dependence upon the Holy Spirit is a carefully worded phrase.

The whole process of preaching and teaching is from beginning to end thus dependent. The Spirit is not a method beside other methods, or a special touch to be achieved by a sudden turning of the mind to the Spirit before or after such other things as study and writing are undertaken. The Spirit is in, with, and under all processes of study, preparation, and action. Nor is the Spirit a substitute for the full use of human powers, as if grammar or philology or clear sentences were inferior to or independent of the Spirit.

The aim of preaching and teaching, or proclamation and instruction, is that the people hear the word of God and accept and follow Christ. Preaching and teaching, thus, are instruments and devices, or pieces of equipment by which a task is completed. Approximately the same was said in the concluding section on the Bible. God's word is spoken to his church today where the Scriptures are faithfully preached and attentively read in dependence on the illumination of the Holy Spirit and with readiness to receive their truth and direction (¶ 30).

An easy misunderstanding of preaching, not so common for teaching, is that the character of announcement or proclamation makes it something peremptory, one-sided, that can be done without full attention to the hearer. But it matters not that the word has been spoken in words that sound in the air unless they are in a known tongue and arrive in the mind of the hearer. None of the gifts result in ceremonial acts, repeated for their own sakes, but have their function among those who hear, see, and respond. An obtrusively pious woman in one community was known to toss folded Scripture verses from her car to pedestrians, even hitchhikers, as she whizzed by. This version of the "foolishness of preaching" does truly appear foolish, but it is questionable as preaching. Polished homiletical pellets tossed from very stylish pulpits are sometimes not far removed from this caricature in either relevance or effect.

The message is addressed to men in particular situations. There is much experimentation today with dialogue sermons, television spots, jazz liturgies, even the provisional dropping of all obvious sermon and worship for other kinds of communal experience.

However strange and exotic the forms may often appear—and some are certainly less relevant than what they are meant to replace—the principle is sound that **hearing** belongs to **preaching and teaching,** and the preacher and teacher cannot dodge the need to find an idiom that can be grasped.

Therefore effective preaching, teaching, and personal witness require disciplined study of both the Bible and the contemporary world. Karl Barth's remark that the Christian should have the Bible in one hand and the newspaper in the other is a good symbolic statement of this teaching of the Confession. Missing, however, in his remark, is **disciplined study.** Casual knowledge, or even the diligently pursued interests of laymen, in neither area will suffice for the church. The everyday reader of the Bible, like the man-in-the-street voter, can learn a lot if he half tries, and his judgment will be valuable and important. But a treadmill of superficiality results in both instances if finely trained minds and good leadership are not forthcoming. Specialized Bible studies will never be ended. Some decades and some centuries will be poorer and others richer in bright new insights or archaeological finds, but unless fresh, firsthand work continues to inform **preaching and teaching,** the message of the church will quickly have the quaint sound of old phonograph records. The Reformation began in the universities, its greatest leaders were learned teachers, and it was a rare bird among the minor Reformers who was not a competent scholar.

There is a second reason why **the contemporary world** also is part of the **disciplined study** required for **effective preaching, teaching, and personal witness.** There may be no shrinking back or covering up of anything that describes and helps understand and evaluate current developments in history. There is truth in the cliché that human nature never changes. But this can be also a cheap dodge to avoid changes that are actually taking place. Changes in society are automatically changes in the church. The church thus needs to understand the contemporary world even to comprehend its own life. Two elements of this statement require separate mention.

First, the **contemporary world** belongs to the providence of

God and may not be treated with contempt. The four-hundred-year-old words of Calvin are quite up to date: "If we regard the Spirit of God as the sole fountain of truth, we shall neither reject the truth itself, nor despise it wherever it shall appear, unless we wish to dishonor the Spirit of God" (*Institutes,* II.ii.15). Then he goes on to praise pagan culture in a series of rhetorical questions. "What then? Shall we deny that the truth shone upon the ancient jurists who established civic order and discipline with such great equity? Shall we say that the philosophers were blind in their fine observation and artful description of nature? Shall we say that those men were devoid of understanding who conceived the art of disputation and taught us to speak reasonably? Shall we say that they are insane who developed medicine, devoting their labor to our benefit? What shall we say of all the mathematical sciences? Shall we consider them the ravings of madmen? No, we cannot read the writings of the ancients on these subjects without great admiration. . . . Those men whom Scripture [I Cor. 2:14] calls 'natural men' were, indeed, sharp and penetrating in their investigation of inferior [that is, earthly rather than revealed truth] things. Let us, accordingly, learn by their example how many gifts the Lord left to human nature even after it was despoiled of its true good." (*Ibid.*) Any twentieth-century man can increase this list almost indefinitely. We are still to "raid the Egyptians as the Israelites were commanded to do" if we are to make a successful journey.

Secondly, there is another reason for **disciplined study . . . of the contemporary world,** and that is to discover where the church is rightly "in" the world and where it must see itself as not "of" the world. The gospel, too, can become a cliché of culture. The church, too, can become just one institution along with others, indistinguishable from its milieu, if it does not constantly examine its own actual life in the society in which it exists. Like the historical researcher who looks into the well of history and manages to see only his own face looking back at him, or the artist who, seeking to express subjectivity, succeeds only in putting on canvas the walls and corners of the garret in which he has sequestered himself, the church that is uncritical of its own life in the world and the world's penetration of the church will have crippled and deformed its own mission. If the church is truly oriented toward the future, animated by hope, and confident of God's providence, it will not and cannot be—what it so often appears to be—a fortress for the defense of everything old-fashioned.

The last sentence of this paragraph does not add much to the foregoing, except to focus on **public worship** in the setting we have just been describing. What it is aimed against is regarding worship as a kind of oasis in life, a moment of elevation, set apart from either worldly work or churchly mission. It may have something of this character, and so may a symphony concert or a view of the Alps, and such experiences in worship and otherwise are not condemned. When this tempting aspect predominates, however, it steals away from rather than contributes to **responding with fitting obedience in the particular time and place.**

PRAISE AND PRAYER

The church responds . . . in **praise and prayer.** The psalms of Israel are the prototype and pattern of all praise and prayer. Throughout the Scriptures are hymns of praise in many forms among the writings of the prophets, in the epistles of Paul, and elsewhere.

Adoration is here called **acknowledgment,** a rather prosaic term for so elevated a response. But **acknowledgment** is helpful, for it means both recognition of a state of things and acceptance of it. **Acknowledgment of the Creator by the creation** owns up that the Creator is Creator and the creature is creature. In pure **adoration** there would be no usurping of the divine, no rebellion, and no undue self-abnegation. The Confession of 1967 reads **by the creation** rather than merely by man, because man is seen as the representative of creation, praising God on behalf of all things.

Confession of sin is a movement within adoration by which the sinful creature acknowledges and deplores his sin and owns the need for forgiveness. No one man is a sinner all alone, but lives in solidarity with others and thus admits **all men's guilt before**

God. The sequence is quite important. **Confession of sin** does not precede **adoration,** because sin is always secondary to the fact of God's creation and his consummation of all things. Sin is something which comes in between. Although it destroys and disrupts, it is never the first fact or the last, but always in the parentheses between **adoration** and **thanksgiving. Confession** is the least independent element of praise and prayer because sin itself is not independent, but is the deprivation or destruction of something else which has independent existence. It, nonetheless, cannot be omitted. **Confession** is the acknowledgment of it and at the same time acknowledgment of the **need for his forgiveness.** The occasion for the whole drama of salvation is man's sin: it is always present as that which has been and is to be overcome, but it is always present in the second rank of praise and prayer, not the first.

Thanksgiving is rejoicing in God's goodness. The creature-sinner, forgiven, rises again to give thanks. The undeserving recipient praises the One from whom all blessings flow for his **goodness,** for **healing,** and for **deliverance.** Thus thanksgiving embraces both the gifts of creation and the gifts of redemption. In public worship, **thanksgiving** is uttered with words and with gifts. But the worship "service" is but part of the total "service" or ministry of the Christian. While all elements of public worship live on in the daily life of the worshiper, **thanksgiving** preeminently is the posture, the mien, of the Christian life.

Closely related to **thanksgiving**—not its opposite or its unfortunate companion concept, but its completion—are **petitions and intercessions.** Very often the prayer of petition is thought of as a selfish prayer, and it easily becomes that. When prayer degenerates to repeated begging for things desired, it may reflect an infantile personality. But request lies close to the center of prayer, and when rightly expressed, reflects the Biblical childlikeness that is very different from infantilism. In the Heidelberg Catechism, prayer is the "chief part" of thanksgiving, and petition is the chief part of prayer. Thanksgiving projected into the future is petition, for it means that not only in the past and present but forever the creature is dependent upon, expectant of, and will be grateful for, the gifts of the Creator and Redeemer. These gifts of God are not capital to be taken over and privately owned and increased by effort or ingenuity, but they are *daily* bread and *daily* forgiveness, expected and confidently requested as by children from parents. "The steadfast love of the LORD never ceases, his mercies never come to an end; they are new every morning." (Lam. 3:22-23; cf. Deut., ch. 8.)

The arts, especially music and architecture. Back toward the beginning of the Confession (¶ 17) we read that **man is free . . . to use his creative powers for the fulfillment of human life.** The creative arts are there mentioned in a brief but important way. Here, specifically, artistic creation is seen as a contribution **to the praise and prayer of a Christian congregation.** These two aspects, **the fulfillment of human life** and **praise and prayer** are completely harmonious yet not identical. It would be a mistake to try pedantically to define and relate the two. It would be utterly deplorable to try to parcel out works of art between them. The point here made is simply that the doors are open and the air is free for the creative artist to make his contribution to the praise expressed by the community in common worship. It could scarcely be open more widely or more freely than in the proviso with which the sentence ends: **when they help men to look beyond themselves to God and to the world which is the object of his love.**

The mention of **music and architecture** and the setting in this paragraph of **praise and prayer** causes one to think immediately of church buildings and public worship—and that is its purpose—but it is not meant to present a general theory of the relation of gospel and church to the arts.

BAPTISM AND THE LORD'S SUPPER

Baptism and the Lord's Supper are each a large and complicated subject matter in history and theology. They have been profoundly restudied in recent decades in many Christian communions. They do not, however, comprise a major emphasis of the Confession of 1967, nor is there a fresh contribution made to the subjects in what is here printed. The chief accomplishments are two:

First, as with other parts of Section B, Baptism and the Lord's Supper are set in the perspective of the church's mission. They are not allowed to swirl into a side eddy of specialized interest or effete concern with costume and pageantry. They are gifts of God essential to the upbuilding of the church, joyful and exhilarating reminders that the **new life** has begun and the **kingdom** is promised. They set forth the same message of reconciliation and the same promise of consummation as do the words written and spoken, but in the quite physical power, sparkle, crispness, color, and flavor of bread, water, and wine that have nourished and gladdened men from prehistoric times. These gifts of Providence are here presented as gifts of grace by the Lord who is both Redeemer and Creator.

Secondly, as is already apparent in the writer's enthusiasm, both are celebrations of the **renewal of the covenant** and the **reconciliation of men with God and with one another.** Both look forward, both imbue men with hope, and both embrace the whole gathered and dispersed community and invigorate it for its mission in the world.

Jesus' baptism by a surprised and unwilling John was the prototype of the baptism he was later to command for all his disciples. In this act he allied himself with the needs of all men and received the power of the Spirit to enter upon his public ministry. As the event that inaugurated Jesus' ministry it might be called the first rite of the Christian faith as the Lord's Supper, instituted just before his death, was the final one. It is appropriately the ceremony of entry into the Christian community.

The Spirit is what distinguishes baptism from all other practical kinds of washing or, as Luther said, from ordinary bath water. The Spirit's role is presented in three Biblical figures that appear in the next sentence—cleansing, rising with Christ from death, and the spiritual birth by which the **new life** begins.

John had preached a water baptism for repentance and promised that another would come who would baptize "with the Holy Spirit and with fire" (Matt. 3:11). The cleansing from sin, or the purging and purifying of the Spirit, continues to be the readiest at hand of these figures, probably because of the daily use of water for cleansing of all kinds. Probably the practice of total immersion of the one to be baptized contributed to the interpretation by the apostle Paul of baptizing as being buried and raised from the dead as Christ was raised (Rom. 6:4). It is, as the Confession puts it, a joyful rising that "we too might walk in newness of life." It would be hard to find a more dramatic public ceremony to make this significance clear. It commits all Christians to die each day to sin and to live for righteousness. Historically, from the earliest times, there has apparently been baptism by the pouring and sprinkling of water as well as by immersion. The method is not prescribed, so long as water is used, but undoubtedly the conscious and unconscious effects of the various methods and surrounding ceremonies are a strong influence on the various Christian communions.

In baptism the church celebrates the renewal of the covenant. Baptism belongs within the assembled people. It should not be a private or even a family ceremony. Although the centuries-long custom of having a baptistry near the entrance to a church has an obvious appropriateness for a rite of entry, it is even more appropriate that baptism take place entirely within and among the assembled people. The whole church celebrates renewal with each new baptism, child or adult.

As already mentioned, by baptism individuals are publicly received into the church. But as natural life is both gift and task (¶ 17) the Christian life has the same qualities and the newly received persons are expected to share in its [the church's] life and ministry. The responsibility is mutual. The church becomes responsible for their training and support in Christian discipleship.

A quaintly worded question of the Westminster Larger Catechism puts the matter splendidly. The question is, "How is our

Baptism to be improved by us?" The word "improve" formerly
meant "to use" or "employ." The answer is, in part: "The needful
but much neglected duty of improving our Baptism is to be per-
formed by us all our life long, especially in time of temptation,
and when we are present at the administration of it to others, by
serious and thankful consideration of the nature of it, . . . by
growing up to assurance of pardon of sin, . . . by drawing
strength from the death and resurrection of Christ; . . . and by
endeavoring to live by faith, . . . and to walk in brotherly love"
(Q. 167). It would be fitting to say that both the individual and
the whole church should "improve" every baptism through training, support, and when those baptized are infants, by Christian
nurture. Baptism is not so much the end and the dying off of the
old as the beginning of the new. Both children and adults should
be strengthened throughout their lives to make, by a public profession, a personal response to the love of God shown forth in
their baptism. Although the last words refer obviously to the
receiving of the young into full church membership, presumably
the broader interpretation given is also agreeable to the text.

The last supper together of Jesus with his disciples, which was
also the first Lord's Supper of the church, was a solemn meal,
prelude to the crucifixion. Nonetheless, it contained a thanksgiving (Luke 22:19) that was so prominent as to give the name
"thanksgiving," or "Eucharist," to the future rite. While it was
a meal of parting and of dimly feared threatening events just
ahead, it also contained a promise that they would eat together
again in the Kingdom (v. 16).

The early celebrations of the church, "the breaking of bread,"
for instance (Acts 2:42, 46), and the memories recorded in Acts
10:41-42, show that the primitive church not only looked back to
Jesus' death, but celebrated his resurrection and looked forward to
his coming (I Cor. 11:26). There are problems as to which of the
early assemblies correspond to the Supper, but it is clear that in
Corinth a common meal of the church culminated in the Lord's
Supper. Paul's account of the proper celebration is given because
the occasion had become both boisterous and divisive. He re-

viewed the correct celebration and correct bearing of those participating (I Cor. 11:17-34). At least we are sure that the early observances of the church were not memorial services for a dead man, but occasions of praise and thanksgiving for the resurrection, for salvation accomplished, and for the lively expectation of his promised coming. The Confession of 1967 sums it up in these words: **The Lord's Supper is a celebration of the reconciliation of men with God and with one another, in which they joyfully eat and drink together at the table of their Savior.**

The meal is, of course, a remembrance of his dying (I Cor. 11:24-25). The crucifixion and the complicity of all men in it is brought vividly into the present at the Communion Service. This excludes careless and superficial observance. At the same time, in various periods in the life of the church, especially the Western Church and often in today's Protestantism, the cross and the conviction of sin so predominate that many a congregation appears remorseful and comfortless at the Lord's Table. Unrelenting self-examination and fear of profaning the Sacrament by unworthy eating suppress the joy and hope that the Lord's Supper is meant to engender.

According to the older confessions (below, Chapter 21) as well as in the present statement, **Christ himself is the active present agent in the communion with him and with all who shall be gathered to him.** Those asembled, partaking in faith, **receive from the risen and living Lord the benefits of his death and resurrection.** This Confession does not deal with problems of how Christ is present, how grace operates, or the like. Recent study and considerable common agreement on these matters appears in the Arnoldshain Theses prepared by European Lutheran and Reformed churchmen and in reports of more recent discussions in America published under the title *Marburg Revisited*. All these studies reject efforts to pinpoint the presence of Christ by one formula or another, and stress his work through the whole liturgy. One of the errors of the Reformation time was too great preoccupation on all sides with the manner of Christ's presence. The present statement is not naïve, but it is wholesomely simple when it says partaking in him as they eat the bread and drink the wine in accordance with Christ's appointment. The questions about how the communion differs during the Lord's Supper from some other time do not appear to be of ready enough solution to find place in a confessional writing.

Having received, they rejoice. The final thanksgiving prayer is the expression of the common rejoicing of the people that should be their spiritual posture day in and day out. At the end they go out. The going out is part of the same fellowship. The members are now renewed in courage and hope for the service to which he has called them.

One of the Arnoldshain theses sums up the past, present, and future reference that is also in this paragraph. "In the communion we commemorate the death of Christ, through which God has reconciled the world to himself once and for all. In it we confess the presence of the Risen Lord in our midst and joyfully await his return, as those called to share his glory in the final consummation."

The Lord's Supper is a foretaste of the kingdom. Appropriately, we now turn to the final part of the Confession, "The Fulfillment of Reconciliation" which is the rule of Christ in his Kingdom.

CHAPTER 13

FULFILLMENT OF RECONCILIATION
(¶s 53-56)

It is not inappropriate to designate the three chief parts of the Confession of 1967 by the names of Faith, Love, and Hope. Part I dealt chiefly with what God has done in redemption and creation and how men receive the benefits of these works through Christ in faith. Part II and, of course, the paragraphs on the new life showed faith active in love toward other men. Part III looks forward to the fruition of God's work in eternal life and the Kingdom, which is the dimension of faith and love called hope.

Hope is not a coda fastened on to the end of a long composition to show that it is over. It is itself one of the movements of the symphony. Or again, like the roof on a house, it is integral to the whole building and makes all the rest habitable. The quickest way to recall that this expectation has been present throughout the Confession is to note that the section on Jesus Christ and that on new life both culminated in paragraphs on eternal life (¶s 11 and 26). It was stated on the strength of ¶ 32 that the church's mission derives both strength and humility from its hope rather than its achievements, and again that the strength of individual emissaries of the gospel is in their confidence that God's purpose rather than man's schemes will finally prevail (¶ 25). And of course the last paragraph on the Lord's Supper spoke of rejoicing in a foretaste of the Kingdom (¶ 52).

God's redeeming work in Jesus Christ embraces the whole of man's life. Not only man and his works, but man's natural environment as exploited and despoiled by sin shall be brought into

155

harmony with divine purpose. The apostle Paul writes that "the creation was subjected to futility, . . . [but will itself] be set free from its bondage to decay" (Rom. 8:20, 21). It is the ultimate unity of the purpose of God in creation and redemption (¶s 15-17) that enables the Christian to hope that God's purpose for human life shall be fulfilled under the rule of Christ and all evil be banished from his creation. "For he must reign until he has put all his enemies under his feet." (I Cor. 15:25.)

The visions and images of the rule of Christ listed in the second paragraph on fulfillment, drawn from The Psalms, the teachings of Jesus, and the Apocalypse, are said to culminate in the image of the kingdom: "Then comes the end, when he delivers the kingdom to God the Father after destroying every rule and every authority and power" (I Cor. 15:24). The political imagery of power and harmony and the pomp and glory of the throne are prominent in the Old Testament as well as the New, summing up the culmination of salvation.

Again, as we have noted many times throughout this commentary, hope is not a detached fragment of imagination expressed by the futile song of the prisoner, "If I had the wings of an angel, o'er these prison walls would I fly." Hope is not an extension of human desire any more than are the gracious gifts of faith or love. It, too, grows from a work of the Spirit in men and in the world. Already God's reign is present as a ferment in the world, stirring hope in men and preparing the world to receive its ultimate judgment and redemption. It is strange, at first glance, that the panoply and glory usually associated with a kingdom should be compared to the working of a ferment, a yeast (Matt. 13:33). This Kingdom, however, is ruled by the one who chose to make his power known in weakness and has promised that the meek shall inherit the earth. It is not a kingdom according to the present order of things (John 18:36), but it will bring about a new reign and a new order in the world.

This hope yields urgency and striving for a better world. Neither optimistic nor pessimistic in ordinary terms, it refuses to say, "Lo, here is the Christ!" or "There he is!" (Matt. 24:24). It does not identify limited progress with the kingdom of God on earth, nor does it despair. . . . In steadfast hope the church looks beyond all partial achievement to the final triumph of God.

"Now to him who by the power at work within us is able to do far more abundantly than all that we ask or think, to him be glory in the church and in Christ Jesus to all generations, for ever and ever. Amen." (Eph. 3:20-21.)

Part Two

Part Two

CHAPTER 14

THE NICENE AND APOSTLES' CREEDS

The Nicene Creed was written in the fourth century after Christ. It was the first universal confession of Christendom and has held the highest honor and authority ever since. By contrast, the favorite creed of European and American Christianity, called the Apostles' Creed, dates in the form in which we have it from late in the sixth century, and is not used by the Eastern churches. For these reasons, the Nicene Creed is placed first in *The Book of Confessions*. This is as it should be, but because the Apostles' Creed is simpler and its core is older, we shall now discuss it first.

THE APOSTLES' CREED

A pious legend of the early church tells us that the apostles, after Pentecost, were preparing to preach in all parts of the world in the languages taught them by the Holy Spirit (Acts, ch. 2). To keep agreement in their message while separated they compiled the Creed. In the Middle Ages the legend was believed and embellished by naming each of the apostles as the author of one clause. Yet, in the fifteenth century, the Eastern Orthodox Church had no knowledge of an "Apostles'" creed. A Renaissance scholar showed the legend to be spurious, and the Reformation churches rejected it but continued to honor the Creed as containing apostolic teaching.

The legend is important because it records the age-old desire of the church to found its teaching and worship on highest authority. The near-truth of the story is that the nucleus of the Creed is very ancient. It stems from a summary of the faith found in Rome in the late second century. The material was used in two forms, one a declaration ("I believe in . . .") to show that a candidate was instructed and ready for baptism. The other and older form was a series of questions and answers. The baptizand, standing in the water, was asked, "Do you believe in God the Father Almighty?" He answered, "I believe," and was immersed. A question and an immersion accompanied each of the three articles of the Creed: Father, Son, and Spirit. The Trinitarian form is derived from the Great Commission of Matthew 28:19, "Baptizing them in the name of the Father and of the Son and of the Holy Spirit." The answer, "I believe" (Latin, *credo*), gives us the word "creed" and is the reason for the singular pronoun "I," still used, although "We believe" seems more appropriate for public worship.

There were many local creeds, confessions, and longer "rules" of faith that summarized Christian teaching. Some are preserved, but we shall probably never know how many there were or what their relations were to one another. For two or three centuries a rule of secrecy prevailed in the church to keep the Sacraments and the Creed from public view. Writing down the Creed was frowned upon. It was "delivered" by the bishop to an advanced candidate for baptism, who memorized and "returned" it by reciting it publicly, as mentioned above. The Apostles' Creed, one of many variations on the old Roman Creed, was very likely developed in southern France. In the early ninth century under Charlemagne it was promulgated in standard form and then "began to enjoy a practical monopoly in Western Europe" (J. N. D. Kelly). The Apostles' Creed was used not only for catechism and baptism but in various orders of prayer and worship, public and private. The Nicene Creed, however, prevailed as the creed recited during the Mass.

The classic "three articles" are shown clearly in the three paragraphs of the Creed as printed in *The Book of Confessions*. We see at a glance that the short first article is about God and creation. The longer second article contains a sequence of events concerning Christ. The third begins with the Holy Spirit, but its contents appear somewhat miscellaneous unless seen as a summary of the Spirit's action. We are told that the second article was expanded when a separate creed about Christ was added to a very brief Trinitarian formula and that the third article did have a rather piecemeal growth.

Unlike the Nicene and some other creeds, the Apostles' Creed avoids theological explanations. It does not give the meaning of **only Son** or why the Son was **conceived, . . . born,** etc. Sin is not mentioned except under forgiveness, and there is nothing about obedience or ethics. It is a spare, objective, liturgical recital of truths of the faith, without interpretation or elucidation. Yet the Creed is the basis for thousands of volumes of explanation as varied and even contradictory as the ways of belief and schools of thought among Christians. The following few pages, aimed to help a modern reader, are written from within a Reformation heritage.

I believe refers to faith. It is unfortunate that we cannot say in English, "I faith in God . . ." as is done in New Testament Greek or in German. The trouble with "believe" is that it is too mental or theoretical to represent adequately the trust that is part of faith. If a man says "I believe" a bridge is strong, but fears to step on it, trust is lacking. He believes *that* it is, but he does not believe *in* the bridge. Again, there is a great difference between believing *that* Lyndon Johnson is President, and believing *in* President Johnson. Similarly, John Baillie distinguished between believing with the top of the mind and believing from the bottom of the heart, which is faith. Faith, in the New Testament sense, includes knowing, but goes beyond what can be merely known. A faithful person does not make a guess or hold a theory that there is a God. He trusts that "without the will of my Father in heaven not a hair can fall from my head" (Heidelberg Catechism, Q. 1).

No one, however, can trust God by simply deciding to do so. We are always driven to demand that our security be within ourselves, at least in part. Wholehearted trust as proclaimed in Romans, ch. 8, is not, as Paul himself taught, a cultivated virtue. It is a gift of the Holy Spirit. Nor is it the gift of a credulous mind or an easygoing disposition, neither of which is a help to strong faith. It is the gift of encounter with God, of the realization of Who He Is by Whom our existence is maintained. "I believe" is made possible by the Holy Spirit despite a disposition that is unwilling (Matt. 16:16; John 20:28-29). The apostle Paul, who fought off this conviction for a long time, finally uttered one of the greatest affirmations of faith ever to come from the lips of a man:

> For I am sure that neither death, nor life, nor angels, nor principalities, nor things present, nor things to come, nor powers, nor height, nor depth, nor anything else in all creation, will be able to separate us from the love of God in Christ Jesus our Lord. (Rom. 8:38.)

Article 1. Does the phrase **God the Father** mean the "Father Creator"? Apparently it once did. But two things occurred: (1) As the doctrine of the Trinity developed, this title was increasingly interpreted as the Father of the **only Son** of the second article. Thus there was added later (2) **Maker of heaven and earth** to attend especially to the creative act of God. It would be incorrect, however, to lose entirely the perception that God is not merely an originator or **Maker,** but continues to be a loving **Father** toward his creation, even in the alien territory where his Fatherhood is rejected.

Almighty. This term belongs especially to the Old Testament, where God is the active ruling Lord of his people, of all history, and of all the phenomena of the physical world. Too often when God is called all-powerful or omnipotent, curious theories and quibbling questions are constructed. Can, then, God do anything? Can he make a stick with only one end or a weight so heavy that he cannot lift it? Neither serious speculations nor foolish puzzlings play much of a role in the Old Testament, but the primordial question of Almighty God and actual evil in the world is never far from the center of the stage in Job, Psalms, Isaiah, Jeremiah, and throughout. "As for you, you meant evil . . . , but God meant it for good" (Gen. 50:20); or, the Lord says, "I form light and create darkness, I make weal and create woe, I am the LORD, who do all these things" (Isa. 45:7). The **Almighty** of the Bible is not a puzzle and not an easy answer to man's questions. He is a presence who governs (Dan. 4:34-35) and a Father who cares (Ps. 27:10; 68:5). Despite the transcendence of his ways and the mystery of his being (Isa. 55:8-9), he made known his name and himself to the people of the covenant (Ex., chs. 3 and 6).

Maker of heaven and earth. Again in the Apostles' Creed we have a sheer assertion, this time almost a quotation from Genesis 1:1. **Heaven and earth** is a convenient and dramatic way to say "everything." The more argumentative Eastern creeds (compare the Nicene) suspect that these words mean two parts of the physical universe and that there may be other spiritual realms overlooked. Therefore they use the phrase **Maker . . . of all things visible and invisible.** The import is the same: Everything that exists is God's creation (Rom. 11:36; Col. 1:16). This subject is discussed in connection with "the world of space and time" in analysis of the Confession of 1967.

Article 2. The second article is made up of two parts: the first, a short title for Christ as related to the Trinity **(and in Jesus Christ his only Son our Lord),** and the second, a string of events related to human history **(who was conceived, etc.)**

And in Jesus Christ identifies at once the historical man Jesus by his title as the Christ or Messiah of the Old Testament. The literal man and the time of his death will be more accurately described farther on, but the root in history should not be overlooked even here. To reverse the order would be to start out with the Son and Lord as abstract ideas. In Peter's confession (Matt. 16:16) and the apostles' preaching generally it is "this Jesus" (Acts 2:23) who is called the unique Son of God. The **only Son** belongs emphatically to the first clause of the article. It is not one of the list of saving events that includes a quite different reference to Jesus' birth and Sonhood. The uniqueness of the **only Son** thus has nothing to do with the virgin birth, but belongs to his deity and is to be further clarified by the fuller doctrine of the Trinity. He was the **only Son** from all eternity (John 1:1; 17:5).

Our Lord applies to Jesus an exclusively divine title (John 20:28). To call Jesus **Lord** was to acknowledge him as God. **Lord** here is parallel to and of equal strength with **Almighty** in the first article. If **I believe** in Christ as **Lord**—remembering again the force of belief as faith—then I confess myself a servant and a subject and trust him wholly.

Who was conceived by the Holy Ghost. The remainder of the second article traces the main outlines of the preaching of the apostles as found in the book of The Acts and in our very earliest written records, Paul's letters. This preaching had as its core the announcement or proclamation that certain things had happened and others were expected soon. Peter's sermon in Acts, ch. 2, contains the elements commonly recited as the heart of the apostolic message. The focus is on the mighty deeds of God for the salvation of those who believe.

There is, however, one startling feature. The initial clauses, **conceived by the Holy Ghost, born of the Virgin Mary,** were not a part of the preaching or the letters of the apostles as recorded in the New Testament. Accounts of conception by the Spirit and of the virgin birth are limited exclusively to Matthew, chs. 1 to 2, and Luke, chs. 1 to 2, and are not alluded to again in these Gospels or the other two Gospels, or the letters of Paul, Peter, John, or the rest. The practice of the Creed finds support early in the second century. The silence in the apostolic preaching and writing, however, has caused some doubt (shared by the writer of these comments) about how essential the accounts were and are to the proclamation of the gospel. Later elaborations of the virgin birth stories encouraged the growth of lore and liturgy about Mary, the mother of Jesus, and have sometimes promoted doubts about the true and complete humanity of Jesus.

The import of the virgin birth accounts is that they identify Jesus as one who is a new, creative act by God for the saving of his people. The same is taught in John's Gospel in the language of the Word made flesh and the light shining in darkness, and in Romans, ch. 1, where the one "descended from David according to the flesh" is designated "Son of God."

There is a second feature, this time an omission, in which the Creed differs from the earliest preaching. It moves directly from birth to death, from Mary to Pilate. There is nothing of the travels from Nazareth to Jerusalem or of a ministry in Galilee or Judea. This contrasts with the preaching that told also of his "mighty works and wonders and signs" (Acts 2:22) and in which Jesus' teaching is reflected, sometimes almost verbatim (Rom., chs. 12 to 13).

Under Pontius Pilate enshrines in Christian worship and teaching the name of an otherwise unknown and trivial character in Roman history. This name is important for at least two reasons. The very banality of Pilate, the civil servant or bureaucrat, shows how colorless and routine the killing of Christ appeared from the point of view of the history of the Roman Empire. Secondly, it fixes the date of the crucifixion, and this was probably the reason why it was at first inserted in the Creed. The scope of the Creed is breathtaking: from **Maker of heaven and earth** and **his only Son our Lord,** it has descended to **under Pontius Pilate.** It would be hard to present more unforgettably the central paradox and the depth of the mystery of the Christian story than in this movement from God to the anguished suffering and death that provides redemption.

Article 2, part two, is also divided into two movements: the movement of descent and the movement of ascent—first, humiliation and then exaltation. The former has its goal and focus in the words **crucified, dead, and buried.** The latter tells of victory over death in the words **rose again** and total victory in the judgment of **the quick and the dead** and **the life everlasting,** which follows in the third article.

Article 3. **I believe in the Holy Ghost,** or, the Holy Spirit. The doctrine of the Spirit is the last main division of the Creed and was slower to develop than the others both among theologians and in official doctrinal statements of the church. The doctrine did not keep pace with Articles 1 and 2 even in the great theological systems of the Middle Ages. In fact, so many eccentric developments in Christian history have been attributed to the Spirit (at least by their practitioners) that there has been almost a phobia in the church about the doctrine. Nonetheless, in worship and liturgy from the beginning, Biblical phrases have been used which praise equally Father, Son, and Spirit. Thus the deity of the Holy Spirit has been expressed in Christian worship more adequately than in Christian doctrine. The very freedom and vitality attributed to the Spirit in Scripture is threatened by fixed formulas. At the same time it is utterly false to separate Spirit from Word (I John 4:1-2) or blithely to attribute any unusual enthusiastic religiosity to the Holy Spirit. Rightly, this is a *third* article, proceeding from the other two, although in no way subordinate. The deity of the Holy Spirit, here assumed, is more developed, as we shall see in a few pages, in the Nicene Creed.

The Spirit's work, par excellence, is the church, which is the whole community of men united to Christ and receiving the benefits of his salvation. It is essentially one, universal, therefore **catholic,** church. The adjective **holy** refers not to the moral condition of the church but to the fact that it exists solely because of the Holy Spirit's work. The **communion of saints** is another name for the church, indicating the fellowship among those chosen by the Spirit, which is a personal relationship of love among the members with each other and with God. The concept of "saints" canonized for exceptional piety or unusual deeds has no place here.

The forgiveness of sins is the basis on which the church communion rests. Calvin was fond of noting that this clause follows the one about the **saints,** indicating that they are not perfect people, but are called saints exactly because of God's daily renewed forgiveness. Originally, because of the baptismal use of this Creed, the phrase probably had special significance for baptism. **The resurrection of the body** refers to an early and enduring Christian conviction, based on the resurrection of Christ, that bodily life will be preserved in **the life everlasting.**

THE NICENE CREED

The threeness of God is presented in the Apostles' Creed, but not the oneness, although there is no question that it was taught from the beginning. We must turn to the Nicene Creed for the doctrine of the Trinity, which holds together the three and the one. The purpose of this Creed was to answer more fully the question of the meaning of Father, Son, and Spirit, and to reject and prevent false assertions. It was to take about five centuries for this doctrine to be worked out. During this time some of the finest minds of the ancient world wrestled with Scripture, with philosophy, with superstition, and with each other to produce the basic dogma of Christendom.

Dogmas are explanations, definitions, or declarations by which one or more teachings of the church are given official formulation, usually in the face of opposition. The opposition has sometimes been anathematized as heresy. All dogmas are meant to have their basis in Scripture, and since heretics, too, quote from the Bible, dogmas have the function of protecting Biblical teachings from distortion. Sometimes words are borrowed or new ones invented to clarify and guard the Biblical message. This risks transposing Biblical teaching into strange categories—but an even greater risk is for the church to do nothing and leave the older words, isolated from contemporary language, at the mercy of casual, jerry-built explanations.

In the Greek Orthodox and Roman Catholic Churches, dogma is regarded as infallible and irreformable, although the two differ on how dogmas are formulated. In Protestantism, official statements of doctrine are generally regarded as capable of being revised or reformed under the authority of Scripture. As the Westminster Confession put it, all "councils since the apostles' times . . . may err, and many have erred" (Ch. XXXI). The Protestant Reformation distinguished between true dogmas that clarify Scripture and those which depart from it. But the legitimacy of dogmatic teachings as such was not challenged by Protestant Reformers. They all defended the dogmas concerning the

Trinity and the nature of Christ formulated in the councils of the early church (Second Helvetic Confession, Ch. XI). The church, however, does not worship doctrines or formulas but God the Father, Son, and Spirit. The doctrines are signposts pointing to a reality beyond themselves.

At the root, the doctrine of the Trinity is an answer to the question, Who is Jesus? In the famed confession of Peter the answer given was, "The Christ, the Son of the living God" (Matt. 16:16). This, and the most characteristic answer of the apostolic church, "Jesus Christ is Lord" (Phil. 2:11), were a scandal to both Jews and Greeks of the ancient world. The Jews read in the Torah, "The Lord our God is one Lord," and "Thou shalt have no other gods before me." To apply God's title "Lord" to an obscure, wandering rabbi was blasphemy. Early Christianity had a great struggle about its relation with Judaism, and no part of it was more profound than this. Nonetheless, the heritage of Judaism has remained the chief bulwark against denying the oneness of God, although from the Jewish point of view the doctrine of the Trinity may have done just that.

If Judaism was the womb of early Christianity, the Greco-Roman world was its first school. The Mediterranean lands from Jerusalem to Gibraltar were a melting pot of religions and philosophies, some superstitious and some sophisticated. There were saviors galore and salvations to suit every taste. Christianity was mingled with these cults and schools of thought to produce an astonishing number of sects. The church took steps from the first to preserve the gospel from distortion and falsification, as we see in the New Testament letters. In the second century the official list of Biblical books, called the canon, the restriction of leadership to properly qualified and ordained bishops, and the formation of creedal statements were all part of the constant effort made to keep the gospel from getting lost in the surrounding world. In all these matters, the question, Who is Jesus? was not far from the center of concern. True worship, true obedience, and true belief all depended on the answer.

Since the gospel was a message carried largely by preaching, the doctrinal problems were crucial. To some, Jesus was a prophet and seer, no more; to others, an angel, or a cosmic principle, or an aspect of the divine being, or a formula for escaping from material existence. Some doubted his humanity, others rejected his deity, and still others made him a third something, higher than man but less than God. In the period just before the emperor Constantine called the Council of Nicaea (A.D. 325) to achieve peace in the church, a movement called Arianism was powerful. In defense of God's absolute oneness, Arius, their leader, held that the Son of God was less than eternal. When the "318 fathers" and the emperor pronounced the Son of one substance with the Father, the fullest possible deity of Christ was affirmed. The battle, however, was to continue throughout the century, embroiled often in theological and political confusion and skulduggery. Bishop Athanasius of Alexandria, the hero of orthodoxy, was exiled five times for holding the Nicene teachings.

Full and final recognition of the "Nicene" Creed came a century and a quarter later at the Council of Chalcedon (A.D. 451). But there is another complication: the creed recognized was not the original but a revision that had been accomplished at the Council of Constantinople in A.D. 381. It is this creed, commonly called Nicene, but more accurately, the Niceno-Constantinopolitan, which became the basis for all future creeds and definitions and which is part of *The Book of Confessions*. There are serious doubts about even this account of the origin of our Creed that are not yet resolved by scholars. One thing is clear. This "Nicene" Creed won the day. It is and has been the supreme doctrinal standard of Christian orthodoxy, East and West, since the fifth century.

How, then, does the "Nicene" (Niceno-Constantinopolitan) Creed answer the question, Who is Jesus?

First, we note the same three articles as in the Apostles' and old Roman Creeds, and the remarks already made apply here. Following the common sequence—Father, Son, Spirit—the Nicene Creed first asserts that **we believe in one God**. Nothing that follows can alter this. Also, as noted above, **all things visible and** invisible, a phrase common in Eastern baptismal creeds, is included to make sure that there is nothing at all beside God and his creation. This article reaffirms simultaneously the first chapter of Genesis and the First and Second Commandments.

Article 2. Now follows the distinctive element of the Nicene faith. The problem was to move from the **one God** to the man **crucified also for us under Pontius Pilate,** but not by a step down or by a bridge, for this would imply that salvation was accomplished by someone less than or other than God. Even the idiom of Scripture, "Son of God" (John 1:18), presents problems. Arians, too, agreed to call Christ the Son of God and the Word of God (John 1:14), for both "son" and "word" have as their natural meaning something subordinate and derived. There was, in fact, no one term in the Bible that would summarize Biblical teaching succinctly and ward off the Arian view that the Son is not eternal, therefore not true God. So a word had to be found outside the Bible. As adopted, the term is the key to this Creed and to subsequent Christian doctrine, East and West, including the doctrinal basis of the World Council of Churches.

The **Lord Jesus Christ** is said to be **of one substance with the Father.** The Greek word for "of one substance" is *homoousion,* pronounced hoe-moe-OUS-eeyon. As we have said, no stronger identification between Father and Son could be devised. Taken alone, this term seemed to many early fathers to cure the Arian error by an equally bad one on the other side, namely, destroying the Trinity by too close identity of Father and Son. There had been heresies of this type in the preceding century which made Father, Son, and Spirit mere modes or facets of the one divine life. Had the Council condemned Arius only to fall into the errors of Sabellius? So the debates raged. In the course of the next decades a whole new vocabulary was adopted for the use of theologians before a common understanding of **of one substance** was achieved. The intention of all was to interpret and to protect Scripture. But clear heads and pure hearts are rare, too, among church fathers. Diversity of training and piety, suspicions about the use of words, imperial politics and regional rivalries, saintliness and cussedness, all entered the process. When the whole is seen in a long view, however, it appears that Scripture was interpreted with massive consistency. Given the kind of problem presented to the church by the Greco-Roman world, the Nicene solution appears almost inevitable. Whether these same formulas can function in the same way in the millennia to come is certainly open to question. That they can be lightly dismissed is out of the question.

Also, in the second article, Christ is called **the only-begotten Son . . . , begotten of the Father before all worlds, . . . begotten, not made.** The word **only-begotten** strengthened by **not made** repudiates the Arian contention that the Son was created or "made" by the Father. It also avoids the idea that the Son is only a mode of the Father's existence. Also, **Very God of Very God,** or, more accurately, "true God from true God," attributes Godhood to the Son in the same sense as to the Father. These phrases, together with **of one substance,** are the most important phrases in the Nicene Creed for establishing the deity of Christ against the Arian heresy.

The same Council of Chalcedon (A.D. 451) not only reaffirmed the Nicene Creed but produced a formula for relating the human to the divine within Christ. According to the Definition of Chalcedon, Christ is made up of two "natures," divine and human, "without confusion, without change, without division, without separation," and yet he is one divine "person" or "subsistence." These terms and others, like the Nicene wording, are a technical vocabulary worked out through many generations of theological thought. Although Nicaea is basic, the Chalcedon statement has a practically equal place in the foundation of the structure of Christian doctrine. The formula of Chalcedon was not included in *The Book of Confessions,* but the teaching is repeated several times in the Reformation Confessions and these are commented on at the appropriate places, for instance, in the Scots Confession, Ch. VI, or the Second Helvetic, Ch. XI.

Other parts of Article 2 will not receive special comment here, for they are close to the Apostles' Creed and the same remarks generally apply.

In the third article, the deity of the Holy Spirit is affirmed, although the special technical term of one substance is not used. The Spirit is called **Lord and Giver of Life,** and the one who with the Father and the Son together is worshipped and glorified. These terms are all of Biblical origin. The Spirit is called **Lord** in II Corinthians 3:17 and **Giver of Life** in John 6:63. In the original Nicene Creed of A.D. 325, the Spirit had been dealt with only in the words **and in the Holy Spirit.** But at the time of the Council of Constantinople, thanks in part to heretical teachings similar to Arianism about the Spirit, there was a clear purpose to develop the doctrine of the Spirit in a way parallel to that of the Son. Originally, the third phrase of the article contained only the words **who proceedeth from the Father,** in agreement with John 15:26. In the early Middle Ages the Western Church added the words **and the Son** (Latin, *filioque*). The profound differences within Trinitarian doctrine that emerged during several centuries of debate and polemic over this term will not occupy us here. But the added phrase **and the Son,** by which the West hoped to avoid any subordination of the Spirit, contributed heavily to a schism between Rome and the Eastern Orthodox Church that continues in the present day.

Chapter 15

THE SCOTS CONFESSION, 1560

"Long have we thirsted, dear brethren, to have made known to the world the doctrine which we profess and for which we have suffered abuse and danger: but such has been the rage of Satan against us, and against the eternal truth of Christ now recently reborn among us, that until this day we have had neither time nor opportunity to set forth our faith, as gladly we would have done. For how we have been afflicted until now the greater part of Europe, we suppose, knows well."

These noble words begin the Preface of the finest document of the Scottish Reformation. It was composed upon request of Parliament by John Knox and five associates, within the space of four days in August, 1560. The General Assembly adopted it immediately and it remained the confession of the Church of Scotland until superseded in 1647 by the Westminster Confession. The change then was made to foster uniformity in the one Reformed Church that it was hoped (in vain) would extend throughout the British Isles. The Scots had already by that time demonstrated their oneness with the Reformed Churches of the Continent by giving formal recognition to doctrinal standards from Geneva, Zurich, and Heidelberg. One patriotic Scot has written that "the Scots Confession was the banner of the church in all her wrestlings and conflicts, the Westminster Confession but as the camp colors which she hath used during her days of peace—the one for battle, the other for fair appearance and good order."

The strong dramatic language of the Scots Confession reminds us that its authors were no strangers to persecution and martyrdom. Knox himself had been an exile and for two years a galley slave for the sake of his faith. Small wonder that when the Reformation was finally established, its confessional banner should be militant, victorious, and exultant in tone, culminating in words from Psalm 68, **Arise, O Lord, and let thine enemies be confounded.** Also, the battle of the Christian life is much to the fore, whether the battle between flesh and spirit (Ch. XIII), against sectarian heresy (Ch. XX), or against Rome, **the horrible harlot, the Kirk malignant**—softened in the modern English version to **the false Kirk** (Ch. XVIII). We must regret this vituperation even while understanding the embattled condition of the church when it was written. The same vigor put to better use yields some brilliant passages: **For by nature we are so dead, blind, and perverse, that neither can we feel when we are pricked, see the light when it shines, nor assent to the will of God when it is revealed** (Ch. XII). If the Confession bears some marks of haste and the violence that go with strong emotions, its chief characteristic is a tremendous prophetic vigor that might well have been refined away had it gone through a longer process of composition and editing.

The quickness of writing does not mean that Knox and his associates were unprepared. They knew well, and Knox had already participated in the writing of, other similar documents. Indeed, the First Helvetic Confession was brought to Scotland by the martyr George Wishart and published there in English (1548) before it was ever printed in English on the Continent. Haste in the composition of the Scots Confession probably shows more in form and style than in content. The document does not have much symmetry. The terse, compact early chapters give way to more diffuse, repetitious, argumentative later ones. Several times, here and there, the subject matter changes abruptly in the middle of a chapter. Chapter VII, one sentence long, has a title that certainly applies more accurately to Ch. VIII. The friendliest admirer could scarcely consider Chs. XVI to XX well organized. Three marks of the church are named in Ch. XVIII, but only two of them are explained in what follows. And so on. We are not picking flaws, but showing that this great Confession is as craggy, irregular, powerful, and unforgettable as the hills of north Scotland.

Any good confession or creed of the church will in some respects be dated and datable by its contents and style. More like a sermon than a mathematical theorem, it speaks the language and reflects the history of the time of writing. We would not today repeat the slight against women's role in the church (Ch. XXII) or the statement that **the preservation and purification of religion is particularly the duty of kings, princes, rulers, and magistrates** (Ch. XXIV), although Biblical proof texts can be found to support both views.

It has been suggested that the Scots Confession is organized on the pattern of the Apostles' Creed. In a general way most creeds, confessions, and theological systems are so ordered. That is, they follow the sequence of Father, Son, Spirit, and church. This may be said of the Scots Confession with passable accuracy,

Chapter	*Outline*	
I	God the Creator	FATHER
II-V	The History of the Church: Adam to Christ	
VI-VIII	The Person of Christ and Election	SON
(VIII) IX-XI	The Work of Christ	
XII-XV	Faith and Good Works	SPIRIT
XVI-XVII	The Church Universal and Invisible	CHURCH
XVIII	Marks of the Visible Church	
XIX-XX	The Authority of Scripture	
XXI-XXIII	Sacraments	
XXIV	The Civil State	
XXV	The Consummation	CONSUMMATION

although several exceptions are evident. The outline of chapters on page 175 with the chief articles of the Apostles' Creed in the right-hand margin, may help the reader to find his way more easily. The whole can also be differently divided, and it is a good exercise in critical reading to attempt alternate schemes.

God the Creator, Ch. I. Beginning with the very first words of the Scots Confession, God is a living power among men, no mere idler or distant cause of things. At once, **we confess and acknowledge one God alone, to whom alone we must cleave, whom alone we must serve, whom only we must worship, and in whom alone we put our trust.** The repeated "alone" derives more from the First Commandment, "Thou shalt have no other Gods before me," than from the Genesis creation story. We hear in it echoes of Luther's paraphrase of the First Commandment, "We should fear, love, and trust God above all things," and Calvin's motif, "It is with God we have to do in all the circumstances of life." The attributes that then follow and the brief statement of the Trinity are nothing unique, but there is unusual force in the relation of men to this transcendent Creator who rules and guides all things by his **inscrutable providence to the manifestation of his own glory.** Finally, he is not only the one **to whom,** but **by whom we confess and believe** that these things are true.

The reader should compare the similar but more personal first question of the Heidelberg Catechism, and the formal doctrine of God in the Westminster Confession, Ch. II, with the beginning here made by the thundering Scots. These confessions are all first cousins, with strong family resemblances, but they cannot be mistaken for identical twins or triplets.

The History of the Church: Adam to Christ, Chs. II to V. One of the most unusual, profitable, not to mention Biblical, features of the Scots Confession is the historical sequence, today called "salvation history," which orders the next four chapters. Man is said to have lived before God in a series of historical epochs leading to the coming of Christ, who fulfills the **joyful promise** of Genesis 3:15 that **the seed of the woman should bruise the head of the serpent** (Ch. IV). At the beginning is life in paradise, followed by the fall from perfection, after which men became by nature hostile to God, slaves to Satan, and servants to sin (Ch. III), an expression that contrasts unforgettably with the alone[s] of Ch. I and the lordly, free Adam of Ch. II. In Chs. II and III the story rushes forward so rapidly that the Fall is described under "The Creation of Man" and salvation under "Original Sin." This may be a sign of hurried composition, but it also shows a bona fide characteristic of the Christian faith, which is rightly more interested in the condition of man than in his origin, and is joyous over salvation rather than morbid about sin.

The rapid forward movement brings us in the final sentence of Ch. III to a remarkable summary of the central teachings of the Christian faith, lacking only mention of the church. It is a valuable exercise to hunt through the Confession and find in various places the fuller treatment of each of the phrases here used.

It may surprise some to read of the church (Kirk), a word that does not occur in the Old Testament, in the days of Adam and Noah (Ch. V). But this language characterized all the older theology, which recognized Genesis 3:15 as the first announcement of the gospel, and according to which the community of the faithful were never absent from the human race from the beginning of the world. This way of thinking in historical sequence, in which the promise was repeated and made clearer from time to time, was especially developed in the theology of Bullinger of Zurich, author of the Second Helvetic Confession. Later it contributed to the covenant theology which was important for church, state, and society in the English-speaking world. This feature of the Scots Confession, agreeing also with a prominent modern movement in theology, places it in some respects closer to the covenant type of theology than the Westminster Confession, which is a classic form of the covenant scheme. The down-to-earth quality of this short recital of Old Testament events (Chs. IV to V) affects the whole Confession, and contributes forcefully to later Chs. XVIII, XXIV, and others.

Not the least important feature of this historical recital is that

it culminates in Christ and in the doctrine of election, as follows:
The Person of Christ and Election, Chs. VI to VIII. Human
history and the redeeming will of the eternal God not only inter-
sect but become identical at the incarnation, as expressed in Ch.
VI: **When the fullness of time came** [history] **God sent his Son,
his eternal wisdom, the substance of his own glory** [eternity],
into this world. This world is the world fallen under divine wrath
through deception and disobedience. These two lines come together in a remarkable way, uniting in the cardinal teaching of
Chs. VI through VIII: Jesus Christ as **true God and true man,**
after the pattern of the ancient orthodox formula of Chalcedon
(A.D. 451). The catholic trustworthiness of the Reformation is
underscored by condemning four ancient heresies, long on the
blacklist of Christendom, East and West.

If the story of human history dominates Chs. II through V,
the dogma of **two perfect natures united and joined in one person**
controls those which follow. It occupies all but the first sentence
of Ch. VIII, answering the implied question in "Why the Mediator Had to Be True God and True Man" (Ch. VII)—a reflection
of Anselm's famous title, *Cur Deus Homo?* The answer, as in
the case of Anselm, is derived from an account of the central
paradox of grace, **Because the Godhead alone could not suffer
death, and neither could manhood overcome death, he joined
both together in one person, that the weakness of one should
suffer . . . and the infinite and invincible power of the other
. . . should triumph** (Ch. VIII). Fascinating for historians and
theologians is the way in which in Ch. VIII the "work" of the
Mediator is used to contribute to understanding the "person" and
vice versa. Then both are expounded through some more "salvation history," namely, the life of Jesus from birth (Ch. VI)
through passion (Ch. IX), resurrection (Ch. X), ascension, and
judgment (Ch. XI).

So far, so good. But why is Ch. VIII titled "Election"? Apparently because the union of Godhead and humanity arises from
the eternal **decree** or decision of God (Ch. VII) **who by grace
alone chose us in his Son Christ Jesus before the foundation of**

the world was laid (Ch. VIII). Here is distinctive Reformed or Calvinistic teaching in purest form from the period of the Reformation itself. If man is saved "by grace alone"—that is, not by his own work but as a result of a divine gift to him—then he is saved by divine choice or "election." And since God's eternity is not cooped up within the historical process—indicated here by the phrase **before the foundation of the world was laid**—his eternal decision or **decree** is finally that **from which all our salvation springs.** This close identity of the doctrine of Christ and salvation with election, or decree, is found in all the early Reformed confessions as well as in the theology of Calvin, Bullinger, and others. In the next century, when scholastic theology had developed, the doctrine of the **decree,** or predestination, not only changed in content but moved in its location into the doctrine of God proper, where it is an expression of divine omnipotence (Westminster Confession, Ch. III). So developed, it runs the risk of becoming a fatalistic determinism, as the various cautions in the Westminster Confession, Chs. III and V, betray. Here in the Scots Confession, as in the Second Helvetic, Genevan, Belgic, and other Reformation documents, election expresses the theme **grace alone** (Ch. VIII) **without respect to any merit proceeding from us** (Ch. XII) with clarity and consistency.

The Work of Christ, Chs. (VIII) IX to XI. The traditional phrase "work of Christ" is here used to group three, really four, chapters together. Chapter VIII is included again in this section because it showed the "why" of the person of the Mediator in terms of the mission he accomplished, just as the following Chs. IX to XI name the events through which the mission was carried out. Altogether these make up Christ's "work." They are not common deeds upon which an explanation is embroidered, but deeds that are themselves freighted with meaning because of who the doer is and what his purpose is. This Confession does a good job of avoiding division between the "person" and the "work," which are really two aspects of a single, once-for-all event, separated only to make discussion possible.

Much of what was said in Ch. VIII concerning Christ suffering in our stead and for our transgression is repeated here but with the difference that, as mentioned, the events themselves are listed. The list begins with the birth of Jesus (Ch. XI) and carries through to the Last Judgment and the eternal destiny of blessed immortality for some men and the dungeon of utter darkness for others.

The preaching, teaching, and healing ministry of Jesus is not mentioned here, despite unusual emphasis on the literal body of the true man: The selfsame body which was born of the virgin ... did ascend into the heavens, ... where he sits at the right hand of the Father, ... and shall visibly return for this Last Judgment as he was seen to ascend (Ch. XI).

This section ends with a paean of praise to the same Christ, risen and exalted, the only Head of his Kirk, our just Lawgiver, our only High Priest, Advocate, and Mediator, and our sovereign and supreme Governor. Christ exalted as Lord finally dominates the teaching about Christ stated by these courageous and hopeful Scots, as it does generally in the thought and worship of the Reformed tradition.

Faith and Good Works, Chs. XII to XV. The three strongest emphases in this part of the Confession are (1) that faith is not man's work but God's gift through the Holy Spirit, and (2) that faith issues in good works, which also are not man's work, but God's, and (3) notwithstanding all this, man remains imperfect. We look now at the personal inward aspect of election. God, who by grace alone chose us, does not timidly await some tentative human response, but brings it about. Our faith and its assurance do not proceed ... from natural powers within us, but are the inspiration of the Holy Ghost. Again, The cause of good works ... [that is, works done in faith] is not our free will, but the Spirit of the Lord Jesus, who dwells in our hearts by true faith, brings forth such works as God has prepared for us to walk in.

The obvious and difficult question of what this means for man's response, whether or not he has any part in his own faith and obedience, is not dealt with in the Scots Confession. The sole concern is to proclaim, as did the apostle Paul and the prophets of Israel, that all trust and obedience come from God alone, all praise and thanksgiving belong to God alone. No quarter is given to man's self-esteem—as if to ask, What more can man be than the recipient of divine grace? "For by grace you have been saved through faith; and this is not your own doing, it is the gift of God—not because of works, lest any man should boast." (Eph. 2:8.) The Westminster Confession will introduce necessity, contingency, and secondary causes to help explain the problems that arise.

Just as firmly, the Confession asserts the seemingly contradictory duty of obedience to the law. No sooner is the believer shown to be without merit, without any good of his own to offer, and without a will of his own to be obedient than the demands of the law are set before him. Faith is not idle. It is blasphemy to assert that it can exist at all without holy obedience (Ch. XIII). The holy law was given to man by God to reveal God's pleasure and displeasure with reference both to the honor of God and the profit of our neighbor (Ch. XIV). These two parts correspond to the traditional "two tables" of the law, and the two parts of the "great commandment" (Matt. 22:37-39).

The Confession elaborates these good works of two kinds so as to include the Christian Sacraments and a rich variety of ethical maxims, followed by a shorter list of bad works, which specifies among other things private invention in the field of worship. Despite the perfection of the law and the prompting of the Spirit, sin continues even after we are reborn. And God continues to pursue the work of salvation: For as God the Father beholds us in the body of his Son Christ Jesus, he accepts our imperfect obedience as if it were perfect, and covers our works, which are defiled with many stains, with the righteousness of his Son (Ch. XV). This is probably the finest brief account of justification by faith in the whole Book of Confessions, although the term is not used. In fact, "justification" occurs only once (Ch. X) in the Scots Confession.

The dominant quality of the Christian life here presented is the battle which is between the flesh and the Spirit and the fight against sin (Ch. XIII). In fact, conflict is said to belong to believers' lives only, for other men do not share this conflict since they do not have God's Spirit, but they readily follow and obey sin and feel no regrets, since they act as the devil and their corrupt nature urge (Ch. XIII). One may be permitted to doubt if the road to hell is always so smoothly paved or the life of the reborn is always so battle-scarred as pictured in Ch. XIII. Curiously, the myth of much contemporary American piety practically reverses the two pictures. It would be valuable to compare the quality of the Christian life in the Heidelberg Catechism, Part III, or in the Confession of 1967 with this persistently embattled view in the Scots Confession to gain a broader outlook.

The Church Universal and Invisible, Chs. XVI to XVII. The church is catholic or universal, including the elect of all ages and places. Outside of it there is neither life nor eternal felicity, regardless of virtue or religious practice. And this church is invisible, which is to say, known only to God (Ch. XVI). Within the catholic or universal church are particular, local, visible churches at such places as Corinth, Galatia, Ephesus, . . . [and] the realm of Scotland (Ch. XVIII). The notes or distinguishing marks of the true church are found in these visible, local communities.

We must pause a moment to note that this pair of concepts, the universal church and the particular church, are drawn together for analysis from the early part of Ch. XVI, and the middle of Ch. XVIII. In between is a short, separate chapter on the immortality of the soul and a critique of the "sleep of the soul" idea held by various sects. Again, Ch. XVIII begins with an intemperate polemic against Satan's pestilent synagogue that stretches out in history from Cain to the Church of Rome. The traditional arguments for Rome's claim to be the true bride of Christ are peremptorily refuted. It is all clear enough, if one studies carefully, but the sequence and the interrelation of ideas are not very well worked out.

Marks of the Visible Church, Ch. XVIII. Three marks are

given for the true church: the true preaching of the word, the right administration of the Sacraments, and ecclesiastical discipline uprightly ministered. These are common enough in Reformed confessions, but it is unique among them that the doctrine of Scripture is introduced in support of right preaching as a mark of the church. It may well be that the practice of the Scots Confession is the preferable one.

There is no doubt that from the beginning the Scots Confession is meant to be Biblical interpretation. The Preface contains the engaging invitation: "If any man will note in our Confession any chapter or sentence contrary to God's Holy Word, that it would please him of his gentleness and for Christian charity's sake to inform us of it in writing . . . [and] we shall alter whatever he can prove to be wrong." The story of the church from Adam to Christ, the teaching of how salvation comes and what is the meaning of faith and works had, at least in intent, no other source but the Bible. But the actual doctrine of Scripture enters at the point where the Bible functions in the church for teaching and preaching. It may seem a small point, but primary concentration on *what* Scripture teaches and *what* the church believes, rather than *how* this book or church derives its authority, might have saved much spiritual bloodshed in the generations since the Reformation. The Scots Confession and the Heidelberg Catechism are good teachers of this way of doing, and the Second Helvetic Confession is another, although less clearly so. By analogy, the whole matter might be compared to demanding a man's credentials before being willing to meet him, as against looking him in the eye first, then, insofar as is necessary, establishing his history and record. If faith is primarily legal and cerebral, the former way is correct. If faith is primarily personal encounter and trust, then the way of the Scots Confession is the better one.

The second mark of the church, the Sacraments, is treated below in Chapter 21, where the sacramental views in all the confessions are brought together.

The Authority of Scripture, Chs. XIX to XX. The plain Word

of God written is sole authority for the church in all matters of faith. The antiquity of some other authority is no criterion of truth: Cain was older than Abel! Nor are pretensions to a splendid title, or linear succession, or a special location, or the support of great numbers of people to be received as valid. These all could apply to the Jerusalem where Christ was not honored, but crucified (Ch. XVIII). The canonical Scriptures alone, where all things necessary . . . for the salvation of man are sufficiently expressed, is the court of appeal for controversies of faith. Accordingly, the interpretation of Scripture does not derive from men or from any church, but pertains to the Spirit of God by whom the Scriptures were written. Controversies are to be resolved by attention to passages where the Holy Ghost uniformly speaks within the body of the Scriptures and what Christ Jesus himself did and commanded. Since the Spirit, as all must agree, cannot contradict himself, the appeal to Scripture is taken to be self-evidently satisfactory.

Great care is exercised in the Confession neither to rashly condemn nor receive uncritically what general councils of the church teach. Since their rightful purpose is not to propound articles of faith, but to refute heresy and give public confession of faith, councils are to be held firmly on a Scriptural tether. In such matters as church polity and ceremonies, councils may take actions appropriate to various ages, times, and places.

The authority of the Holy Spirit through the Scriptures (Ch. XVIII) and the proper role of church councils (Ch. XX) are elucidations of the otherwise too brief Ch. XIX which carries the title "The Authority of the Scriptures." The Confession asserts bluntly and reiterates several times the authority of the plain word which comes from God, but does not touch problems of interpretation such as are mentioned in the Second Helvetic or Westminster Confessions. The principles of faith and love (end of Ch. XVIII) are usually taken in the sense that Augustine used them, namely, as guides for resolving problems of obscure or apparently contradictory texts. The stress here, however, on the plain text seems to belittle the importance of such considerations.

It should be noted that the emphasis on Christ, comparable to that found in the doctrine of election and the earlier chapters on Biblical history, appears here also in the statement that the true church in Scripture **always hears and obeys the voice of her own Spouse and Pastor.**

The Sacraments, Chs. XXI to XXIII. The second mark of the church, the sacraments, is treated below in Chapter 21 where the sacramental teachings in all the confessions are brought together.

The Civil State, Ch. XXIV. The divine establishment of all levels of government from vast empire to local city authorities is first stated without condition or inhibition in Ch. XXIV, as it had been more succinctly in the second table of the law, in Ch. XIV. All who rebel or overturn civil powers **are not merely enemies to humanity but rebels against God's will.** Typically, a Reformed confession and Reformed leaders and people assert the legitimacy of government as part of God's law. But these same leaders and people were often part of movements that upset the existing order. The whole discussion of what this means and meant cannot be undertaken here, but attention must be called to provisos in the Scots Confession that condition the statements just pointed out. Among good works toward neighbor, the first is **to honor father, mother, princes, rulers, and superior powers; to love them, to support them, to obey their orders if** they are not contrary to the commands of God (Ch. XIV, emphasis mine). The same passage goes on, **to save the lives of the innocent, to repress tyranny, to defend the oppressed** (same passage, emphasis mine). What then, if the ruler is tyrannous or oppressive? Can he be so, **acting in . . . [his] own sphere** (Ch. XXIV)? There is no clear answer in the Confession, but the direction is evident, and the life of Knox and the story of the Covenanters show that they knew how to obey God rather than man, even when the man or woman was one of **his lieutenants.**

The theological basis of the state, and the relation of Christian obedience to the state, was one of the most vexing problems for the churches of the sixteenth and seventeenth centuries. Their teaching and practice, what they learned from the Bible and from experience, helped build the nations in which their descendants still live. The same sources in a new age have also brought about fresh responses. Comparison should continue throughout *The Book of Confessions* with the Westminster divines, the German churchmen under Hitler (Barmen Declaration), and the problems of tyranny and oppression in the twentieth century as reflected in the Confession of 1967.

The Consummation, Ch. XXV. Except for the title, "The Gifts Freely Given to the Kirk," the last chapter of the Scots Confession is a rather typical doctrine of "last things." The church visible is a mixed body in which the reprobate live among the elect until the end. Only the elect, those who **unfeignedly believe** and **boldly confess,** receive the fruits of Christ's work. In this life they receive forgiveness and faith, and in the life to come, resurrection, glory, honor, immortality, reigning with Christ forever. The reprobate shall be **tormented forever, both in body and in spirit.** The end is a doxology with a verse from Psalm 68 and includes the appropriate appeal, **Give thy servants strength to speak thy Word with boldness, and let all nations cleave to the true knowledge of thee. Amen.** The Reformation Scots did not fail to speak boldly.

CHAPTER 16

THE HEIDELBERG CATECHISM

The first Protestant confession to arrive in the New World with the European explorers was the Heidelberg Catechism. In 1609, less than fifty years after it was written, it was brought to Manhattan Island by the discoverer of the Hudson River. Afterward it was taught in the Dutch settlements of New Amsterdam and the Hudson Valley. A hundred years later it came again with the German settlers to Pennsylvania and moved west with the Dutch and Germans who became prosperous farmers and merchants throughout the Midwest. The current history of the Heidelberg Catechism in America is crowned by a new English translation published in 1963 on the four-hundredth anniversary of its composition. The practical pocket-size edition evidences that it is still widely used.

The sixteenth-century Heidelberg theologian Zacharias Ursinus was chiefly responsible for this Catechism. It was first adopted into the church order of the Palatinate under the pious Elector Frederick III. The life and mind of the Reformed Churches of Hungary, the Netherlands, and Germany have been shaped by it as well as the churches that grew from the immigrant stock of these lands, both in America and around the world. The Catechism was widely used in Scotland, and was approved for use in American Presbyterian congregations by the General Assembly of 1870. When we recall the courage and faith of the embattled churchmen of the Barmen Synod (Chapter 20), we should remember that many were nurtured on this still vital confession.

The Heidelberg Catechism has been uncommonly well loved and much used by its adherents. Not only did young and old know it by heart, but pastors were prescribed to preach from one of its fifty-two sections each "Lord's Day" of the year. Theological lectures followed the course of its teachings, and a small mountain of commentaries, handbooks of devotion, and guides to practical piety have been based on it. It has been translated into a dozen or more languages.

As with most catechisms, this one was expected to include instruction in the Ten Commandments, the Apostles' Creed, the Lord's Prayer, and the Sacraments. Luther's catechisms simply follow them line by line. The Westminster Shorter Catechism explores these materials in part, then appends their texts at the end. The Heidelberg Catechism integrates the four elements, text and all, ingeniously into a seamless outline that is as comprehensive as it is easy to remember.

The Catechism has three divisions: Sin, Salvation, and Thanksgiving. In more detail, Part I describes the misery of man's condition from which he cannot rescue himself. Part II presents God's provision for man's need in the form of an exposition of the Apostles' Creed and the Sacraments. Part III, "Thankfulness," is the response to God's gift of salvation. The guides to thanksgiving are the Ten Commandments and the Lord's Prayer! This sequence shows dramatically that the Christian does not obey or pray in order to gain God's favor, but out of gratitude. In broadest terms this structure is also the outline of the letter to the Romans, and the lengths of the sections are approximately similar: "Of Man's Misery" corresponding to the first three chapters, "Of Man's Redemption" to the middle section, and "Thankfulness," to the last four.

The renowned first question of the Heidelberg Catechism contains the whole content in a nutshell and communicates as well the spirit that prevails all the way through. By contrast with the Scots' more belligerent stance and the Westminster Confession's lofty abstractions, the tone here is personal and confident, although not sentimental. The outline of the Answer follows the

Persons of the Trinity named in the same sequence—Son, Father, Spirit—that is followed in Part I of the new Confession of 1967. By contrast with all other confessions it begins with the believer at his home address. It starts off with **your** life and death, faith in Christ, and trust in God's providence, rather than the origins of Scripture (Westminster Confession), Creator and creation (Scots), man's "chief end" (Shorter Catechism), and the like. From the here-and-now it harks back to the work of salvation and anticipates eternal life, all the while looking unblinkingly at the realities of the present.

The language of Romans, ch. 8, several sayings of Jesus (Matt. 10:29-31), and Psalm 46 resound in the words of the first Question. These are the setting in which to understand **comfort**, which is the catchword summing up the whole Catechism (Q. 2). This **comfort** is not a quiet state of mind resulting from a spiritual sedative, but a well-founded response to the reality of divine care. The root of the English word "com*fort*"—from the Latin *fortis* ("strong") as in "a mighty *fort*ress" (Ps. 46)—is more agreeable to the meaning given here than thoughts of comfortable armchairs and cushions. Questions 21, 27, 60, and 61 show comfort related to faith, trust, and justification. It is almost a synonym for the word "salvation." The Christian man, "comforted" by Christ's work and God's providence, is **wholeheartedly willing and ready from now on to live for him** (Q. 1). The same man shows a "hearty joy and delight in living according to God's will" (Q. 90, my translation). This comfort would seem to be a stimulant rather than a sedative, and to issue in a life of delight and endeavor, not passivity.

"Of Man's Misery," Qq. 3-11. Close attention to this brief, simple section yields some features of unusual value. Just as Q. 1 had its starting point in the life of the believer, Qq. 3-6 begin with the actual present individual existence of the sinner, not with Adam's fall or a general definition of sin, but, **Where do you learn of your sin?** The answer, too, is direct, **From the Law of God.** The law is then stated in its purest and most devastating form as the love of God and neighbor. A man might squirm out from under the commandment, You shall not kill, by never having committed a murder. But You shall love . . . overwhelms him, and he must abjectly admit to hatred of God and neighbor.

Since it is God's law that convicts him, the sinner knows that he is not a sinner by God's will, so God cannot be blamed. But he needs to understand more than his private experience. Now follows the general teaching about the image of God and the story of the original Fall so that man can appreciate his present condition, can in fact appreciate how utterly helpless he is (Qq. 6-9). This unique order, proceeding from individual predicament to a general account of sin is obviously not presented in a historical sequence. We have not yet come even to the doctrine of creation! It is, rather, the order determined by personal Christian experience.

Again, it must not be lost on the reader that the teacher of the law is Jesus Christ (Q. 3), who has already been designated as my faithful Savior (Q. 1). He propounds the law in a summary that comes from The Gospel According to Matthew. It is not Moses who raises the lash of the law, but Christ. Nor is it Satan who ultimately threatens man with eternal punishment of body and soul (Q. 11), but God. Before the law, there stood the holy gospel, which God himself revealed in the beginning in the Garden of Eden (Q. 19). The law itself is a gift of the merciful God to his own people of the covenant, to discourage them from trying to save themselves (Qq. 13-14). The only rescue is from God (Qq. 16-17).

When we observe the sequence from "Misery" in Qq. 3-11 to "Redemption," Qq. 12-21, we see two elemental powers emerge: justice and mercy, God's justice which punishes and God's mercy which forgives. God is divided rather more sharply between justice and mercy in this Catechism than in Scripture. We make this comment with great confidence, because it is a comment widely shared, and it applies not only to this Catechism but to most theology since the late Middle Ages, Catholic and Protestant. Justice and mercy are so pitted against each other that a transaction has to take place between them. The rather crass language of **payment** and **debt** (Qq. 12-16, and throughout, even stronger in the German than in this moderating English translation) describe the transaction by which one satisfies the other. These words, of course, occur in Scripture, but in Scripture they are not so radically divided, as if God were paying his right pocket out of his left.

The word for God's "righteousness" in the Old Testament came down through Greek and Latin translations as "justice." Justice in civil law means giving each his due, treating all equally. The goddess with the balance on the courthouse frieze is blindfolded. Her justice is exact and impersonal. In such a setting, mercy may violate justice. But the righteousness of God as taught in the Bible is both more mysterious and more personal than this. God's righteousness both demands perfect obedience and offers free forgiveness. God is as righteous when he forgives as when he punishes. Indeed, God's righteousness and salvation are sometimes interchangeable terms, used together in poetic parallels such as Isa. 45:8, 21. The letter to the Romans, especially chs. 3:21 through 4:25, teaches the righteousness of grace: "But now the righteousness of God has been manifested apart from the law, although the law and the prophets bear witness to it, the righteousness of God through faith in Jesus Christ" (Rom. 3:21-22; also, ch. 4:5, and throughout, or Rom. 1:17, or Phil. 3:9). This view, despite the criticism we have offered of the language of the Catechism, finally emerges. As it is Christ who teaches the law and Christ who pays the debt and satisfies God's justice (Q. 34), so, when at the end of all things the terrible **Judge from heaven** appears, he is no other than the One who **has already submitted himself to the judgment of God . . . and has removed all the curse from me** (Q. 52). The punishment due the sinner is crushing, but his comfort is that the Judge is the Redeemer himself. (Compare the development of this theme in the Confession of 1967, ¶s 9-11, which end with a near-quotation from Heidelberg Q. 52.)

"Faith," Qq. 20-22 (and Qq. 32, 53, 59-61), is the meeting place where mercy replaces justice, where Christ's work overcomes the

work of Adam (Qq. 20, 60-61) as in Romans 4:5. Faith comes
from the Spirit, causing a man to share in Christ and all his
benefits (Q. 53) by means of the gifts of knowledge and trust
(Q. 21). Since this particular aspect of faith is typical and rather
clear, we shall not expand on it here. Fruitful comparisons can
be made especially with parallel teachings in the Second Helvetic
and Westminster Confessions. Three thoughts only: First, as the
introductory question contains the whole Catechism in a nutshell,
so Qq. 2-21 contain the whole again in a somewhat fuller form.
The focus continues to be on the same personal subject. Second,
the body of the Catechism begins uniquely with a discussion of
sin. Or we might say, taking Qq. 2-21 together, that the starting
place is man's life before God in the two conditions of sin and
faith. It is a very satisfactory way of putting the question of the
knowledge of God with inescapable force and clarity. Third,
since the Apostles' Creed follows immediately, it might not be
amiss to understand Q. 21 as an explanation of the first two
words, I believe.

The full text of the Apostles' Creed now appears in Q. 23 and
is explained, bit by bit, through Q. 64. Our task is not to write
again of the Creed, but to point to the particular emphases of
the Heidelberg Catechism. Looking ahead, we note that just as
the Creed is introduced by questions about faith (Qq. 20-22), it
is followed by more on the same subject (Qq. 59-64). The Creed
itself contains the content of the faith, *what* is believed. The
prelude and postlude tell *how* we believe, or the way the content
of faith is effective for us. Questions 20-22 present faith more
subjectively as knowledge and trust, while Qq. 59-64 present faith
more objectively in relation to justification.

There is, strictly speaking, about as little of the "doctrine" of
the Trinity in this highly Trinitarian confession as there is in
the Apostles' Creed. What there is skirts the risk of being understood as an "economic" or administrative Trinity. That is to say,
Q. 24 relates the Father to creation, the Son to redemption, and
the Spirit to sanctification. That there is no intent to reduce the
persons to a mere working arrangement is shown in Q. 25, but

rather skimpily, where **three distinct persons** are said to be the **one, true, eternal God.** The Nicene distinctions are doubtless presupposed (above, Chapter 14), but they are not stated.

"Of God the Father," Qq. 26-28. The old puzzler about whether "Father" in the first article refers to God as Trinitarian Father of the Eternal Son or as Father of men through creation is solved neatly and ingeniously by combining the two in Q. 26. Altogether, Qq. 26-28 are primarily about providence. This is quite right, for there is not much to say about creation **out of nothing** except to assert it (Q. 26). It yields little to speculation. Moreover, the providential stress is not on **his eternal counsel** but on the down-to-earth, active government of God in the world.

What is said about divine rule from the middle of Q. 26 through Q. 28 can hardly be surpassed for simplicity, clarity, mystery, and concreteness. If we grant that the language sounds today somewhat quaint and pastoral, failing to mention midair collisions and nuclear war, it is nonetheless pointed enough to puncture the delicate tissue of sweet and good things that many of us call "providential"—a nice day for a picnic, a passed examination, a promotion, or a narrow escape. God's works listed in Q. 27 are not all "good." God brings on **rain and drought, fruitful and unfruitful years, food and drink, health and sickness, riches and poverty, and everything else.** Does sickness include cancer? And drought, a great famine? And unfruitful years, mass unemployment? And everything else, the mass butchery, the poverty, the race hatred of the twentieth century? The answer, if we dare, is yes. When stated so brutally, however, we shall find the cosmic dimensions of the language of the apostle Paul more nearly adequate to comfort the terror that racks the human race today. "For I am sure that neither death, nor life, nor angels, nor principalities, nor things present, nor things to come, nor powers, nor height, nor depth, nor anything else in all creation, will be able to separate us from the love of God in Christ Jesus our Lord." (Rom. 8:38-39.)

"Of God the Son," Qq. 29-52. This section throughout gives an appropriate slant to the language of the Creed by emphasizing the function or work of Christ more than the classic dogma of his person. Since the title "Christ" is the Greek translation of "Messiah," "anointed one," the Catechism explains it with reference to the three anointed offices in Israel: prophet, priest, and king. (This is a familiar device among theologians taught by Calvin.) Then in a striking tour de force, a play on the words "Christ" and "Christian," the special offices of Christ are transferred to every Christian. First, **Why is he called Christ?** Then, **Why are you called a Christian?** He is called Christ because he is anointed a prophet or revealer, a priest or sacrifice, and a king or ruler (Q. 31). The Christian, who is "by faith a member" of Christ, is anointed as an organ of Christ's anointed body. (The translation **share in Christ** loses the analogy.) The offices that were once reserved to specially anointed people now fall upon all, so that they become as in I Peter 2:9, "a royal priesthood, a holy nation, . . . that you may declare the wonderful deeds." In the Catechism, the three parts of Q. 32, although not so labeled, exactly parallel the offices of Christ. The believer as a member of Christ shares the offices by confessing his name (prophet), offering a living sacrifice of gratitude (priest), and ruling with him (king) (Q. 32).

The remainder of the teaching on the second article continues in the pattern just observed in Qq. 31 and 32, moving back and forth between Christ and ourselves. Consistently, although not mechanically, a word or event in the Creed is followed by the question, **What benefit do you receive . . . ?** The bulk of the list is made up of a sequence representing the incarnate life as **conceived . . . born . . . suffered . . . crucified . . . dead . . . buried . . . rose . . . ascended.** The movement back from the objective happening to ourselves is clearly seen in Qq. 32, 34, 36, 42, 45, 49, 51, and 52. Of special note is the consistent carrying out of the payment theme, and the firm reassertion of the Nicene formula, **true man and true God** (Q. 47), as an integral part of the theme.

"The Holy Spirit," Qq. 53-58. Only one question in the entire Catechism is devoted exclusively to the Holy Spirit, in spite of the fact that the Spirit is one of the three capital articles of the Apostles' Creed. Now, when we look closely at this question, Q. 53, we discover that even here there is no unique content. The first part has already been stated back in Qq. 24-25, and nothing more is added. The second part, about the Spirit's work, faith, which makes me **share** in Christ and his **benefits** is, as we have already seen, the subject matter of Qq. 29-52, although the sequence is not fully completed until Q. 64. The rather minor sector that is marked out for the Spirit in all Reformed confessions results from the nature of the teaching. The Spirit is not thereby isolated in life or in the Creed but is expressed throughout all aspects of the work of providence and salvation. To study fully the doctrine of the Spirit in the Heidelberg Catechism would be to study the entire document.

The clearest expression of the doctrine of election in our Catechism is Q. 54, related to a work of the Spirit, the holy catholic church. The church is a **congregation chosen for eternal life.** Its members are elsewhere called **elect** (Q. 52), and the same is the implication of the phrase in Q. 21, **out of sheer grace solely for the sake of Christ's saving work.** Through Christ this redemption is based on **the secret purpose and will of God** (Q. 31) and is rooted in **his eternal counsel and providence** (Q. 26). There is not a fully developed teaching about predestination in this Catechism, not even so full as in other sixteenth-century Reformed statements. Enough is present, however, to indicate agreement with the others. The special nuance of the Heidelberg Catechism is a particularly intimate confidence in the providence of God growing out of the promise of salvation. This in turn issues, as we shall shortly see, in a hopeful and courageous style of Christian living.

"Justification by Faith," Qq. 59-64. Question 59 is rather disarming. Referring back to the elaborate treatment of Christ and his benefits in the Creed, the question is, **But how does it help you now that you believe all this?** The answer (Qq. 60-64) contains a teaching that Calvin called the hinge of the Reformation, —justification by faith. All the benefits of Christ are summed up in this one: his righteousness has taken the place of our un-righteousness (Q. 61). The guilty man of Qq. 5-7 now goes scot-free, as if I had never committed a single sin or had ever been sinful (Q. 60).

This does not appear to be fair. It is certainly not equitable according to ordinary justice. But the righteousness of God, which the Heidelberg writers call "gospel" or "evangelical" righteous-ness, is, as we have seen, another kind. It is not achieved by effort, but received as a gift. How this takes place is one of the great dividing watersheds in theology. Roman Catholic and Reforma-tion teachings agree well enough about the predicament of man, his helplessness, and his need for God to provide the way out. Also, they agree that God provides this way through Jesus Christ. But at the point of how it all happens a difference appears that is so decisive and divisive that it reflects doubt upon some of the other areas where we have just noted near agreement.

Generally, Catholic teaching has held that faith must be com-pleted by obedience in order to be truly saving. Reformation teaching held for faith alone. But how is it received? How does Christ's righteousness get to the Christian? In Catholic doctrine there is a cooperative work between the Spirit of God and the human will. In Reformation teaching, nothing that the will of man contributes is effective for salvation. In both cases faith in-volves obedience. But in the former, obedience is part of the work of faith and in the latter, obedience follows faith as part of man's gratitude. The issue is this: Is faithful obedience a partial *cause* of salvation or is it the *result* of salvation? Luther learned from the apostle Paul and his own experience that if salvation depends upon obedience, then the grace of Christ is incomplete, and Christ is a lawgiver after all. The burden of having to maintain by one's own discipline the state of righteousness before the Holy God, of having to earn the love of such a Father—when the stakes are so high—is intolerable. It leads either to superficial con-fidence or, as in the case of Luther, to utter despair.

The difference might be illustrated in this way. Does a child have to obey a parent *in order to* be loved and accepted in return?

Or does the parents' love precede obedience, and does it embrace both obedience and disobedience? Again, is marriage basically a free, unreserved self-giving or is it basically a matter of calculation and the performance of mutual services? The first part of each of these examples is meant to point to "salvation by works" and the second to "grace alone." Clearly, the Heidelberg Catechism belongs with the latter. As Ursinus wrote in a commentary on the Catechism: "This beggar is enriched only by receiving alms, all works and merits are excluded therefrom, yea, even the very acceptance of alms, in as far as it is viewed as a merit. It is for this reason that Paul always says that we are justified *by faith, and through faith, . . . and never on account of faith.*" For the Protestant Reformers, one of the decisive texts of the entire Bible was Ephesians 2:8-9, "For by grace you have been saved through faith; and this is not your own doing, it is the gift of God—not because of works, lest any man should boast." On this basis, the Heidelberg Catechism will introduce the "good works" of the law under the heading of "Thankfulness" in Part III, Q. 86, and those following.

Now, a caution. Although "salvation by faith alone" was certainly the hinge of the Reformation, we cannot so clearly distinguish today between Catholics and Protestants on this issue. First, some leading Catholic thinkers teach in ways that seem closer to Luther than to Luther's Roman opponents. Secondly, the preaching of Protestant pulpits and the piety of Protestant people often reflects law more than grace, striving more than receiving. This only demonstrates that the struggle of the apostle Paul against legalism is a constant one in the life of each individual and of the church in all communions and denominations.

"The Holy Sacraments," Qq. 65-85, are discussed in the separate chapter (Chapter 21), below, hence are omitted here.

Part III, "Thankfulness." The first question of Part III is one that naturally comes to mind: **Since we are redeemed from our sin . . . without any merit . . . , why must we do good works?** (Q. 86). Paul put it more strongly in Romans 6:15, "Are we to sin because we are not under law but under grace?" The reason for obedience is twofold: that we may show ourselves grateful to God; and that we ourselves may be assured of our faith by its fruits (Q. 86). The first reason is basic, for the work of the Spirit brings new life, the dying of the old self and the birth of the new (Q. 88). The second reason is less fundamental and raises some serious problems if it is allowed to play a disproportionate role in personal piety.

Life has a direction and a purpose, namely, to glorify God (Q. 86), and it is to restore this purpose that salvation takes place. The gospel is not meant merely to supply a new vocabulary, or a good cause to work for, or a kind of ultimate fire insurance—but a new life, here and now. Although obedience is not the starting point of salvation, or the condition of it, it is, properly understood, the goal. Hence, it is impossible for those who are ingrafted into Christ by true faith not to bring forth the fruit of gratitude (Q. 64). The gift of faith is responded to by the gift of obedience. This is not strange. The common coin of friendship, love, family life, and Christian fellowship is always a gift rather than a demand. As soon as calculation and payment enter deeply into these close personal relations, they are violated. So also the coin of the relation of God to the world and to men is the coin of gifts freely given. Not to give may rupture the relation, for it is impossible (Q. 64) that love will not bear fruit in gifts—yet when giving turns subtly into payment, or into devices for getting something in return, grace is no longer present. A legal or a commercial relation has replaced love.

The second reason for good works is reassurance and influence on others (Q. 86). Neither of these play a part in the Catechism at large, but are comments upon the first reason, gratitude. Kept in a subordinate place, they enhance thankfulness. But if reassurance takes the form of tabulating one's own good works, then law and calculation can easily return. A common criticism of Reformed Christianity is that this does happen. If so, it occurs by departing from, not by following, the teaching of the Catechism. See the discussion under the Westminster Confession of this important issue.

"The Ten Commandments," Qq. 92-115. The law first appeared at the beginning of the Catechism to condemn the sinner. Now it reappears in more detail as a guide to obedience (Q. 91, as well as a convictor of sin, Qq. 114-115). To that end, the familiar "two tables" are divided according to the Reformed custom into four commands concerning duty to God, and six concerning duty to men. The interpretation goes well beyond the letter and the words to the spirit of each command.

Particularly notable are Qq. 94-95, where idolatry is defined as misplaced trust. The "Sabbath" Commandment includes Jesus' emendation of helping those in need (Luke 13:10-17) and extends even to Christian education. The honoring of parents in the Fifth Commandment is treated as a symbol for "all who are set in authority over me," and the vocabulary is reminiscent of the honor of God in Q. 94. **You shall not kill** is expounded in three questions which proceed from the prohibition of murderous acts (Q. 105), and the **hidden murder** committed by evil intentions (Q. 106), to the requirement of **patience, peace, gentleness, mercy, friendliness** to neighbors, and **also to do good to our enemies** (Q. 107). Chastity includes **actions, gestures, words, thoughts, desires** (Q. 109). The forbidding of robbery becomes a sharply stated and timely business ethic, including the Golden Rule and responsibility for **the poor in their need** (Qq. 110-111). The words **deceptive advertising or merchandising** are apparently an interpolation of modern translators—to which no one can really object. **False witness** applies to **judicial and all other matters** such as gossip, slander, and twisting words, and failing to **defend and promote my neighbor's good name** (Q. 112). The final command against coveting is used, after the manner of Augustine, as a summary prohibition against all immoderate and impure desire (Q. 115).

The last small section of the Catechism presents **the chief part of gratitude,** which is prayer. Curiously—at first glance, curiously—literal thanksgiving is not mentioned again after Q. 116. The whole is dominated by the language of asking, begging, beseeching. **Help us . . . grant that . . . be pleased to provide,** runs throughout, but there is no list of blessings acknowledged. Thus conceived, the chief part of gratitude is asking for more. So the Catechism in fact teaches. It should not surprise us that we acknowledge best that God alone is the giver of all things by petitioning him for all things. Accordingly, the Lord's Prayer is constructed wholly of petitions. The first three petitions are treated in the Catechism chiefly as pleas for the gift of obedience. The last three are construed as petitions that cover all the needs of man within God's providence: bodily (Q. 125) and spiritual (Qq. 126-127). The final three questions echo noticeably the opening lines of the Catechism and transpose the language of the first answer into the form of childlike petition.

CHAPTER 17

THE SECOND HELVETIC CONFESSION

The highest authority among Reformed confessions has generally been granted to the Second Helvetic (Swiss) Confession. It was so evaluated in the late Reformation and also in nineteenth-century America by those sturdy adherents of Westminster theology, the Hodges of Princeton. This high regard comes not only from the general excellence and fullness of the Confession, but from the wide recognition it received among European Reformed Churches. When these churches wished to show the consensus among their various existing confessions, they prepared a harmony (1581) in which the Second Helvetic Confession received the place of greatest honor and influence.

One man, Heinrich Bullinger of Zurich, wrote the Confession single-handed on his own initiative. He intended to attach it to his will as a legacy to the city in which he had labored so long. Bullinger had become head of the Zurich Church in 1531 after Zwingli's death in battle. This occurred before Calvin's conversion to the gospel, and Bullinger continued as leader until his death in 1575, eleven years after the passing of Calvin. His public life, thus, spanned three generations of the Reformation and his vast personal correspondence spanned the Continent from the British Isles to Hungary and Poland. Bullinger's theological treatises, Biblical commentaries, and sermons were among the most widely read of his time. He was a major influence in the formation of early English Puritanism. The first preacher in New Amsterdam, later New York City, was ordered by church au-

201

thorities in Holland to memorize and preach sermons from Bullinger's *Decades* to his New World congregation. The First Helvetic Confession and several other statements of belief were partly his work. In his last years he was in effect senior theologian and senior pastor of the whole Reformed family of churches. Bullinger, thus, was uniquely prepared to embody the theology of these churches in this document, his masterpiece, which he called "a simple confession and exposition of orthodox faith."

A crisis in Germany brought the Confession out into the open and caused it to be published for the first time in 1566. Adherents of the Heidelberg Catechism and their pious sovereign Frederick III of the Palatinate were in danger of being excluded from among the legally acceptable religious communions of Germany. Frederick, through his chancellor, asked for help from other Reformed Churches and received in return the document Bullinger had prepared in 1561. It was received with great enthusiasm. Quickly, other Swiss cantonal churches recognized it, and subsequently it was recognized or adopted in Scotland, France, Poland, Hungary, and Austria. Although it was revoked in Switzerland in the eighteenth century, it had its greatest influence there, and continues to be the living confession of the Reformed Churches of Hungary, Austria, Poland, and Czechoslovakia. The celebration in 1966 of the four-hundredth anniversary of its first adoption and the inclusion in the American Presbyterian *Book of Confessions* in 1967 have brought the Confession back into the mind and life of the church.

The Second Helvetic Confession is longer and more like a treatise than the others we are discussing. Its thirty chapters vary in length from about two hundred to about two thousand five hundred words, and are themselves divided by the important subheadings which Bullinger supplied. In some chapters almost one third of the language is directly quoted from the Bible. Various "holy Greek and Latin fathers" are cited or quoted, Augustine most frequently. In addition to positive teachings, heresies are listed both from the early church and the days of the Reformation. By and large the tone is peaceful, the thought mature, and the whole informed by a profound catholic (or as we prefer to say today, ecumenical) spirit.

The most remarkable achievement of the Confession is the way in which Biblical and technical theological materials are expressed simply and always with a view to their practical significance for daily life. The doctrine of God, for instance, is as lofty as that of Westminster, but never abstract or separated from the life of men. The teaching about Scripture has more to do with the word preached, read, and heard in the church than with theories of origin. Probably the second most notable quality is the way the Confession reflects the wholeness and oneness of the **assembly of the faithful called or gathered out of the world**, the church. Over against all sectarian divisions, Ch. XVII offers one of the strongest sustained passages on the oneness of the church to be found in Christian literature. Small wonder that the Confession helped when the Reformed Churches with their various confessions were being regarded as sectarians by both Lutherans and Roman Catholics. This document from the heart of the Reformation establishes better than any other that to be "Reformed" is to be nothing but the ecumenical or catholic church, reformed according to the word of God. Again, the doctrine of the church includes more about the daily life, administration, and teaching activities of the church than is found in other confessions.

The excessive length of the Second Helvetic Confession may scare away some readers. It is, however, generally easy to understand. The following outline may be of service.

Chapter	Outline
I-II	Scripture and Preaching
III-V	God and True Worship
VI-VII	Providence and Creation
VIII-IX	Sin
X-XI	The Work of Salvation
XII-XVI	Receiving Salvation, the New Life
XVII-XXI	Church, Ministry, Sacraments
XXII-XXX	Various Church Ordinances
XXIX-XXX	The Family and the State

Another helpful way to analyze the Confession for study is to note that Chs. I to II present the source and authority for Christian teaching. Chapters III to XI contain doctrines common to ancient catholic orthodoxy, richly supported by references both to the ancient church and ancient heresies, and closing with the words, **And in this way we retain the Christian, orthodox and catholic faith whole and unimpaired.** From Ch. XII through XVI the particular Reformation teachings on how man is saved come to the fore. Here there are practically no references to the early church or the fathers. From Ch. XVII to the end of the Confession the *one* catholic, Reformed Church is the subject of discourse, concluding with a short statement on the home and the political order, Chs. XXIX to XXX.

Scripture and Preaching, Chs. I to II. The Second Helvetic Confession opens with a typical Reformation assertion of "the Bible alone"—without a doctrine of revelation in nature, history, or conscience—and a typical Reformed concern to identify the canonical Scriptures as the word of God. But in addition, uniquely among all confessions, we are told also that **the preaching of the Word of God is the Word of God.** The opening sentences move rapidly and confidently from the origin to the function of Scripture: **For God himself spoke to the fathers, prophets, apostles, and still speaks to us through the Holy Scriptures. In preaching, the very Word of God is proclaimed, and received by the faithful. The inward illumination of the Spirit,** remarkably, is affirmed rather of the preached than the written word. The living voice of God spoken aloud through the living words of men is emphasized, as it was in Luther's teaching. Bullinger is more interested in the load and the destination than the vehicle. He explains his meaning in a passage from his little book called the *Summa:*

We know very well that the Scripture is not called the word of God because of the human voice, the ink and paper, or the printed letters (which all can be comprehended by the flesh), but because the meaning, which speaks through the human voice or is written with pen and ink on paper, is not originally from men, but is God's word, will, and meaning.

Thus the Bible is called the word of God because of that which it reveals, not in an exclusive and unique sense, but in a sense transferable to another instrument carrying out the same function, namely, preaching. Still, preaching must always conform to the Bible, which is the normative form of the revelation of the word.

In addition, the Bible requires **interpreting** (from the title of Ch. II), and it must be "expounded" and "applied" (Ch. XVIII). To grasp the **genuine** meaning correctly, **private interpretation** (Ch. II) must be excluded and also the official interpretations of the Roman Church. Rather, attention must be given to the original languages of Scripture (Rome at that time held to a Latin translation) and to the **circumstances** or context of each passage. Like and unlike passages are to be compared, and preference given to those which are clearer and to teachings which occur more frequently. Also, a guide to the interpreter is the **rule of faith and love,** which means summaries such as the Apostles' Creed and the love that holds together the communion of the church.

This short passage on interpretation is the only one of its kind among early confessions. It reflects the processes by which the Bible exercised its authority in the reform of the church and in the daily lives of men through preaching and teaching. That a good deal more needs to be said in the light of modern historical studies need not dim our appreciation for this statement, which accords with the scholarship of the sixteenth century. The provision of interpretative or "hermeneutic" principles so that the Bible may be always freshly understood and may not become the captive of official doctrine is a constant task of the church.

God and True Worship, Chs. III to V. No risk is taken that the doctrine of God might become merely theoretical or in a bad sense merely theological. Linked with the doctrine of the Trinity (Ch. III) are two chapters on worship (Chs. IV to V). Reading between the lines, one sees that this means that the doctrine of

God must not be separated from the worship of God. The principle can be seen throughout the works of Bullinger and Calvin, and it certainly is Scriptural, but it is nowhere expressed in a confession, except here. Much more about the actual content of worship will follow in Chs. XVII to XXIII, etc. In the meantime, this broad treatment sets the whole Confession within the context of God and the worship of God. The doctrine of the Trinity is presented in a traditional way, except that the deity of the Spirit alone is here supported by Biblical verses.The deity of the Son is similarly supported in Ch. XI.

False worship includes every kind not prescribed by Scripture. Specifically rejected are images that represent God or Christ. Lutherans, somewhat less strict in reading the Second Commandment, retained Christ's image in the crucifix on the altar. Here, in characteristic Reformed-Puritan style, was the ground for destroying works of art, good and bad, that tempted men to idolatry. The only true images are the living and true creatures of God. Further, the saints are not to be adored, worshiped, or invoked, nor are their relics to be reverenced. At the same time we do not despise the saints, who are living members of Christ and friends of God. All true worship is directed to God alone and takes place through the mediation of Christ. The only acceptable aids or helps are the Sacraments which Christ himself instituted.

Even a first reader of the Confession must by now be thoroughly apprised of its practical character. Not only has the doctrine of Scripture focused on the living, preached witness to us, but the doctrines both of God and of the Mediator first appeared in the setting of worship—and all this has taken place before the author of the Confession has managed to advance in the list of topics to where the world is created!

Providence and Creation, Chs. VI and VII. Now providence appears before creation. If providence were the doctrine of eternal decree such as is found in the Westminster Confession (Ch. III), the sequence would be logical. But here we encounter the teaching that all things . . . are preserved and governed by the providence of this wise, eternal, and almighty God. Only in the next chapter do we read that God created all things. Farther along we shall notice that the doctrine of divine government continues to dominate Chs. VIII and IX. It is again the concentration of the entire document on the actual life of man and the relation of God to human history that has caused the author to reject the logical order of Chs. VII and VIII and teach providence first.

God's rule, Bullinger hastens to say, does not cancel out man's purpose. God does govern all creatures: Nevertheless, we do not spurn as useless the means by which divine providence works. Men may not resign their own responsibility, for God's providence functions through their deeds and purposes to achieve his ends. Bullinger, by the way, always held back a bit from some of Calvin's statements that sounded as if God's omnipotence canceled man's initiative. Men, angels, and devils were all created free and good, and it is of their own free will that they became disobedient. In passing, the practice of inserting "angels" and "devils" in the account of creation (Ch. VII) was traditional from early centuries, although lacking in direct Biblical support. In the sixteenth century practically everyone accepted the existence and influence of such beings as a matter of course.

Sin, Chs. VIII to IX. The creation of the physical world, angels, and man were very briefly dealt with in Ch. VII. But man and his condition are lengthily described in terms of the divine image (Ch. VII), the Fall and the nature of sin (Ch. VIII), and man's free will (Ch. IX). The latter is a very comprehensive treatment which gives a synopsis of the threefold condition of man as created, fallen, and reborn. It then leaps ahead to discuss the Christian life in a way that presupposes the contents of Chs. XII to XVI. The main issue continues to be the question of how to express the relation of God's good "government" of all things to man's ability to exert his own will.

Man fell at the instigation of the serpent and by his own fault. God, at the same time, ordains all means and ends in creation. But the problem of whether or not God willed the Fall is abruptly rejected as an overcurious, irreverent question. Some godly teachers have been forced by heretics to discuss this subject (Calvin, no doubt), but the Second Helvetic Confession affirms the paradox and leaves it unresolved: What things are done are not evil with respect to the providence, will, and power of God, but in respect of Satan and our will opposing the will of God.

Before the Fall, man's will was free; after the Fall it was enslaved. Here the reader should compare especially the Westminster Confession (Ch. VI) for the variety possible between two statements that are in general agreement. Man reborn by the Spirit has his will again freed so that it is able to do the good of its own accord (Ch. IX). This new freedom, however, is weak because sin continues to exert its power, and even regenerate men may not boast of their goodness.

The Work of Salvation, Chs. X to XI. The salvation of men by "election" and "free grace" is discussed under two topics, "predestination" in Ch. X and "Jesus Christ" in Ch. XI. Like the Scots Confession, the Second Helvetic treats these two topics together—and this is unlike the Westminster Confession (Ch. III) which first erects the superstructure of the divine decree. Predestination, like providence, is not a speculation about how God thinks or acts, but it is the answer to the question of how men, helpless through sin, are introduced to God's grace. The bulk of Ch. X dwells upon the relation of the elect man to Christ, the confidence this gives him, the errors from which it protects him (libertinism, fatalism, scorn of admonition, temptation to false confidence), and the root of the whole relation in faith. Men are not to puzzle about election: If you believe and are in Christ, you are elected. Even the reprobate are treated with pastoral concern. We must hope well of all, and not rashly judge any man to be a reprobate. The center, as always, in this Confession is Christ in whom and on account of whom we are elect.

Christ himself was predestinated or foreordained to be the Savior of the world. So begins Ch. XI, which is the doctrine of Christ in the Confession. The long first part of the chapter repeats with extensive Biblical support the ancient doctrine of Nicaea and Chalcedon that Christ is the Eternal Son, True God and True Man, two natures in one Person, that he truly suffered, died, and rose from the dead. The stress upon the same flesh of Christ located in heaven at a certain place after the ascension is to be understood as a rejection of Lutheran and Roman Catholic teachings about the presence of Christ in the Lord's Supper and the Mass. The ascension is also the place where this Confession speaks of the resurrection of all the dead, eternal life, and eternal punishment. The beginning and the end, predestination and eternal life, are here quite literally united, brought together in the single chapter on Jesus Christ, who is called alpha and omega.

The fruit of Christ's death and resurrection was reconciliation and salvation. The fruit was reaped by those who lived before the law and under the law, as well as by all under the Gospel, for there is no other Savior of men than Christ. The final lines of the chapter contain an encomium to Christ the sole Redeemer and Savior of the world, the King and High Priest, the true and awaited Messiah, and also a reaffirmation of the decrees of the first ecumenical councils and the orthodoxy of the faith Reformed.

Receiving Salvation, the New Life, Chs. XII to XVI. The one term that encompasses all of what is taught in these chapters is faith, defined in the first lines of Ch. XVI. The law (Ch. XII) was given to expose man's weakness, so that despairing of our strength, [we] might be converted to Christ in faith. But since the law contains the whole will of God and all necessary precepts for every sphere of life, it continues to be useful to the Church . . . when explained by the Gospel. The condemning function is abrogated, but the guiding function (given at length in Ch. XVI) never ends.

Even before the advent of Christ, the promise of his coming (Ch. XIII) removed the curse of the law for those who received it. Salvation through Christ, thus, was effective in the days of patriarchs and prophets, yet the gospel properly speaking consists of the history of what things Christ taught and did. This point, taken up again in the last paragraph, is meant to rebuff the charges of Rome that the Protestant faith was "scarcely thirty years old." The use of predestination to shore up the point is an oddity, to say the least.

The contrast between evangelical repentance and the Roman

Catholic sacrament of penance is the hotly disputed point behind
Ch. XIV. On this issue the Reformation had ignited fifty years
before with the preaching of Luther and Zwingli against indul-
gences. Here, **repentance is conversion,** a turning to God and the
recovery of a right mind in sinful man. It is a sheer gift of God
and not a work of our strength. Nor is it a sacrament. Ministers
remit sins and absolve sinners when they preach the Gospel of
Christ. Repentance and conversion issue in new obedience out of
gratitude for the gift of salvation.

The by now familiar doctrine of justification (Ch. XV) differs
in no important way from what we have seen in the Scots and
Heidelberg documents. The definition that opens the chapter and
the lucid explanations of the last three paragraphs, however, are
valuable complements to the teachings of other parts of *The Book
of Confessions.*

Faith is the underlying theme of this series of chapters. The
most characteristic phrase concerning faith is **through faith.** Faith
is that through which law is forsaken, spirit triumphs over letter,
men repent and are converted, renewed, and justified; in short,
through faith Christ is received and a new life begun and constantly nourished. It is all summed up in the definition given in
the first two paragraphs of Ch. XVI. Then in the third and
fourth paragraphs we turn to faith **active through love,** which is
the threshold for entering on a life of **good works.** The burden
of the remainder of the chapter is to insist upon good works as
the natural and expected outgrowth of faith while holding that
they in no way merit God's grace or recompense him for it. God
owes nothing to anyone, nevertheless [he] promises that he will
give a reward to his faithful worshippers. As written in the preceding chapter on the Heidelberg Catechism, grace freely given,
not merit, law, or payment, is the sole medium of exchange provided by the gospel.

Church, Ministry, Sacraments, Chs. XVII to XXII. We have
reached approximately the middle of the Second Helvetic Confession, only to discover that all the rest of it is devoted to the
church, Sacraments, and various church ordinances. The ven-
erable Reformation teachings on Scripture Alone (Chs. I to II)

Grace Alone, Christ Alone (Chs. III to XI), and Faith Alone (Chs. XII to XVI) now culminate in an equally important but often less well appreciated theme, "One Church." The oneness of the church (already mentioned as a leading motif of this entire document), set against a Trinitarian background, is derived from its one head, Christ, the sole Mediator. This is the unceasing refrain of the entire seventeenth chapter. With striking emphasis the word "one" recurs nine times in a single sentence: one God, one Mediator, one Shepherd, one Head, one Spirit, one salvation, one faith, one covenant, one church. Twice again in this chapter after the citing of diversities of time, place, and status, and also while the marks of the church are being discussed, the refrain is repeated. The parallel, almost identical, theme of universality or catholicity is introduced at the beginning of the chapter by identifying the doctrine to be expounded with the Apostles' Creed and again at the end by affirming that the **truth and unity of the Church** consists in the **truth and unity of the catholic faith**, derived from Scripture, of which the Apostles' Creed is a summary.

The major purpose of Ch. XVII, thus, is to identify the church "governed and reformed" by the word (also, Ch. I), as the one, holy, catholic church of which Christ alone is the head, to the exclusion of sectarians who scorn Scripture and of Rome which displaces Christ by an earthly head. So far as the structure of the Confession is concerned, the achievement of Chs. XVII through XXVIII is to focus full attention upon the actual contemporary life of the **assembly of the faithful.** Agreeing with the emphasis on means in the doctrines of providence and predestination, the entire latter half of the Confession is devoted to the *means* by which God through the Spirit acts both to create and to preserve the church. The means, however, are not devices that man uses to achieve something, but God's instruments to carry out his purpose.

That Christ alone is head of the church is not meant to exclude but to strengthen the means through which he works, namely, preaching and Sacraments carried out by **lawful** ministers (Ch. XVIII). Preaching has priority over the Sacraments. Although no one chapter is devoted to preaching in this or any confession, the

Second Helvetic Confession contains a full treatment if all the parts are drawn together from Chs. I and II, XIII and XVIII. Further material will appear when the reader realizes that preaching, teaching, doctrine, exposition of Scripture, and a few other expressions are used almost as synonyms. Whatever the precise term, preaching is the communication or proclamation of the gospel in words, and it is the chief medium or means that relates Christ and faith. **Faith is the gift of God** which he gives **by the Holy Spirit by means of the preaching of the Gospel and steadfast prayer.** (Ch. XVI.)

Added to preaching **from the beginning** are Sacraments. These are certain **mystical symbols, . . . holy rites, . . . sacred actions** of which God is the author and Christ the sole institutor. The Sacraments are discussed, as already noted, in Chapter 21 of this volume.

Various Church Ordinances, Chs. XXII to XXX. In order that public preaching and prayer, the Sacraments, and offerings for the poor may take place, regular times of assembly are required by the church, as well as appropriate buildings with modestly clothed, sober Christians in attendance. Public prayer should be proper in style and length, and above all, **poured forth to God alone, through the mediation of Christ only, out of faith and love** (Ch. XXIII). These and other concerns for holidays and fasts, education and ministering to the sick, burial and other rites and ceremonies, and the care of church property occupy Chs. XXIV through XXVIII. All may be construed as relating to the work of the ministry in the general care and government of the church. This, in turn, bears out the practical, down-to-earth quality of the Second Helvetic Confession. These are not addenda, but direct implications of the teachings of the early chapters.

The Family and the State, Chs. XXIX to XXX. The fullest treatment of marriage and family in any of the confessions of the church is found here. Celibacy, with which the chapter begins and ends, was regarded as the highest and most meritorious estate in life before the Reformation. But here, marriage, **which is . . . continency itself,** is upheld as **instituted by the Lord God himself.** In marriage **man and woman . . . cleave one to the other**

THE SECOND HELVETIC CONFESSION

inseparably, and live together in complete love and concord. Marriages are to be lawfully contracted, **kept holy,** and guarded **against quarrels, dissensions, lust and adultery.** The "Matrimonial Forum" or court, was a unique Zurich institution for counseling and judging cases of troubled marriages. Further, this chapter tells of raising children, educating them both in faith and **honest trades or professions.** The domestic duties of parents **are in God's sight holy and truly good works.** Bravo Bullinger!—who owed his large family and hospitable home to the former nun, Anna Adlischweiler, his wife. Not since has a Reformed confession dealt with marriage and the family in such a sympathetic and positive way. It must do so again, but in more contemporary terms. Bullinger concludes this chapter with a small fillip against monastic vows of poverty: **We do not disapprove of riches or rich men, if they be godly and use their riches well.**

The state (Ch. XXX) is from God, and it rightly should hold **the chief place in the world.** The purpose of the state is to **secure and preserve peace and public tranquillity.** For this the state makes laws and bears the sword to control criminals and heretics (!) and, if it is necessary, to wage war. Subjects should **honor and reverence the magistrate as the minister of God;** . . . **love him, favor him, and pray for him as their father;** . . . **obey** . . . **commands [and]** . . . **pay** . . . **taxes.** All sedition and rebellion is condemned. There is nothing here on forms of government, rights of the oppressed, or other themes that force themselves on modern men. Such teaching certainly cannot be transferred directly to a present situation. But here, again, appears the concrete, practical concern of the Second Helvetic Confession for all aspects of the life of men. The teachings do not hold in their precise form, but the relevance they show for the days in which they were written must remind the church of the breadth of its task.

To conclude: unlike several Reformed confessions, the Second Helvetic Confession does not end with a chapter on eternal life, which was treated in Chs. VII and XI. Rather, it is brought to a close among the practical affairs of the church, the state, and the Christian life in a world **preserved and governed by the providence of this wise, eternal and almighty God** (Ch. VI).

CHAPTER 18

THE WESTMINSTER CONFESSION

The Westminster Confession was written by a congress of Puritan clergymen of the Church of England that met in 1643 by order of the Long Parliament. Their wider task was to construct a Presbyterian church order for the entire British Isles. Parliament had agreed to this in a Solemn League and Covenant concluded with the Scottish church and nation. One hundred twenty-one ministers were appointed to membership together with thirty members of Parliament named, as one of them said, "to overlook the clergy, lest they spoil the civil work." Six able Scottish advisers, seated prominently, exerted strong influence among the "threescore" in average attendance

England in the 1640's was in a state of revolution, and the Westminster Assembly was a power and a pawn in the struggle. Before its 1,163 sessions had ended in 1649, the Archbishop of Canterbury and the king had been beheaded. The Presbyterian Parliamentarians lost out to Cromwell's Independents, and their program was never widely established in England. With the restoration of monarchy and bishops after 1660, Presbyterian clergy were ejected from the church, so despised that the body of Twisse, the Assembly moderator, was exhumed from Westminster Abbey and thrown into a pit. With the Act of Toleration, 1689, they obtained freedom, but Presbyterianism practically died out as a free church. It is remarkable that the Westminster Confession, offered as "Humble Advice" to a revolutionary Parliament in a tumultuous age, is the most patiently constructed,

214

the most massive and intricate, of Reformed confessions—also, that it was to have its influence not in England but Scotland and, more curiously, in an America where no parliament could convene a church synod.

Although political conditions were revolutionary, the theological work of the Assembly was not. The Westminster divines were not breaking new ground, but consolidating the intellectual work of three quarters of a century since the last comprehensive confessions had been written. These years of English and continental church history included bloody wars of religion, synods for the extirpation of heresy, decades of reflection and teaching, and an immense volume of theological writing. The drive for stable doctrine, worship, and order in the face of rival claims to catholic orthodoxy and rival national destinies had brought into being the ponderous way of thought called Protestant orthodoxy. "Orthodoxy" is perhaps the best name for it, because the highest zeal was to demonstrate "right belief," which is the meaning of the term. Some prefer to call it scholasticism, because it was largely the work of teachers and because in some ways it resembles the theological science of medieval Schoolmen more than the Protestant Reformers.

Thanks to the Reformed theological consensus, it could happen that on matters of doctrine there were no grave differences among the Westminster fathers. Their battles royal concerned church organization. A thirty days' "Grand Debate" took place over whether or not presbyterian order is sanctioned by "divine right." Still, they devoted more than two years to drafting and debating the Confession. Their lasting achievement was to refine a predestinarian, two-covenant system of theology into confessional form. What this rather ponderous description means we shall, hopefully, explain in the following pages.

The political defeat of the Presbyterians practically ended, as we have already mentioned, the influence of the Westminster divines in England. The present-day English Presbyterians derive chiefly from Scots who moved to England in the eighteenth century. The Confession was first officially put into service by the General As-

sembly of the Church of Scotland in 1647, and has remained in
force there ever since. Various Congregational assemblies adopted
it with minor changes in Old and New England, as did some
Baptists in England and America. The mainstream of influence
in America, however, followed adoption by the Presbyterian General Synod in Philadelphia in 1729, and later by the newly
founded General Assembly in 1788. Through two and a half
centuries marked by migrations of people, shifts in theology,
regional divisions, schisms, and reunions, it has continued to be
the confession of the several American Presbyterian churches. A
revision movement in the largest Presbyterian group, the Presbyterian Church in the United States of America, produced some
modifications of the Confession in 1903, and the United Presbyterian Church of North America replaced it with the Confessional Statement of 1925. When these two united in 1958, Westminster was the basis, and a new contemporary statement was
projected. A new phase in the history of the Westminster Confession began with the creation of *The Book of Confessions* in
May, 1967, by the union church. The Presbyterian Church in the
United States (largely in the Southern States) holds the Confession, including most of the changes made in 1903.

The text printed in *The Book of Confessions* is not exactly that
prepared by the Westminster divines, but the form received in the
Presbyterian church union of 1958. All changes are indicated in
footnotes. The chief alterations are: (1) those of 1788 concerning
the civil magistrate (Ch. XXIII) and church councils (Ch.
XXXI), which recognized the separation of church and state on
this side of the Atlantic; (2) new chapters on the Holy Spirit
(Ch. XXXIV), the love of God and missions (Ch. XXXV), and
a mild modification of predestination (Declaratory Statement)
were added in 1903; (3) the present chapter on marriage and
divorce (Ch. XXIV) was newly written and adopted in 1953;
(4) among other smaller changes of varying importance, several
served to remove expressions offensive to good taste concerning
the "popish" church. When the Presbyterian Church in the
United States added the 1903 chapters (in 1942), they quite

properly inserted them after the present Ch. VIII. This changes the chapter numbers from that point on in editions published by that church.

The structure of the Confession is reasonably plain through Ch. XVIII except for Ch. IX, the location of which is not self-evident. Chapters XIX through XXIV are quite partial and ad hoc, but hopefully the suggestions made for grouping them in the following outline are not far from the intent of the authors. The outline is meant as a help for the contemporary reader and a guide to study groups.

Chapter	Outline
I	Holy Scripture
II-V	God the Creator
VI	Man's Sin (with IX, Free Will)
VII-VIII	Salvation Provided
IX-XVIII	Salvation Applied
XIX-XX	God's Law and Liberty
XXI-XXII	Duty Toward God
XXIII-XXIV	Duty Toward Man
XXV-XXXI	The Church
	Sacraments, Discipline, Government
XXXII-XXXIII	The Consummation
(Added in 1903)	
XXXIV	The Holy Spirit
XXXV	The Love of God and Missions
—	Declaratory Statement

The special prominence of the Westminster Confession in American Presbyterianism invites more extended comment than the older confessions. Beyond this the reader should consult Prof. George S. Hendry's *The Westminster Confession for Today*. Our plan is to present an analytical survey followed by special comments on its three controlling themes: Scripture, Divine Sovereignty, and the Two Covenants.

Chapter I, which we shall discuss in more detail below, is in a class by itself. It is meant to establish the authority of the Bible from which everything else in the Confession is to be drawn. Furthermore, the Bible's authority is derived from the Bible itself, and not lent to it from elsewhere. To put it briefly, God inspired Scripture (Ch. I, Sec. 1), the Spirit persuades of Scripture's truth (Ch. I, Sec. 6), and Scripture is its own interpreter (Ch. I, Sec. 9). Three other ways of knowing or reasoning about God are mentioned in the Confession: the manifestation in nature, which leaves man inexcusable (Ch. I, Sec. 1); deductions made from Scripture (Ch. I, Sec. 6); and the light and the law of nature within which men apparently agree with and supplement Scripture (Ch. I, Sec. 1; Ch. XXI, Secs. 1, 7). But these are peripheral to an almost exclusive concern for the Bible's teachings about God's glory, man's salvation, faith, and life.

Holy Scripture, Ch. I. The first chapter, thus, tells *how* the Christian knows God, and all the rest tell *what* God reveals and *what* the believer learns from Scripture.

God the Creator, Chs. II to V. These chapters which also will be discussed more in detail below, present God the Creator, or more carefully put, God in himself (Chs. II to III), then God in his works of creation and providence (Chs. IV to V). As Ch. I gives the principle of knowing, these chapters present the principle of being. Everything *known* of God in the Confession follows from Ch. I, and everything that *is* derives from the Triune Creator.

Man's Sin, Ch. VI. This chapter does not appear unexpectedly. It is implied in the **inexcusable** condition of man in the first clause of Ch. I, and in the doctrine of God (Ch. II, Secs. 1-2). The "Eternal Decree" shows how God both brings about and deals with sin (Ch. III), and sin is again a focal point of the doctrine of providence (Ch. V, Secs. 4-6). The direct treatment of Ch. VI fits in a historical sequence—creation, fall, salvation— and begins appropriately with "The Fall of Man" as a historical event.

Our first parents, tempted by Satan, **sinned in eating the forbidden fruit.** This act is described variously in the history of Christian thought as motivated by pride, sensuality, doubt, or disobedience. Here it is lawbreaking: a transgression of the righteous law of God (Ch. VI, Sec. 6). This is identical with saying in another idiom, a violation of the covenant of works (Ch. VII, Secs. 2-3; Ch. XIX, Sec. 1), and in still another, destruction of the divine image (Ch. IV, Sec. 2; Ch. VI, Sec. 2). The result of the first transgression was defilement and corruption of human nature at the root. The Larger Catechism says Adam sinned "as a public person, not for himself only" (Q. 22) and the Shorter, that "all mankind . . . sinned in him, and fell with him" (Q. 16). Guilt was imputed, corruption passed down, and punishment both temporal and eternal was pronounced on all their posterity, descending from them by ordinary generation (Ch. VI, Sec. 3). The doctrine here presented without one word concerning remnants of goodness remaining in man is generally and rightly called "total depravity" (Ch. VI, Sec. 2).

Free will, described in Ch. IX, might very well have followed here, because the subject matter is the effects of sin on the human will. The scheme of the chapter is like Augustine's three stages of man's history: first, the stage of innocence in which man had the power and freedom not to sin at all (Ch. IX, Secs. 1-2); second, after the Fall, when man's will cannot avoid evil and is incapable of turning to God (Ch. IX, Secs. 3-4); and third, eternal life, when man shall no longer sin, because he will be immutably free to good alone (Ch. IX, Sec. 5). The whole of ordinary history takes place within the second stage, and even the regenerate are not free of sin. Perhaps this chapter was placed where it is to reinforce a basic premise of the Confession that in matters of salvation the sinner is a slave and can do nothing to aid himself.

Salvation Provided, Chs. VII and VIII. The title "The Covenants and the Mediator" might also have been given to these chapters. Covenant is the historical principle of the Westminster Confession, comparable to the principles of knowledge (Ch. I) and being (Chs. II to V) in its importance for the entire system. The infinite distance between God and the creature is spanned by God's voluntary condescension, called covenant (Ch. VII, Sec. 1). The word "covenant," not defined in the confession, means a formal agreement or pact between two parties. In this case the terms of agreement are conditions freely laid down or promises freely given by God, together with obligations laid upon the elect human partners. "Testament," another translation of the same word (Heb. 9:15-17), teaches the same thing under the figure of a will and the inheritors (Ch. VII, Sec. 4). The violated covenant of works or law was followed by a covenant of grace or forgiveness, culminating in the coming of the Mediator of the covenant (Larger Catechism, Q. 36). Christ's obedience fulfills covenant conditions on behalf of men who have excluded themselves by disobedience. All human history is encompassed by the two covenants, and by the two stages, law and gospel, of the covenant of grace. From the latter, the Biblical writings are named Old and New Testament or covenant (see below).

The particularly notable features of Westminster's doctrine of Christ (Ch. VIII) are, first, the thoroughness with which the doctrine of Christ's person is integrated with that of his work. The classical language of Nicaea and Chalcedon is present (Ch. VIII, Sec. 2) and, as usual, comes first. Then it is commingled with that of atonement or reconciliation. The effect of Christ's work is that he satisfied the justice of his Father and purchased . . . reconciliation and an everlasting inheritance (Ch. VIII, Sec. 5). We recall here the teaching and the critique of the Heidelberg Catechism, which, like Westminster, places Christ in the position of making a purchase from his Father (Chapter 16, above). The questions we raise are not concerning whether this language is Biblical, but whether it is used in a Biblical way.

Secondly, the effect of Christ's work is limited by the doctrine of the decree in Ch. III. The satisfaction and the purchase price are not for all men, but for all those whom the Father hath given unto him (Ch. VIII, Sec. 5). Did Christ die for all, or only for the elect? Since the Confession holds that some men are foreordained to everlasting death . . . particularly and unchangeably . . . and their number is . . . certain and definite (Ch. III, Secs. 3-4), it cannot affirm that Christ died for all. While there is some disagreement about how severely Westminster teaches "limited atonement" (the word "atonement" is not used, but "reconciliation"), it seems to the present writer that there is no way to avoid the conclusion that it does so teach, although in irenic, moderate form. This problem plagued the Reformed theology, because many held that such Biblical texts as John 3:16 point to God's wider will to save. The teaching was modified, or muddled, in the additions made in 1903. Coming at the problem, not from the doctrine of the decree, but from a consideration of the love of God, the revisers speak of God's **gift of his Son to be the propitiation for the sins of the whole world** (Declaratory Statement). Again, God through the covenant and Christ's sacrifice provided a way of salvation **sufficient for and adapted to the whole lost race of man** (Ch. XXXV, Sec. 1). If the drift of the modifications had been taken seriously by the majority of the church, a much more far-reaching revision of the Confession would have developed back in the year 1903 (further comments below).

The dominance of the doctrine of decree in the doctrine of Christ, we should have noted, is already clear in the opening paragraph (Ch. VIII, Sec. 1), which is a capsule of the whole of redemption (cf. also, Ch. III, Secs. 5-6). The concluding paragraph (Sec. 8) of Ch. VIII repeats (observe carefully!) the three offices of Christ named in Sec. 1 and summarizes the group of chapters which immediately follow.

Salvation Applied, Chs. IX to XVIII. We have now learned about the fatal disease of man (Ch. VI), and also about the cure (Chs. VII to VIII). But medicine is useless unless it reaches the sick man. So with salvation **God did . . . decree to justify all the elect; and Christ did . . . die for their sins . . . ; nevertheless they are not justified until the Holy Spirit doth . . . actually apply Christ unto them.** (Ch. XI, Sec. 4, emphasis mine, and cf. Ch. VIII, Sec. 8.) The same is said in the 1903 addition, in similar prickly prose, **The Holy Spirit . . . is the only efficient agent in the application of redemption** (Ch. XXXIV, Sec. 3). The eternal decree takes effect in time when it is "applied" in the ways now to be described.

The titles of these chapters can be found in all the older theological systems. The series was called the "order" or "way" of salvation, or the "dispensation" of salvation, or the "application of grace." One problem was to achieve the right order and the correct interrelation among these closely connected themes. Does repentance come before faith, or follow it? What is the relation of Christian obedience (sanctification) to justification by faith and to the new birth, and of all these to the decree of God? Should the order be logical, biographical, Biblical—and if the latter, according to what passage?

The Westminster solution, as demanded by the doctrine of eternal decree, moves from eternity to time (Ch. X, Sec. 1), from decree through effectual calling, to the effects that follow in the believer. We should remember again that Ch. IX was a last reminder, before the effectual call, that man by himself is guilty, helpless, and lost. He cannot move himself; he has to be moved.

"Effectual calling" (Ch. X) is the historical underside of the eternal decree. Reduced to its basic elements, the decree is a cause and we now observe its effect. God calls effectually those, and those only (Sec. 1), whom he has predestined. And these are altogether passive therein, until, by the action of the Spirit, they are enabled to answer this call (Sec. 2). The sheer cause-and-effect mechanics of this chapter, which dominates those following, raises problems that are discussed more fully below in the pages on God's sovereignty. Three remarks will suffice to expose the structure of the Confession, which is our present task. (1) The first paragraph contains in advance summary most of what follows all the way through Ch. XVIII. This occurs because everything that happens has a kind of preexistence in the decree. (2) Throughout, the active subject is God, who acts with or without means. Elect infants and other elect persons, who are incapable of being outwardly called are saved by a special work of the Spirit (Ch. X, Sec. 3, emphasis mine). (3) The exclusiveness cannot be missed: Others, not elected, even though called by the ministry of the Word, and having some common operations of the Spirit . . . cannot be saved, nor can men not professing the Christian

religion, however diligent in practicing their own way. To assert
that such may be saved is very pernicious, and to be detested.

Some flesh is put on the bare bones of causality by the language
of justice and of family life in the next two chapters. The language of justification, from the apostle Paul, invokes the legal
aspect, which is also the covenant aspect, of the eternal decree.
It is the transaction by which God receives the elect, accepting
their persons as righteous (Ch. XI, Sec. 1) through the instrument of faith (Sec. 2) and by substituting Christ's satisfaction
(Sec. 3). Then, in a set of images drawn from the family idiom
of both John's Gospel and Paul's letters, the justified are
"adopted" among the children who call God Father (Ch. XII).

Chapter XIII is a turning point in the series on Salvation
Applied. In Chs. X through XII, the action is wholly God's, but
from Ch. XIII through XVIII we learn what the Spirit enables
man to do. This is the inward, subjective side of calling. The
same Word and Spirit (Ch. X, Sec. 1) now bring about changes
in the elect person so radical that he is called regenerated or
reborn. This is only the beginning of a lifelong process (Ch.
XIII, Sec. 1) which, however, is never complete in this life, but
introduces a continuing war between flesh and spirit. In this
warfare, although the remaining corruption for a time may much
prevail, yet . . . the regenerate part doth overcome (Sec. 3).

Now at last we arrive at the topic "faith," whereby the elect
are enabled to believe to the saving of their souls (Ch. XIV, Sec.
1; cf. Ch. XI, Sec. 2). The definition of faith in Ch. XIV, Sec. 2,
is divided into two parts. The first sentence tells the elect man's
response to the Bible (whatsoever is revealed in the Word), and
the second sentence contains his dependence on Christ alone, for
justification, sanctification, and eternal life. Faith has been practically absorbed into the two dominant themes of the Confession.
The knowledge aspect has been taken up into the doctrine of
Scripture, and the trust aspect has been transposed through the
"way" of salvation (Chs. X to XVIII) into the key of the effectual call and eternal decree. Faith is demoted to a relatively minor
role. The watchword of the Reformation, "By faith alone!" has

been practically replaced with another, "By divine decree!" In saying this we risk exaggeration. For Westminster does speak of faith as **accepting, receiving, and resting upon Christ alone.** But let the reader, then, compare the subject "faith" in the Scots, the Heidelberg, and the Second Helvetic documents, and also Calvin's formulation: "Now we shall possess a right definition of faith if we call it a firm and certain knowledge of God's benevolence toward us, founded upon the truth of the freely given promise in Christ, both revealed to our minds and sealed upon our hearts through the Holy Spirit" (*Institutes,* III.ii.7).

Parenthetically, Calvin in his *Institutes* takes an opposite course from that of the Westminster Confession. He begins with faith and repentance. Then follow the new life and justification, then Christian liberty and prayer, and last of all—the last implication of the gift of faith—predestination. Thus Calvin moves *up from below,* from faith to predestination, while Westminster moves *down from above,* from decree, through call, to faith. Many of the words are the same, and both belong to the same family of theology, but the great-grandsons of Calvin at the Westminster Assembly were letting logic and system dominate Biblical teaching.

Repentance follows faith (Ch. XV). This sets it off from all other kinds of regret and remorse because, like faith, it is an **evangelical grace,** a gift of the Spirit. The title of Ch. XV, "Repentance Unto Life," is a good deal more Biblical than the body of it. **Unto life,** the positive aspect of repentance, is found only at the end of Sec. 2. The New Testament Greek word for it means "a transformation of the mind." One sentence in the Shorter Catechism, Q. 87, describes it better than this rather unsatisfactory chapter.

Good works are **fruits and evidences** of faith produced by an **actual influence** of the Spirit (Ch. XVI, Secs. 2-3). They differ from the most admirable **works done by unregenerate men** because the latter lack the source (faith), the pattern (the word), and the purpose (God's glory) of true good works (Sec. 7). The motive for and the function of the believer's good works is described in Sec. 2 and merits careful study as the root of Christian ethics in the Confession. The subject will be greatly enlarged upon in chapters on the law (Chs. XIX to XXIV) and in the catechisms.

Perseverance (Ch. XVII) and assurance (Ch. XVIII) complete the "order" of salvation series. Perseverance means that because of the **immutability of the decree of election** (Ch. XVII, Sec. 2), the elect can never fall away. Nonetheless, because of continuing sin, their lives may show some rather scandalous lapses from the holiness to which they are called (Sec. 3). So also, while believers *may* possess an **infallible assurance of faith** (Ch. XVIII, Sec. 2), this does not belong to the essence of faith, and may be lacking. Assurance may be **shaken, diminished, and intermitted** through sin, temptation, or **by God's withdrawing the light of his countenance.** The preventive and the cure for this uncertainty and the way of possibly achieving **infallible assurance** is prescribed. **It is the duty of everyone to give all diligence to make his calling and election sure. (Ch. XVIII, Sec. 3.)**

One of the most famous problems concerning Reformed theology arises from this suggested reassurance. Where does certainty rest? Is it wholly in the **promises of salvation** and in the evidences of the Spirit's work (Ch. XVIII, Sec. 2), or is it transferred to the believer's own **diligence** (Sec. 3)? Further, since the same chapter teaches that there may be **false hopes and carnal presumptions . . . of salvation** (Sec. 1), some additional anxiety is likely to arise, tempting the believer to convince himself by his own Christian performance. If *re*assurance plays the major role in a believer's life, then law and conditional salvation have returned, in effect, for faith's confidence is transferred to obedience, and removed from God's free grace. Many volumes have been written taking the view that the diligence of the Puritans in worldly callings was a form of reassurance of salvation, hence the "Protestant ethic." Secular good works take the place of ascetic obedience that two centuries earlier drew men into monasteries. This tortuous chapter betrays, at least, the kinds of uncertainties that develop when the love of God is subordinated to the inscrutable decree.

God's Law and Christian Liberty, Chs. XIX to XX. If God's decree dominates the Westminster Confession from the divine side, God's law controls the historical dimension. The life of man within the covenant scheme is always surrounded by law. God's law, a perfect rule of righteousness (Ch. XIX, Sec. 2), was given to Adam as a covenant of works, by which he bound him and all his posterity to personal, entire, exact, and perpetual obedience (Ch. XIX, Sec. 1; Ch. VII, Sec. 2; Ch. IV, Sec. 2). Neither doth Christ in the gospel any way dissolve, but much strengthen, this obligation (Ch. XIX, Sec. 5). The unalterable moral law stands firm from creation to consummation. It was given special form in the Ten Commandments, and temporary supplements in the ceremonies and civic laws of Israel. Always it has been accompanied by the promise of life for obedience and the threat of death for violation. Since all men are violators, they are cursed by the law to die. Only the justified (Ch. XIX, Sec. 5) shall live, that is to say, those who receive as a gift Christ's legal obedience to take the place of their own unrighteousness. (Cf. Chs. VII to VIII, XIX to XX, and concluding remarks.)

Nonetheless, the law continues to have uses for the justified man. It provides a rule of life, discloses sinful pollutions, and demonstrates the need for Christ (Ch. XIX, Sec. 6). No longer does law threaten the believer as a covenant of works on which his salvation depends, for these uses of law sweetly comply with the gospel. Also, the Spirit enables the wills of men to do freely and cheerfully what law requires (Ch. XIX, Sec. 7). The liberty of a Christian is not exemption from obedience, but freedom from having to earn his salvation, and from the guilt, wrath, and curse of failing to do so. The famous words God alone is lord of the conscience (Ch. XX, Sec. 2) mean that man is free from the prescriptions of other men in matters of faith and worship, but he is free, not for sin or lust, but to serve the Lord without fear (Ch. XX, Secs. 2, 3). For the political application of these words, see the comments on Ch. XXIII.

The chapter on Christian liberty concludes with a grim and severe warning that this liberty may not oppose any lawful power, or the lawful exercise of it, and that those spreading about opinions contrary to the light of nature or to the known principles of Christianity are liable to prosecution by both church and state. This is a prescription for intolerance. The Westminster fathers were not so at ease with ideas of liberty and freedom as with law and duty, whether theological or political. The subject of Christian liberty is not mentioned in the Shorter Catechism at all, and it is difficult to find in the Larger one. Apparently it was a dangerous concept for children and laymen. Almost the same can be said for the love of God and neighbor love. All three documents reverberate with the thunder of divine power and justice and with "the duty which God requireth." The sounds of love, liberty, and gracious human relations are nearly drowned out. The Westminster statement on Christian liberty is cautious and fearful compared to the exultant freedom of the Christian in Galatians, chs. 3 to 5, in Luther's writings, or the Heidelberg Catechism, Qq. 86 and 90.

Duty Toward God, Chs. XXI to XXII. The Ten Commandments were divided in Ch. XIX, Sec. 2, into two tables. Four commands concern duty toward God and six contain duty toward men. The full analysis of the commandments was placed in the Westminster Catechisms (see Chapter 19), but three important topics were selected for a place in the Confession: worship, the state, and marriage. Puritan worship, rather plain and with remarkably long prayers and sermons, was regularly observed on fast days by the Westminster Assembly together with members of Parliament. The contents of such worship are here described (Ch. XXI). More detail was given in the Westminster Directory for Worship. Most of this material is clear enough not to require comment, except for several elements that will strike the contemporary reader as antiquated. First, the internal light of nature (Sec. 1) and the external law of nature (Sec. 7) are credited with producing a rather detailed knowledge of God and even a prescribed period of worship. Secondly, a rather rigid view of the Puritan Sabbath was adopted. This had been the subject of painful and acrimonious debate during nearly a century before the Westminster Assembly met. Again, the full chapter devoted to oaths and vows might seem excessive. But oaths and vows were more common in the seventeenth century. By denying oaths the sectarian movements threatened the state, and the lifelong vows of the monastic orders were considered a threat to justification by faith. Hence Ch. XXII is a defense both of theological and civic principles.

Duty Toward Man, Chs. XXIII to XXIV. The state or civil magistrates are part of God's law. They are ordained by God to be under him over the people, they are rightly armed with force, and it is lawful for Christians to be among them. The state has a definite sphere of activity, the public good, which includes maintenance of piety, justice, and peace, and the waging of just war. The magistrate is to be prayed for, paid taxes, honored, and obeyed, even if he is faithless or adheres to a difference in religion. One thing the state may not do is undertake the ministry of Word and sacraments.

So far we have agreement between the original Westminster Confession and the revision that was made in 1788 to adapt it to the American scene. So far it presents a conservative, *status quo* picture with no mention of appeal against injustice, let alone rebellion or revolution. This may surprise us in view of Huguenot experience and theory, the works of the Long Parliament, and the strong Presbyterian role in the American Revolution. However, it would admittedly have been difficult, even were the desire present, to plant seeds of rebellion in an established church, and do it when responding to the command of Parliament.

The original Confession gave the magistrate the power to call, attend, and influence church synods, to keep order in the church, and to suppress blasphemies, heresies, and abuses. The American revision breathes quite a different spirit, and no longer reflects the Westminster Assembly's dependence on Parliament. On this side of the Atlantic, the state, although recognized as established by God, may not in the least interfere in matters of faith. It is to protect the church without giving the preference to any denomination. All people are under the state's protection and are not to suffer indignity, violence, or abuse, either upon pretense of religion or of infidelity. In short, a pluralistic society. The first chapter of the Form of Government goes even farther. It was prepared at the same time probably by the pen of John Witherspoon, the only clergyman to sign the Declaration of Independence. It reads, in part:

> They [the Presbyterian Church] consider the rights of private judgment, in all matters that respect religion, as universal and inalienable: they do not even wish to see any religious constitution aided by the civil power, further than may be necessary for protection and security, and, at the same time, be equal and common to all others.

These thoughts indicate the arrival within the Reformed scheme of a concept of freedom that arose out of political experience, including severe persecutions, and took shape chiefly among the sectarian movements and in the philosophy of Enlightenment. The reader should analyze both versions of Ch. XXIII, if possible with the Biblical proof texts (in Schaff) marshaled in support of each view. It may be instructive for understanding the way in which historical change enters into Biblical understanding even where the Bible is claimed to be its own interpreter (Ch. I, Sec. 9).

Next to the state, the other divinely established institution of mankind to have a place in the Westminster Confession is marriage. One wishes it might have been a chapter on the family, but this is not the case, for family life is not mentioned. The original Westminster chapter on marriage was, to say the least, rather joyless. Nearly all of it was devoted to prohibitions and to the conditions of divorce. The positive values of marriage were limited to "mutuall help," the "increase" of mankind and the church, and "for preventing uncleannesse." Neither here nor in the Catechisms is there much about the relations of parents and children. The subject, even in a comment on the Fifth Commandment, is abstracted to relations among "superiors, inferiors, and equals" (Larger Catechism, Qq. 123-133; Shorter Catechism, Qq. 63-66). The old chapter was replaced in 1953 by one made up in part of the marriage service. A much richer conception informs the new statement. Happiness and love are at least mentioned, and the household—this is still the only reference to children—is to be provided for in honesty and industry. There are great resources in Scripture and in experience that were not, and still are not, brought to play on the increasingly critical problem of the family. The Confession of 1967 makes a small beginning in this direction.

The Church, Chs. XXV to XXXI. True to pattern, our Confession begins the doctrine of the church with the divine decree and then descends to history: first, the church invisible, . . . the whole number of the elect (Ch. XXV, Sec. 1), then the church visible on earth (Secs. 2-6). The catholic and visible church, identified as Christ's Kingdom, is endowed with means used by the Spirit to call men into the household and family of God. The church on earth is imperfect and impure, for sanctification is not complete, yet it shall never vanish from the earth. Christ alone, and not an alleged vicar of Christ, is head of the church. With the next chapter on the communion of saints (Ch. XXVI) we come upon perhaps the least legalistic and duty-ridden paragraphs of the entire Confession. Faith, grace, love and communion, mutual help and accord, mark the life together of those who have fellowship with Christ. This fellowship is the inner bond of the churchly institution. Two common sensible warnings at the end of the chapter remind us that we are still in Puritan England: lest enthusiasm carry away the saints, as it was then currently doing among the flourishing sects, both union with God and communal holding of property are repudiated.

The Sacraments, Chs. XXVII to XXIX, are dealt with in the general chapter on the Sacraments in the Reformed confessions (below, Chapter 21).

Censure, Ch. XXX, is but one negative aspect of the more general subject, discipline. The Book of Discipline is the full account of the administrative and judicial procedures to which "censure" belongs. Just why the Confession begins in Ch. XXX with the single function of censure, then proceeds to the general structure of government in Ch. XXXI, is not wholly clear. Most likely, the close relation between the Lord's Supper and the discipline, expressed in suspension and exclusion from the Supper (Ch. XXX, Sec. 4), provides the link between the two. In any case, "discipline" is the more proper term, and it, in turn, is primarily positive in practice rather than merely dealing with offenders as the term "censure" implies (Sec. 3).

The church government here presented (Ch. XXXI) is by representative assemblies of overseers and other rulers of the particular churches. The right of the civil ruler to call and consult with such synods was stricken from the text in the American adoption. Since synods and councils may err, and many have erred, their pronouncements are not to be made the rule of faith and practice, but are to be used as a help in both. The Form of Government is the full exposition and practical application of this chapter.

The final stricture against "intermeddling" in civil affairs agrees well with the status of the Westminster Assembly as a creature of Parliament and reflects the suspicions that Parliament entertained of organized ecclesiastical power. At the same time, the strictures against "intermeddling" are not absolute: unless by way of humble petition in cases extraordinary, is a clear provision for a direct communication with the government should an issue require it. The sermons of various Westminster divines before Parliament during the Assembly years deal with all kinds of current affairs. As for humble petition, the Confession itself was officially titled "The Humble Advice of the Assembly of Divines . . . ." The phrase indicates respect, not timidity. Since this paragraph was widely discussed in connection with the adoption of the Confession of 1967, it might be well to compare ¶ 43 of that document on "particular problems and crises through which God calls the church to act." The two are clearly not contradictory, and with allowances for the changed historical situation, the new statement may be seen as an extension and revision of the older one.

The Consummation, Chs. XXXII to XXXIII. The drama of human history, which plays out on earth what God has eternally decreed, reaches final consummation in the next two chapters. The former deals with the ends of individual lives, and the latter with the end of human history. Awkward problems have always plagued Christian theologians who have tried to relate these two sets of "last things." Did Old Testament prophets have to wait after their deaths for Christ's work to take place before they could go to heaven? When the body dies, does the soul go to sleep until the resurrection? Is there a place of purifying (purgatory) for those needing it, and a permanent limbus for unbaptized babies? The Westminster Confession answers these standard old questions with an unqualified "No" (respectively, in Ch. VIII, Sec. 6, and Ch. XXXII, Sec. 1). The scheme it does adopt, however, answers the same kind of questions and arrives at a single time sequence.

Westminster teaches that only bodies die. Souls live on. Those of the **righteous** go at death immediately to the **highest heavens and behold the face of God in light and glory**, and the **wicked are cast into hell.** But they do not stay there. All are awaiting a **day** appointed by God for judgment. On that day, the **selfsame bodies of all the dead shall be raised and be united again to their souls forever.** Then, **all persons that have lived upon earth shall appear before the tribunal of Christ, to give an account of their thoughts, words, and deeds.** Finally, all are reassigned in bodily existence to where their souls formerly were, the elect to experience fullness of joy and the reprobate **eternal torments.** Like the resolution of a mighty baroque fugue, the divine attributes of righteousness and mercy (Ch. II, Sec. 1) and the twofold predestination to life and to death (Ch. III, Secs. 3-8) with which we began, and which mingle in human history, are manifested on Judgment Day, showing, for all to see, **the glory of his mercy, in the eternal salvation of the elect; and of his justice, in the damnation of the reprobate.**

First, some questions, then four remarks.

Is there not something awkward also in this solution? What is the function of the Last Judgment, especially since heaven and hell have begun already at each individual death? Does this not imply that judgment is really pronounced individually at death? Are we to believe that the whole human race, billions of people from countless millennia of life on the planet, will **appear** and individually **give an account?** And what will it mean that the majority may have lived outside the Christian religion, and that even the visible church has mixed in with it the damned? Even if all Christendom were saved, would not the proportions be appalling?

Now the comments. First, the questions about time and space (**waiting** and **shall appear**) may come from a too direct equating of eternity with endless continuation of a single line of time. It may be that **waiting** has no translatable meaning in an eternal dimension, and the same may be true of space, which is something of a mystery even as we occupy it. It may be that instead of fitting together the parts of an incomplete jigsaw puzzle, it would be better modestly to extract the meaning from each image individually. Secondly, the Westminster Confession focuses wholly on the theme of judgment and is comparatively free of the fantastic apocalyptic fireworks and the millenarian musings that so frequently mark this type of discourse. It is notable that in the proof texts for Ch. XXXIII, the book of Revelation is cited only once—as the source of the final words, **"Come, Lord Jesus, come quickly."** These, of course, are the final words of the Bible, except for a benediction. For this Confession, then, judgment is significant rather than maps and timetables for the future. Thirdly, while the theme of judgment serves in the Confession to manifest the glory of God (Ch. XXXIII, Sec. 2) and to keep men alert, **because they know not at what hour the Lord will come** (Sec. 3), its wider function is to vindicate all that it has taught about the ultimate seriousness of man's life before God, about good and evil, about sin and salvation. Fourthly, and apart from the specific Westminster statement, the Christian hope is founded in Christ's work, not in a blueprint of the future. The many images that tell of "last things" are valid as they enhance the gospel and show its significance. But to literalize and fit together fragments of parable, prophecy, and apocalyptic may distract from the bona fide judgment of God now taking place. "This is the judgment, that the light has come into the world, and men loved darkness rather than light, because their deeds were evil." (John 3:19.) "The last day should not be thought of as the day judgment *begins;* it is the day on which it *ends."* (Hendry, *The Westminster Confession for Today,* p. 250.)

The Holy Spirit, Ch. XXIV. This chapter was added to the original Westminster Confession in the year 1903 to overcome the lack of a sufficiently full doctrine of the Holy Spirit. It succeeded for the most part in repeating content from earlier sections of the Confession under the new rubric of Spirit. The four sections relate the Spirit, in order, to the Trinity (Ch. II), revelation (Ch. I), the way of salvation (Chs. X to XVIII), and the church (Chs. XXV to XXVI). The first and second sections make use of language taken partly from the Nicene Creed. The one sentence on Scripture leans, as is remarked more fully below, in a rather reactionary direction. Section 3 appears to differ from the old Westminster treatment of the same subject in the more generously stated gift of salvation to **all who ask him.** The final section is the least needed part of the chapter, thanks to the fine account of the communion of saints in Ch. XXVI.

The Love of God and Missions, Ch. XXXV. Two related motives were at work in this chapter. First was the desire to express the love of God for all men, unhampered by the rigid predestinarian limits of Chs. III, VIII, and X. Second, and closely related, was the desire to show the theological basis for world missions, which in 1903 were rounding out their greatest century of expansion. The former motive shows especially in the assertion (Ch. XXXV, Sec. 1) that Christ's sacrifice is **sufficient for and adapted to the whole lost race of man.** Also, a changed spirit produced a changed idiom throughout, found in the phrases **whole lost race . . . to all men . . . all men . . . all who truly repent . . . all to embrace . . . everyone—**"all" this without a word about predestination, decree, the elect, or such a forbidding condition as opens Ch. X, **All those whom God hath predestinated . . . and those only . . . .**

The additions cannot be said clearly to have changed the substance of the earlier Westminster teaching, but they offered a palliative mildly satisfactory both to progressives and to those who wanted no revision at all.

The extension of the Kingdom of Christ throughout the whole earth is the kind of language used by those who lived after the opening up of the continents by ship and railroad in the nineteenth century. The Westminster divines, with all the problems they faced in England, could hardly have been expected to think extensively of missions "from Greenland's icy mountains" to "India's coral strand." Already deeply committed to missions in all the world, the Presbyterian Church in 1903 wrote missions into the Confession of Faith, soundly based on the Great Commission.

Declaratory Statement. The first section of this appended Statement implies that the Statement itself may be unnecessary because the ordination vow **requires the reception and adoption of the Confession . . . only as containing the system of doctrine taught in the Holy Scriptures.** Then it continues with, **nevertheless . . .** and proceeds to disavow **certain inferences . . .** and make **more explicit statement . . .** in the following two paragraphs. The implication is that **only as containing** means "only insofar as it contains," which would allow an individual to make an alternative interpretation of Scripture even without the Declaratory Statement to support him. This is a perfectly good principle and has in fact been the guarded practice of the church at least since 1870. One cannot help feeling that it should have been stated more clearly and courageously.

The force of the first numbered paragraph of the Declaratory Statement is to assert the harmony between Ch. III and the new (1903) Ch. XXXV, that is, between the old statement that **by the decree of God, . . . some men and angels are predestinated unto everlasting life, and others foreordained to everlasting death** (Ch. III, Sec. 3), and the new statement that salvation is **sufficient for and adapted to the whole lost race of man.** A second paragraph treats the related subject, the salvation of those dying in infancy. The phrase **elect infants** (Ch. X, Sec. 3) carries the implication that some infants might not be elect, against which the addition holds, **We believe that all dying in infancy are included in the election of grace,** . . . **regenerated and saved by Christ.**

The logic of the two new statements is as hard to follow as that of the older ones is reprehensible. The real difficulty comes from a patchwork approach to the problem. A genuine new beginning in which the gracious and holy love of God would take the place of the **eternal decree** would have brought about, as we have pointed out elsewhere, a greater change in the confessional standards than is represented by the three additions. However, the move for more thorough revision had already failed before the turn of the century. The church had in some measure departed from the theological premises that made the eccentric question of **elect infants** a bone of contention, but it had not departed far enough or seen clearly enough another option to take a larger step. The action was generally in the direction of broadening the church's theological base, but it does not seem to represent a comparable deepening of its understanding.

THE LEADING THEMES

In the survey just finished, "Scripture," "Divine Sovereignty," and the "Two Covenants" were said to control the remainder of doctrinal topics. Another way to say the same thing would be to call them the basic systematic elements of which the Confession is constructed. By analogy with architecture, God and his sovereign decree would be the foundation of the building, the covenants would be the rooms and halls where men live and do business, and Scripture would be the road of access and the guide for use. These three subjects were included in the outline just given, but rather than have the survey too detailed at the beginning, we have chosen to deal with them more fully and critically here.

Holy Scripture, Ch. I. The Westminster chapter on Scripture,

even without the listed names of books of the Bible, is the longest
in the Confession, and perhaps the most carefully worded. Its
special characteristic is that it rests the authority of the Bible more
heavily than the other confessions do on a view of the origin and
inspiration of the written text. The overall scheme is as follows:
Secs. 1-4 show both the origin and authority of Scripture to be
based on divine inspiration; Secs. 5-6 make **full persuasion** of this
authority and **saving understanding** of the truth of Scripture
dependent on inward illumination by the Spirit; and Secs. 7-10
show the source of authoritative interpretation: **the Holy Spirit
speaking in the Scripture,** which was **immediately inspired** in
the Hebrew and Greek that God has **kept pure in all ages.** Scripture contains within itself its own **infallible rule of interpretation.**

Inspiration is not defined in the Confession, but its meaning
appears in the use of the term **immediately** (Ch. I, Sec. 8), which
signifies "directly," without means or media. Nothing intervenes
between God's revelation and the written text. Accordingly, no
human writers, not even apostles and prophets, are mentioned.
It pleased the Lord . . . to reveal himself, and . . . **to commit
the same wholly unto writing.** (Ch. I, Sec. 1.) Again, **The authority of the Holy Scripture . . . dependeth . . . wholly upon
God . . . , the author thereof; and therefore it is to be received
because it is the Word of God** (Ch. I, Sec. 4), or the **Word of
God written** (Ch. I, Sec. 2). The typical language of the Confession is to call the Bible **Word** or **Word of God** (about thirty
times). These terms are generally used as synonyms for "Scripture" (Ch. I, Secs. 2, 4) and are much preferred to the term
"Scripture," which appears infrequently after the first chapter.

There is, further, no explanation in Ch. I of the **inward work,**
or **illumination** (Ch. I, Sec. 6) by the Spirit, except that it bears
witness by and with the Word in our hearts (Ch. I, Sec. 5). Some
have held that **illumination** consists in being convinced by the
arguments for Scripture that are so eloquently stated in Sec. 5.
But the prominent words **notwithstanding** and **nevertheless** (Ch.
I, Secs. 5, 6) seem to exclude that view. We must be satisfied
with concluding that this illumination is part of the total work

of the Spirit (Chs. X to XVIII, especially Ch. X, Sec. 1; Ch. XIV, Sec. 2) by which the elect are effectually called. The outer work, including inspired Scripture and the preaching of the Word (Ch. VII, Sec. 6), and the inner illumination are the means ordinarily (exceptions, Ch. X, Secs. 3-4) used in communicating what God has revealed for the purpose of salvation.

Concerning the interpretation of Scripture, the Confession grants that all things in Scripture are not alike plain in themselves, nor alike clear unto all, yet the things necessary to salvation are so clearly propounded and opened in some place of Scripture or other that both unlearned and learned may sufficiently understand them (Ch. I, Sec. 7). When there is a question about the true and full sense of any Scripture, the meaning may be found in other places that speak more clearly (Ch. I, Sec. 9). The reader is to look within, not outside of, Scripture for clarification, because the infallible rule of interpretation of Scripture is the Scripture itself (Ch. I, Sec. 9). The Supreme Judge of all controversies in matters of religion can be no other but the Holy Spirit speaking in the Scriptures (Ch. I, Sec. 10).

Thus, divine origin, divine authority, divine preservation, a divinely given persuasion and illumination of Scripture's authority and saving truth, and an inherent rule of interpretation are all affirmed of Scripture in the first chapter of the Westminster Confession. The Bible appears as a supernatural book, the contents of which are supernaturally grasped. Its character is not qualified in the Confession by historical or accidental traits.

At the same time we must observe that the Westminster Assembly was in some respects moderate for its day. It did not go to the extremes of teaching the inspiration of punctuation and Hebrew vowel points, although some of its members represented this extreme view. Also, it held back from using such terms as "dictation" by the Holy Spirit, although the term immediately inspired was used by people holding that view. The Confession did not go so far in this direction as some later American fundamentalist interpreters would have it. For these, the language of Westminster needed additional fortification against nineteenth-century science and historical criticism. The words "verbal" and "plenary" were commonly used as adjectives with inspiration, and "inerrancy" was paired with infallibility. The new Ch. XXXIV of the year 1903 seems to reflect the influence of this view. Whereas Westminster proper speaks of the **infallible truth** of Scripture, but does not give details about the writing process, the addition links infallibility with it: **All the writers of the Holy Scriptures [were] inspired to record infallibly the mind and will of God.** The difference is not great, but if anything, the later statement is nuanced in the direction of "inerrancy." This means that the church in 1903 was not yet responding positively to some of the advances in Biblical studies that it today takes for granted.

All told, the Westminster Confession reflects the exaggerated concern for the authority of Scripture that characterized the orthodox theology of that time, even if it does not descend to the untenable extremes of modern fundamentalism. Generally, with the coming of the new sciences of man and the world in the century after the Confession was finished, its adherents could only ward off, they could not take advantage of new knowledge that was, in God's providence, enriching the life of men.

The Westminster view of Scripture, however, was not a view of authority for authority's sake. The formal considerations were made primarily to protect the content of Scripture to which all the remainder of the Confession is devoted. This is a gratuitous remark, probably, since no theology ever was purely formal; it is all aimed toward salvation, toward Christ, and toward the actual work of the Holy Spirit in the life of men. But when the history of theology is surveyed, and comparisons made (as the reader may do, in part, by comparing the other parts of *The Book of Confessions*), formal questions about authority are seen to play a larger role in Westminster than in the Reformation confessions. Narrow interpretation of the Westminster teaching on Scripture cost Presbyterianism the services of the eminent scholar Charles A. Briggs about the turn of this century. In the decade after World War I, the tide turned toward more moderate and progressive understanding.

The Sovereignty of God, Chs. II to V. The infinite . . . immutable . . . almighty God (Ch. II, Sec. 1), not standing in
need of any creatures, . . . nor deriving any glory from them
(Ch. II, Sec. 2), did freely and unchangeably ordain whatsoever
comes to pass (Ch. III, Sec. 1). God not only created out of
nothing, the world, and all things therein (Ch. IV, Sec. 1), but
doth uphold, direct, dispose, and govern all creatures (Ch. V,
Sec. 1) according to his infallible foreknowledge, and the free
and immutable counsel of his own will (Ch. V, Sec. 1) and for
his own glory (Ch. II, Sec. 1). All things come to pass thus
immutably and infallibly (Ch. V, Sec. 2) and yet neither is God
the author of sin, nor is violence offered to the will of the creatures, nor is the liberty or contingency of second causes taken
away, but rather established (Ch. III, Sec. 1; cf. Ch. V, Sec. 4).

This mélange of phrases from Chs. II to V expresses what is
usually and correctly referred to as the "sovereignty" of God that
dominates Westminster theology. These are the most difficult and
technical paragraphs to be found anywhere in *The Book of
Confessions*. We can here only touch the subject and recommend
the analysis and criticism of Prof. George Hendry in his *Westminster Confession for Today*, Chs. III to V. Also helpful would
be a comparison with the Second Helvetic Confession, Chs. III
and VI to X. We shall proceed to give a brief comment, but first
the reader should find his way through at least one reading of
Chs. II to V.

After these chapters are read, the question certainly comes to
mind: If God did . . . unchangeably ordain whatsoever comes
to pass (Ch. III, Sec. 1), then is not *everything*—creation and
consummation, Satan and Christ, damnation and salvation—
already included in the eternal decree? This is in fact the case,
and it is easy for the careful reader to observe it if he will now
accept further schoolmasterly directives and carry out two tasks:
(1) Read Chs. II to V again and note how many major topics
dealt with later in the Confession are included here; (2) skip
through the entire Confession and note how often it refers back
to these chapters, especially Ch. III.

To show exactly what is meant by the first task, we give as examples the appearance of the following topics: Christ (Ch. III, Sec. 5); grace, love, faith, calling, justification, adoption, perseverance (Ch. III, Secs. 6-7); sin, wrath, dishonor (Ch. III, Sec. 7). Note well! All this which will be presented in detail in following chapters is part of the **eternal decree** even before we come to the creation of the world in Ch. IV. Again, in Ch. V, which is an extension of the decree topic, we have the **Fall, and all other sins of angels and men** (Ch. V, Sec. 4), the **temptations** and **corruptions** of believers (Ch. V, Sec. 5), as well as the sin, lusts, and the power of Satan among the **wicked and ungodly** (Ch. V, Sec. 6). And this is before we come to the fall of man and sin in Ch. VI and farther on. Suggestions for the second task, aimed to illustrate the way that the entire Confession hangs upon the decree as on a peg, are the following references: Ch. VI, Sec. 1; Ch. VIII, Sec. 1; Ch. X, Secs. 1-4; Ch. XI, Sec. 4; Ch. XII; Ch. XIII, Sec. 1; Ch. XIV, Sec. 1; Ch. XVII, Secs. 1-2; Ch. XXV, Sec. 1. In each case the treatment of a separated topic must be related to the fundamental motif, "divine decree."

These chapters show perhaps the most typical strength and the greatest difficulties in the entire body of Westminster doctrine. The strength is that it refuses finally to make God fit man's ways of reasoning. For example, this combination of foreordination and contingency is a flat contradiction. But, given the Westminster method, to resolve it rationally would weaken divine power and make the human will decisive. The unsentimental virility of such a mode of thinking, and the sense of the awesome transcendence and power of God, compels admiration, most especially in our day when among so many God is little more than the fulfillment of a wish. But is this God of awesome power Biblical? Yes and No. Yes, in that the decree develops from a genuine Biblical theme, "the electing love of God." No, in that it abstracts and separates power from love, justice, and mercy, and God transcendent from God incarnate. It makes an intricate puzzle out of a joyous and confident personal relation. The Declaratory Statement of 1903 modifies the harshness of Ch. III, but scarcely adequately. Not a palliating afterthought, but a proper starting point will make the needed change. Both the Scots Confession, and the Second Helvetic Confession succeed where Westminster fails, by centering on Christ and election, not an all-determining decree. We cannot but prefer the comfort of faith in Christ of the Heidelberg Catechism, and the eloquent confidence of the Second Helvetic: "It is to be held as beyond doubt that if you believe and are in Christ, you are elected. . . . Let Christ, therefore be the looking glass, in whom we may contemplate our predestination. We shall have a sufficiently clear and sure testimony that we are inscribed in the Book of Life if we have fellowship with Christ, and he is ours and we are his in true faith" (Ch. X).

Over against this wholesome confidence, Westminster cautions that the high mystery of predestination is to be handled with special prudence and care (Ch. III, Sec. 8). To this, Professor Hendry comments trenchantly that "there is no suggestion of caution in Ephesians 1 and Romans 8; there, if ever, the apostle is letting himself go" (*The Westminster Confession for Today,* p. 52). The apostle can do this because he is teaching the loving purpose of God to save men through Christ, not an abstract and absolute decree. It was a noble risk that the Westminster fathers ran, and certainly a more Biblical one than the Arminian alternative of complete free will; but there was already a better way than either, as we have pointed out in the Reformation confessions and in Calvin's *Institutes,* Book III.

Now, have we been fair to the Confession? Does not Ch. II say also that God is **most loving, gracious, merciful, . . . forgiving** (Ch. II, Sec. 1), and do not Christ and God's **free grace and love** (Ch. III, Sec. 5) figure in the decree of Ch. III? Yes, they do. But by descending from the abstract decree to particular grace, the proportions as well as the idiom of Biblical teachings on these subjects are markedly altered.

The Covenants and the Mediator, Chs. VII to VIII. "Covenant" is one of the most prominent words and concepts in the Bible. The whole Bible, in fact, is divided into two parts by it: the Old and New Covenants, or Testaments. Strange to say, "covenant" was never a prominent topic of theology until the Reformation. Within a century or so, however, "covenant theology" was almost a synonym for Reformed theology in Europe and the British Isles. The history of this movement in a nutshell might be described as taking place in three stages. First, "covenant" was used prominently to describe God's relation to the patriarchs, to Israel, and to the church (covenant of grace). Secondly, it was extended backward in time to include God's demand of obedience upon Adam in paradise (covenant of works). Thirdly, the term was extended into eternity to designate predestination as a covenant, or pact, among the Persons of the Trinity concerning man's redemption. Only the first stage appears in Calvin and the Reformation confessions; the second was widely held after the Reformation, but the Westminster Confession is the only major confession that expresses the double covenant; the third stage was common in theology but did not receive confessional formulation. The latter stages of covenant theology are generally called "federal" from the Latin word for covenant, *foedus*. The federal theology was coming into its own in Reformed lands about the time of the Westminster Assembly and was to have tremendous influence also in New England. It was fought by some who thought it weakened predestination and divine sovereignty by concentrating too much on man and his history, but finally it became an accepted mode for teaching that same sovereignty. As a theological motif it proved to have tremendous scope, extending from the eternal decree of God, through creation and paradise, and finally embracing all human history and the entire drama of redemption and consummation. Its virtue was that generally it introduced more personal and social idiom into the scheme of decree and predestination. At the same time its disadvantage was that the common meaning of two-sided legal compact was always encroaching upon the theological meaning which centered in grace. What, then, is the status of covenant in the Westminster Confession?

Above, when Chs. VII to VIII were discussed, the meaning of the term was explained and its scope was indicated. The legal side of the covenant was examined as part of Chs. XIX and XX, and still other elements in Chs. XVI and XVIII. Drawing these together, we conclude that the covenant terminology and the covenant concept are effective enough that Westminster can be said to belong to the covenant, or federal, theological scheme. But these materials do not succeed in modifying the arbitrariness of the decree or in introducing a historical focus—as covenant thought is reputed to have done generally in Reformed theology. Further, an inherent tendency to legalism in two-covenant theology is realized in the overemphasis on law in Chs. XVI through XX. Covenant, which we have designated the "historical principle" of the Confession, is thus unsuccessful in bringing historical movement very strongly into it, and it does serve as the instrument of a pervasive emphasis on the law.

To conclude: a formal principle of authority, a metaphysical principle of being, and a strong tendency to legalism in the life of man characterize the Reformed theology of the Westminster Confession, at the expense of historical revelation, grace, love, and free obedience, which it also teaches, but less effectively than it should, because of the predominance of its major themes.

CHAPTER 19

THE SHORTER CATECHISM

The Westminster Assembly fathered two catechisms which present the teaching of the Westminster Confession in question-and-answer form. The Shorter Catechism was to be memorized by children and the Larger Catechism expounded from the pulpit. Both were meant as practical handbooks for the Christian life. For this reason, they bear down heavily on the Ten Commandments, which occupy 45 out of 107 questions in the Shorter Catechism and 58 out of 196 in the Larger.

The Larger Catechism ceased to be part of the Constitution of the United Presbyterian Church with the revision of 1967. It was dropped to keep *The Book of Confessions* within manageable size, and because it was never so widely used and loved as the other two Standards. Lack of popularity probably resulted from the unwieldiness of the question-and-answer method in a document longer even than the Confession. Also, the answers to some questions contain 150 to 175 words strung out in a single sentence. Nonetheless, it is a fascinating and instructive document and reveals penetrating and astute ethical judgments especially in some of the long answers related to the Decalogue. By being more detailed, it is more dated in language and judgment, and sometimes picayune. Strict observance would produce perhaps a classic seventeenth-century Presbyterian Puritan type, a man of impressive stature, zeal, Biblical learning, and moral strength, but somewhat cramped and overscrupulous in his day-to-day life. A typical excerpt reads as follows:

Q. 134. Which is the Sixth Commandment?

A. The Sixth Commandment is, "Thou shalt not kill."

Q. 135. What are the duties required in the Sixth Commandment?

A. The duties required in the Sixth Commandment are: all careful studies, and lawful endeavors, to preserve the life of ourselves and others, resisting all thoughts and purposes, subduing all passions, and avoiding all occasions, temptations, and practices, which tend to the unjust taking away of the life of any; by just defense thereof against violence; patient bearing of the hand of God, quietness of mind, cheerfulness of spirit; a sober use of meat, drink, physic, sleep, labor, and recreation; by charitable thoughts, love, compassion, meekness, gentleness, kindness; peaceable, mild, and courteous speeches and behavior: forbearing, readiness to be reconciled, patient bearing and forgiving of injuries, and requiting good for evil; comforting and succoring the distressed, and protecting and defending the innocent.

There is more extensive precedent for the specific ethical emphasis of the Confession of 1967 in the Larger Catechism than in the other Westminster documents.

The Shorter Catechism, by contrast, is a model of brevity and occasional eloquence. Some answers have the spareness, strength, and clarity of fine ironwork: **Man's chief end is to glorify God, and to enjoy him forever** (Q. 1), or **Sin is any want of conformity unto, or transgression of, the law of God** (Q. 14). The mind or spirit of the Catechism is highly prescriptive and demanding. The Bible is **the only rule to direct us how,** and it teaches **what man is to believe** and **what duty God requires** (Qq. 2-3). Many word pairs or triads such as "glorify and enjoy," "belief and practice," "sin and misery," or "prophet, priest, king," are used skillfully as memory aids for reflection upon important themes. The present-day reader notices language and content from an earlier society (**Q. 64, superiors, inferiors, or equals**) or questionable Biblical exegesis (**Q. 60, on the Sabbath**) which call for updating. But attempts to repair and refurbish by stylistic changes have proved fruitless. It is unquestionably a fine piece of literature and one of the greatest catechisms. Hopefully, renewed study will recover for the church some of its original power, although it hardly seems likely or desirable that the catechetical method will return to prominence in Christian education. Catechism training in days gone by sometimes produced young people who had memorized answers but did not relate them to everyday life.

The general sequence of the Shorter Catechism is roughly that of the Apostles' Creed, followed by the Ten Commandments, the Sacraments, and the Lord's Prayer. The texts of the Commandments, the Lord's Prayer, and the Creed are appended at the end and are meant to be memorized as part of the Catechism. Unhappily, the legalistic and individualistic tendencies of the Westminster Standards are more fully exposed in this manual for youth than in the Confession. Both Christian liberty and the doctrine of the church are completely omitted. It may be helpful to divide the Catechism into sections as follows:

THE RULE FOR GLORIFYING GOD

Qq. 1-3   The Scriptures

WHAT MAN IS TO BELIEVE

Qq. 4-12   God the Creator
Qq. 13-20   Sin and the Two Covenants
Qq. 21-28   Redemption Purchased by the Son
Qq. 29-38   Redemption Applied by the Spirit

WHAT GOD REQUIRES

Qq. 39-84   The Moral Law and the
                        Curse on Sin
Qq. 85-107   Faith (Q. 86), Repentance (Q. 87),
                        Outward Means (Qq. 88-107)

APPENDED TEXTS

The Ten Commandments
The Lord's Prayer
The Apostles' Creed

Since the teaching of the Shorter Catechism is essentially the same as that of the Westminster Confession, the next paragraphs are brief and they assume knowledge of the comments already made on the Confession.

The brief doctrine of Scripture omits all mention of the origin of the Bible and assumes rather than demonstrates its authority. The emphasis is on the function of the Bible and its contents. The doctrine of God presents succinctly the attributes of God, the Trinity, and the decrees, then brings to the fore the covenants, one related to providence (Q. 12) and the other to salvation (Q. 20). God transcendent (Qq. 4-7) not only creates (Qq. 9-10) and governs (Q. 11) but approaches men in these covenants and thereby opens up to them eternal life. The teachings about God, man, providence, sin, and covenant are skillfully interrelated. The historical movement of the Scots Confession is lacking, and so is the personal confidence of the Heidelberg Cathechism, but given the Westminster type of teaching, the Catechism appears superior to the Confession in heightening the themes of sin and grace and leaving to one side the elaboration of divine attributes and decrees.

We should not miss the repeated treatment of sin. First, in terms of the Fall of **our first parents** (Qq. 13-19) there is a formal definition of sin that applies both to Adam and to us (Q. 14). Secondly, more after the manner of the Heidelberg Catechism (Qq. 3-11), the conviction of sin appears as the function of the moral law, which every man **doth daily break . . . , in thought, word, and deed** (Qq. 82-84). There is no significant difference in content between these two, but the care given to treating sin both historically and personally is impressive.

The covenants appear even more prominently here and in the Larger Catechism than in the Confession, as already mentioned, hence the personal quality of man's life before God is heightened. The questions on the nature and the work of Christ are distinguished by their pith and brevity. Christ the prophet is revealer, Christ the priest is himself a sacrifice and a reconciler, and Christ the king subdues, rules, and defends us. So also, the subject matter of Christ's benefits, extensively treated in the Confession, is here compressed into a group of definitions of the chief concepts (Qq. 30-38). Faith plays even less of a role in this familiar list than in the Confession and Larger Catechism, but like sin, it receives another definition after the law has been taught (Q. 86).

The Ten Commandments, which appear in the Heidelberg Catechism under the heading "Thankfulness," here tell what God "requires" and "forbids" to the end that all men are shown to commit sin, and **every sin deserveth God's wrath and curse** (Q. 84). Although these Decalogue questions culminate in a curse upon men, it is quite clear that an equal reason for their being here is to tell what God requires and forbids in the Christian's life (Q. 44). This is as it should be. Yet we note with some disappointment that the Catechism progresses smoothly, without even a change in vocabulary, from the law to the evangelical "requirements" of faith, repentance, and the use of **outward means** (Q. 85). Lacking is the contrast of law and gospel taught by the apostle Paul and the Reformers. There is, as we have noted, nothing on Christian freedom. It is thus not surprising that among the three hundred odd proof texts added to the Catechism in the nineteenth century the great Christian liberty passages from the letter to the Galatians are nowhere to be found. The description of faith in Q. 86 is a gem, although it needs completing from the fuller content of Qq. 30 and 31. **Repentance unto life** (Q. 87) is superb.

The **outward means** must be carefully understood. **God requireth of us . . . the diligent use of all the outward means whereby Christ communicateth to us the benefits of redemption.** (Q. 85.) Men are asked to make **diligent use,** but it is Christ and the Spirit who make the means effectual (Qq. 88-89, 91). The decisive action is divine action, not human obedience. The Sacraments are discussed elsewhere, but special note should be taken of the **reading, but especially the preaching, of the Word** (Q. 89) and the memorable portrayal of "hearing": **We must attend thereunto with diligence, preparation, and prayer; receive it with faith and love; lay it up in our hearts; and practice it in our lives** (Q. 90).

In eight sentences it would be hard to say more on the Lord's Prayer than is found in Qq. 100-107. Yet, since intercession is not mentioned at all as part of prayer (Qq. 98-99), we may supplement the Catechism by a statement from the Westminster Confession: "Prayer is to be made for things lawful, and for all sorts of men living, or that shall live hereafter" (Ch. XXI, Sec. 4).

Chapter 20

THE BARMEN DECLARATION

The Barmen Declaration dates from the early years of the church struggle during Adolf Hitler's dictatorship in Germany. The struggle was not primarily against the government but against destructive forces within the church itself. From this derives both the greatness of the Barmen Declaration and its chief shortcoming.

Catastrophic defeat at the end of World War I left in Germany a political, military, economic, and spiritual vacuum. The void was filled by as evil a power as ever overwhelmed civilized men. The largest, most gifted and energetic nation of Western Europe became the terror of mankind. Towering over every other horror was the methodical murder of 6,000,000 Jews, whom madness had blamed for national disaster. Looking back in time, across the sea, and remembering the concentration camps, the refugee hordes, and the destroyed cities of World War II, an American may be tempted even now to vent his wrath and pride himself on not being German. However, this is to ignore the deeper historical roots of the conflict and to evade the permanent Christian significance of the Barmen Declaration.

Germany was a nation of deep religious piety and of the highest artistic and scientific, industrial, philosophical, and theological achievements. It was historically as Christian, as civilized, as fun-loving, as rich in family life as any of its neighbors, including the United States of America. The majority of the people of Germany supported the National Socialist regime as the only hope for internal stability and national security. Both bolshevism and democracy were condemned. Protestants and Catholics made up the masses and the elite who joined the roar of "Heil, Hitler!" The Vatican signed a concordat. One of the saintliest of Protestant leaders was for a time Reich bishop under Hitler. Eminent theologians concocted Nazi-Christian ideology, and a theology faculty world famous for scholarship and conservative orthodoxy underwrote the exclusion of Jews from public life and of Jewish converts from church offices.

Traditional harmonizing of "throne and altar," fatherland and church, gospel and patriotism, Christian hope and national destiny, had robbed the church, so it seemed, of critical perspective and prophetic power. The gospel was absorbed in the culture. The salt lost its savor, and the leaven its power to change the lump. The distortion of cross into swastika, which seemed obvious to wise men from afar, was clear in Germany to relatively few.

Among those few were the Protestant churchmen who brought into being and led—not without suffering, slander, prison, and death—the Confessing Church under the banner of the Barmen Declaration. The response to their **common message for the need and temptation of the Church in our day** was a reformation from which Christianity in Germany still draws vitality. This Confessing Church caused Albert Einstein to say: "Only the church stood squarely across the path of Hitler's campaign for suppressing the truth. . . . I am forced to confess that what I once despised, I now praise unreservedly."

The drama of the story, thus oversimplified, should not blind anyone to the tangled motives and cross-purposes at play in the church struggle. Nor should we gloss over the confessional bickering and the large-scale defections that took place as time passed. But the Synod of Barmen, all this notwithstanding, confessed the gospel of Jesus Christ in a time of trial with clarity, force, and courage rarely matched in history.

The movements and events that led directly to calling a synod in the Barmen section of the large city of Wuppertal are very complex. The following religious and organizational factors will show the main lines of development: (1) A Christianity embellished with racial and national overtones took form in Germany even before World War I. It was organized shortly before Hitler came to power as the Faith Movement of German Christians. The gospel was subordinated to "a faith in the national mission that God has given us." Among and near this group were, shockingly, theologians as noted as Gerhard Kittel and Emanuel Hirsch. Opposition was spearheaded by a vigorous theological movement led by the Swiss Karl Barth and deeply rooted in Reformation teachings. There were other forms of theological opposition and other important teachers, some driven early into exile, but none so effective and farsighted as Barth. (2) Constitutionally, a government order of July, 1933, signed by Hitler and leaders of the regional churches created a national German Protestant Church. "German Christian" leaders were soon in the saddle. Opposition crystallized quickly in two ways. Martin Niemöller, of Berlin, founded the Pastors' Emergency League in September, 1933. Several thousand members signed a pledge to be bound only by Scripture and the Reformation confessions and to reject curbs on so-called non-Aryans in the church. Besides the League, several voluntary meetings and a number of independently organized synods in various parts of Germany took action that clashed with the new national administration. The various opposition movements met together in the Confessional Synod of the German Evangelical Church, at Barmen, May 29-31, 1934. The name chosen for the Synod made clear that it was not meant as a protest against the church, but as a claim to *be* the Protestant Church in Germany.

Only two parts of the official documents of the Barmen Synod are included in *The Book of Confessions,* namely, the Appeal, and the Theological Declaration. Materials on the legal status and practical ministry of the church, appointments to offices, etc., were omitted. In one sense these should have been retained to show that the theological articles did not float above events but were part and parcel of them. This, however, would be overly long and uninstructive in detail. Enough specifics are given in the Appeal and the Declaration to make the point. The text printed is that translated by Prof. Arthur C. Cochrane for his book *The Church's Confession Under Hitler* (The Westminster Press, 1962), the best source for further information. All material quoted here can be found in Cochrane's volume.

The title (Declaration) translates a German word that means also "explanation." The Barmen theses were intended both to explain the older confessions of the church in the face of an unprecedented situation, and to declare without compromise that certain lines must not be crossed. In both these aspects as well as others the Declaration qualifies as a confession of the church, although it has been more widely accepted in this category by the Reformed Churches, to whom confessions are always to be written anew, than among Lutheran Churches.

The brief account already given is background for the Appeal and also for the opening paragraphs of the Theological Declaration. Several further facts should be kept in mind. First, the Barmen Declaration was not meant to stand alone. It rested on the historic creeds and confessions already recognized by the churches and churchmen assembled. Secondly, it was a united message and was followed later by the creation of an emergency church polity, but it was not intended to effect a permanent church union. It was a common act of confessing, but it did not resolve traditional confessional differences. For better or worse, Reformed remained Reformed, and Lutheran remained Lutheran, and have functioned separately since the emergency. At the same time great ecumenical gains were registered both among Protestants and between Protestants and Catholics as a result of the crucible in which all were tried. Thirdly, Barmen opposed the nationalized church union as destructive of true union insofar as it rested on **false doctrine, . . . force and insincere practices.** The real enemy was the "German Christian" movement, which is named several times and called the **ruling Church party.** Because of "German Christian" teaching and administration, **the Church ceases to be the Church and the German Evangelical Church, as a federa-**

tion . . . becomes **intrinsically impossible.** The extralegal Confessing Church was, by implication, excommunicating the legal, established, national church.

The end of the Appeal is particularly strong and courageous. The condemnation of **loose talk** was to prove more important as time went along and slander was poured on confessors, Protestant and Catholic. All were defamed for subverting national unity in a period of national emergency. The appeal to Scripture makes sharp alternatives. **If you find that we are speaking contrary to Scripture, then do not listen to us! But if you find that we are taking our stand upon Scripture, then let no fear or temptation keep you from treading with us the path of faith and obedience to the Word of God.**

The main body of the Theological Declaration is made up of six articles, or theses. Each consists of three parts: first, a passage from the Bible, then the thesis itself, and finally a negative thesis that repudiates specific false teachings.

Article 1. The first thesis is basic to all the rest. It repeats the Reformation cry, "Scripture alone!" and "Christ alone!" The preaching of the church comes wholly from Scripture, not from tradition, from nature, or from history—more especially not from current events in national history. By particular emphasis on Christ the article recalls a teaching of the Reformers, namely, that the focus of Scripture and the focus of faith are on Christ. On the other hand, the careful statement that **Jesus Christ, as he is attested for us in Holy Scripture, is the one Word of God** warns that Christ is not an idea to be extracted from Scripture and used at will. Rather, it is the fullness of the Biblical testimony concerning salvation, promised and achieved in the Old and New Testaments, **which we have to hear, . . . trust and obey.** By contrast, the "German Christians" were disparaging the Old Testament, and distorting Christ into a hero of merciless "Aryan" piety.

The reader might well compare the first article with the first question of the Heidelberg Catechism and the first chapter of the Second Helvetic Confession. One of the Ten Theses of Bern

(1528) appears to be the true progenitor of Article 1: "The holy, Christian Church, whose only Head is Christ, is born of the Word of God, abides in the same, and hears not the voice of a stranger." These words had been used verbatim as the first of the Düsseldorf Theses five months before the Barmen Synod.

Those familiar with theology in the 1930's will recognize in the negative statement a rejection of "natural theology," that is, reasoning about God based on nature rather than exclusively on Scripture. Article 1 holds only that teachings based in this way may not be used as a source of . . . proclamation by the church. Such teachings must not be confused with the gospel. The reason is not far to seek. Precisely this kind of "revelation" had been employed by National Socialist apologists to harmonize Hitlerism with Christianity. If God rules history, and if the state is a divine order, then is not what happens in history and the state a sign of God's will? Prof. Paul Althaus, in a book called *The German Hour of the Church,* wrote: "Our evangelical Churches have welcomed the turning point of 1933 in Germany [Hitler's rise to power] as a gift and miracle of God."

The guiding principles of the "German Christians" (1932) illustrate how the case was developed in defense of racial theories: "We see in race, folk, and nation, orders of existence granted and entrusted to us by God. . . . Consequently miscegenation is to be opposed. . . . 'Keep your race pure.' . . . Faith in Christ does not destroy one's race but deepens and sanctifies it." Farther on: "The nation [must] be protected against the unfit and the inferior. . . . As long as the Jews possess the right to citizenship and there is thereby the danger of racial camouflage and bastardization, we repudiate a mission to the Jews in Germany. . . . In particular, marriage between Germans and Jews is forbidden." There is nothing either Biblical or rational in this shameful "German Christian" theology. It is an incredible effort to give Christian baptism to a particularly demonic hatred. Such teaching crowded the gospel of grace from the church wherever it prevailed, except for a few scraps of vocabulary.

The language of the negative thesis aims directly at the above paragraph and others like it. The church may not recognize besides this one Word of God, still other events and powers, figures and truths, as God's revelation. This means other events such as the coming of Hitler and National Socialism, and other powers than the Spirit of Christ, such as the military, political, and economic power of a "divinely ordered" state. The word translated figures yields the same meaning as when Julius Caesar is called a great figure of history. Hence, it sets up the figure of Hitler against that of Christ. The alleged truths are those of blood and soil, racial purity, and the "heroic" and "positive" gospel of Jesus as revised to fit the Aryan myth. This elaborate construct, based on purported revelation in nature and history, accounts for the high emotion and great enmity aroused in otherwise academic debates about natural theology. It was the insight of Barmen that not merely the ideas of the "German Christians" or the Erlangen pronouncement were being condemned, but the poisoned soil from which they grew: natural theology as a basis of preaching in the church.

It takes little imagination to see what Barmen may teach the church in America thirty-five years later. The atmosphere of the world is even more widely polluted with politicoreligious myths of race, blood, soil, and national destiny than it was then. And the church again is tempted by them.

Article 2. In the second thesis we move from form to content. Granting that the message of the church is drawn exclusively from Christ the Word, it is all the more important to know what the Word says. The message has two parts consisting of God's assurance of . . . forgiveness, and God's mighty claim. The first is the free, unearned, consoling gift of the gospel, and the second is the persistent demand of the gospel. These two elements are hardly new to readers of Scripture and the Reformation confessions. Why was it necessary to repeat in the land of the Reformation that Christ is both justifier and sanctifier, Redeemer and Lord? The negative thesis answers our question.

The false doctrine rejected is that there are areas of our life in which we would not belong to Jesus Christ, but to other lords.

The Third Reich wanted the church to keep away from political and social affairs and devote herself to "the inner mind of the German people," and to "maintain a harmonious attitude in the church" as the national church constitution expressed it. In January of 1934 a "muzzling order" prohibited pastors from dealing in the pulpit or in pastoral letters with the church controversy, let alone broader social issues. They were to restrict themselves to "the preaching of the pure gospel." This familiar cry is not limited to Nazism but arises whenever and wherever the gospel translated into deeds becomes "controversial." It becomes controversial and divisive always in some degree or other when it conflicts with prevailing manners, customs, ways of making a living, governing a state, or conducting international relations. The point at issue is not an easy one to resolve and there is no permanent formula for its resolution. In technical terms it is the relation of justification to sanctification, then further the relation of the private and the public or the personal and social ethic within the Christian's obedience. The easy solution is to withdraw and say that faith is a private affair. But to separate the "two kingdoms" in this way into a private spiritual realm and a public worldly realm is exactly to divide Christ and deny his rule, **as though there were areas of our life in which we would not belong to Jesus Christ, but to other lords.**

The Barmen Declaration does not develop a specific form of social ethic. If it had, it would likely be of interest today only in the classroom. But it does lay that task upon the church. Further, it demanded certain negative actions the church had to take against the prevailing social ethics. A memorandum sent to Adolf Hitler in June, 1936, by the leadership of the Confessing Church, condemns anti-Semitism, concentration camps, police power exempt from judicial control, the oath of the Hitler Youth, and an official morality of sheer expediency and power. We shall comment again, below, on this section of the Declaration.

Article 3. Article 1 has said Christ is the Word, and Article 2 that he is both Savior and Lord. The third article proclaims him sole head and ruler of the church, where he **acts presently as the**

Lord. The affirmation is almost a formal definition of the church. It was not intended to be so in the first draft, but the addition of various elements alternately from Lutheran and Reformed members of the Synod gave it its present cumbersome fullness. Perhaps the original draft of this paragraph will help the reader both to appreciate the main point more clearly and to observe realistically how partisan interest may affect the work of a church council. It originally read as follows: "The Christian Church is the congregation of brethren in which Jesus Christ is proclaimed as the Lord. It has to testify with its faith and obedience, with its message as with its order, in the midst of a sinful world and itself as the Church of sinners, that it is solely his property, and that it wants to live solely from his comfort and from his direction." We are told that the suggestions went something like this: "If we mention church, then we must mention sacrament; if we mention sacrament, then the Holy Spirit," etc. The chief urgency of the paragraph, however, was not lost. The church here pictured is not one form of human society among others, but in essence wholly unique. It is **solely his property, and . . . it lives and wants to live solely from his comfort.** At the same time the church does not claim artificial holiness or exemption from life. It speaks not as a church of angels, but as **the Church of pardoned sinners,** testifying **in the midst of a sinful world.**

As with all these articles, the negative thesis brings the point home: the church is not allowed **to abandon the form of its message and order.** This can be fairly paraphrased and pointed up by saying that the form of its message is derived from Christ and cannot be altered into the so-called heroic Aryan piety fostered by the "German Christians." Also, its order may not be changed either for arbitrary reasons within the church or in response to **ideological and political convictions.** Barmen does not hold exclusively for one or another form of church order, but it does uncompromisingly hold that the state may not devise that order, nor may the church itself for reasons unconnected with Christ.

Article 4 continues with the function of church offices and

officers. These offices are not given to the church from outside to rule it. Quite the opposite, they are a method of exercising a ministry that actually belongs to and arises from the whole congregation. Church officers are "servants," not rulers. There is no implication that civil offices should conform to this pattern, but merely that **"it shall not be so among you,"** the church (emphasis mine).

As before, there is nothing theologically new in principle presented in Article 4, and everything taught was already implicit in Article 3. But it needed to be further explained and declared. A separate article was constructed because of the problem of the national bishop, or Reich bishop. All the regional churches—Lutheran, Reformed, and United—had agreed to this office. At first a non "German Christian" was elected, but within a month he resigned, powerless. This article, in the official interpretation of Pastor Hans Asmussen, does not mean to decide for or against a bishop's office in the church. "It is our opinion that in a Christian congregation there can be an episcopal and a presbyterian constitution. But we are also convinced that in a Christian congregation a devilish will to dominion can get in under an episcopal as well as under a presbyterial constitution." This particular bishop's office, however, is rejected as devilish because it is a ruling and not a serving office. The election of the perfidious Ludwig Müller to this post was disastrous to a church government formerly responsible to both pastors and people. Once Müller seized a church headquarters with the aid of troops. It was he who issued the "muzzling order" and curtailed the church press. Further, various devices, both of the state and the church, circumvented or crushed the existing regional administrations. A lion's share of the stenographically recorded debate at Barmen went to these questions of jurisdiction and structure. This only demonstrates the inseparability of message and church order. If one speaks of the gospel, he speaks of the church; simultaneously he must speak of the structure of the church as a society, and this already involves its place and role in society at large.

Article 5. Here is Scriptural warrant for the state. There are

of course other Biblical passages that might have shown more
fully what is implied. But the dramatic form of I Peter 2:17,
"Fear God. Honor the emperor," makes it unmistakable that the
church honors government, despite charges of sedition and sub-
version that have been aimed at it from the days of Jesus to the
present. On the contrary, the State has by divine appointment
the task of providing for justice and peace.

There are weighty matters concealed in the choice of language.
Great care was given not to call the state an "order," or "order
of existence" as found in the "German Christian" articles, and
as shared one way or another by the majority of theologians at
that time. "Order" implies a structure established by God, and
therefore exemption of the state from criticism, in structure if not
in policy. But in Article 5 the state is seen as a function, a means
to an end. Primary is its task rather than its structure. The *task*
is by divine appointment or direction.

This description of the state in terms of its task, function, or
end to be achieved establishes a point of criticism above any
given, existing state. Not divine sanction or divine "order" but
divine direction to the task of providing for justice and peace
is the position stated. The degree to which a state provides for
justice and peace is a measure of whether the state is fulfilling
its function. Toward this end the state legitimately uses the threat
and exercise of force, according to the measure of human judgment and human ability. The whole panoply of state powers and
functions is thereby reaffirmed. Even more: by analogy with the
Kingdom of God, God's commandment and righteousness, there
is reinforced the responsibility both of rulers and of the ruled.
The Barmen Declaration, having in Articles 1 through 4 established the radical uniqueness of the church and set it apart from
human societies of all kinds, now has presented the church's view
of the state. It offers evangelical rather than natural law, or
nationalist, or sentimental ground on which to honor the emperor.
The fifth Barmen article is at once disengagement from an older
view of a state by divine right, and reaffirmation of the state as
devoted to a divinely appointed task.

This Barmen article, thus, neither denies the role of the state within its proper sphere nor denies its divine appointment. But it does deny the National Socialist conception of the state as the single and totalitarian order of human life, thus fulfilling the Church's vocation as well. The negative thesis contains no comment on the form of the state, whether democratic, monarchic, or dictatorial, but it limits the extent of the state's interest in and power over the lives of men. Certain things do not fall within the state's appointment, whatever its form. Not only a dictatorship but also a democracy could be totalitarian if it tried to control the total lives of its people. If in democracy a majority vote determined the religious faith of all, it would be totalitarian. This article has in view the ambitions and achievements of a particular state which set out to provide the whole world view and even the theology of its people. But the message applies beyond the time and place of Germany in the 1930's and to all kinds of ideology, right wing, left wing, or center. Caesar may never appropriate what is God's—nor may any of society's institutions or ideologies, even when inspired by benevolent and pious intentions.

The church, too, has limits. A special statement is devoted to repeating that the special commission or task (Article 5) of the church prevents it from adopting the role of the state. In the background is a critique of the medieval papacy. In view of the traditional quiet of the church in Germany in the face of government policies, this second element might seem not to have been necessary. It was insisted upon by those holding the traditional view. An indispensable thought occurs at the end. Should the church assume the characteristics, the tasks, and the dignity of the State, then the church becomes itself an organ of the State. The church loses its identity entirely if drawn to these other tasks. This is emphatic in the comments of Pastor Asmussen. "When the Church preaches a political kingdom, an earthly law, and the justice of a human form of society, it goes beyond its limits and drags the State down into the mire with it."

Again the precise language must be carefully watched, for we are in an area where the Declaration has been heavily attacked from opposite sides. Is there a conflict between Article 2, **God's mighty claim upon our whole life,** and this division between state and church, as clearly drawn as if life were lived in hermetically sealed compartments? May not **God's mighty claim** ever be expressed through the church's confessing against an evil state or an evil practice in the state as such?

The case in point is anti-Semitism, which was not superficial but elemental in the ideas and practices of Nazism. Persecution was minor in 1934 compared to five years later, but it was already serious and the program had been known for years from the writings of Adolf Hitler. "German Christians" understood and espoused it. They, in turn, are the immediate enemy in the church struggle and are named frequently as such. But the anti-Semitism condemned throughout the church documents is within the church. Even that is not mentioned explicitly in the Barmen Declaration or, to my knowledge, in the debates at the Synod. The implication is unmistakable, probably clearest in Article 2. The inference was drawn and stated clearly in the memorandum to Hitler, already mentioned, condemning "an anti-Semitism . . . forced on the Christian that binds him to hatred of the Jew." It speaks also of the Christian parent combating the penetration "of these anti-Christian ideals in their children's minds."

This is not enough. The church was still being too churchly, too fascinated with and fearful of its own nature and purity. Having correctly disengaged itself from "preaching a political kingdom," it should have gone on to the full significance of **God's mighty claim upon our whole life** and condemned the objective falsehood in state and society of the whole Aryan-anti-Semitic lie. Later this was realized. The Stuttgart Declaration after the war, made by leaders of the Confessing Church, acknowledged this guilt. Niemöller was the frankest of all. Karl Barth, who made the first draft of the Barmen articles, has called the Confessing Church program too defensive, and a "partial resistance" on the narrow front of the church's own life. We shall cite his fuller evaluation below.

It is embarrassing to write and provoking to read such a criticism of the confessors and martyrs of Barmen by and for others who did not stand in that dangerous place. But it reminds us that the church is made up of men, "sinners and righteous at the same time," not angels, supermen, or inhabitants of Utopia. Others will evaluate the wisdom and the courage, or lack of them, of those called to confess their faith in the last third of the twentieth century.

Article 6. The final article reiterates the uniqueness, independence, and freedom of the Word of God, but this time as anchored in a future expectation. Not only what has been done and promised, but the **"close of the age"** is in view. Since hope is entirely fixed upon a coming reality, it may not be hindered by or attached to **any arbitrarily chosen desires, purposes, and plans.** It should not be amiss to set side by side the use of the word **service** in Article 2 and the present article. Above, we read of **the joyful deliverance from the godless fetters of this world for a free, grateful service to his creatures.** And here, in relation to II Tim. 2:9, "The word of God is not fettered," the false doctrine is rejected that the **Word and work of the Lord** might be placed **in the service of any arbitrarily chosen desires, purposes, and plans.** The utter freedom of the word *from* the latter does not end the story. It is also an unfettered freedom *to* the service of **his creatures.**

In summary, an evaluation of Barmen and the Confessing Church written by Karl Barth appears balanced and instructive not only as an account of recent history but as offering suggestive ways of understanding present history and the function of the Barmen articles within American Presbyterianism.

"In 1933 and the years immediately following—at the time the National Socialists 'seized power'—there was no struggle of the German universities and schools, of the German legal profession, of German business, of the German theater and German art in general, of the German Army, or of the German trade-unions. Many individuals, it is true, went down to an honorable defeat. But in no time at all, those large groups and institutions were subdued and made to conform. On the other hand, from the very first months on there was a German *Church* struggle. Even it was not a total resistance against totalitarian National Socialism. It restricted itself to repelling the encroachment of National Socialism. It confined itself to the Church's Confession, to the Church service, and to Church order as such. It was only a partial resistance. And for this it has been properly and improperly reproached: properly—in so far as a strong Christian Church, that is, a Church sure of its own cause in the face of National Socialism should not have remained on the defensive and should not have fought on its own narrow front alone; improperly—in so far as on this admittedly all too narrow front a serious battle was waged, at least in part and not without some success. At any rate, the substance of the Church was rescued and with a better understanding of it than it had had before. If at least as much had been done in other areas as was done at that time in the Church, National Socialism would have had a hard time of it in Germany right from the start. In proportion to its task, the Church has sufficient reason to be ashamed that it did not do more; yet in comparison with those other groups and institutions it has no reason to be ashamed; it accomplished far more than all the rest." (Quoted by Cochrane, *The Church's Confession Under Hitler,* p. 40.)

CHAPTER 21

SACRAMENTS IN THE
REFORMED CONFESSIONS

"Sacrament" is a word that does not appear in the Bible. It began to be used in the Christian church about the turn of the third century after Christ in connection chiefly with baptism. Later it was a general name for a large and indefinite number of churchly ceremonies which were eventually reduced to seven. Baptism, penance (confession), and the Mass were central. The Catholic Middle Ages were a full flowering of sacramental religion. The Mass, especially, occupied the chief position in worship and piety both secular and monastic. The great cathedrals known throughout the world as well as parish churches were built primarily as houses around the altar on which the "sacrifice of the Mass" took place and in which the body of the Victim was retained day and night. Here was the place and here were the means through which saving grace was made accessible to mankind. The preaching of the word, correspondingly, played a lesser role, to the point at times of practically disappearing from regular public worship.

By contrast, the Protestant Reformers aimed to reduce the relative importance of sacraments and bring back the preaching of the word of God as an equal or more often dominant feature of Christian life and worship. They reduced the number of sacraments to the two clearly instituted by Christ, Baptism and the Lord's Supper. These changes brought on some of the most virulent debates of the period, not only between Protestant and Roman Catholic or Protestant and sectarian, but within the camp of classic Protestantism itself, between the Lutheran and Reformed Churches. The changes were not only those concerned with a reduction of pomp and ceremony, but they went to the heart of sacramental dogma and the whole question of how man is saved. Still, a study of the Reformers shows them heavily occupied with the same problems that had exercised the church at least since the days of Augustine; hence, they were not so far removed from their opponents as we sometimes like to think. Since these old problems cannot be raised in a brief discussion and since they are no doubt very strange to the many Presbyterians who take the sacraments as audio-visual aids to personal remembrance of Christ's sacrifice, the following comments may be quite unsatisfactory.

All Reformed confessions treat the sacraments under the doctrine of the church. In the Scots Confession they were ranked among the "notes" or signs of the true church along with preaching and the discipline. A further characteristic is that the treatment begins with a presentation of the general definition of a sacrament, then proceeds to separate analyses of Baptism and the Lord's Supper. It has often been argued that the creation of this one category for the two actions, Baptism and the Supper, tends to distort one or both. With this in mind, the Confession of 1967, while offering no polemic against the older method, omits the word and the class of sacrament and deals with each separately in its own terms.

In what follows we shall make the Second Helvetic Confession the basic document and treat the others in relation to it. This is justified because it was recognized as the leading Reformed confession of the Reformation period, it represents an agreement between diverging tendencies in Geneva and Zurich, and it is the fullest treatment to be found in *The Book of Confessions*.

Preaching and the sacraments have the same basic function of communicating effectively the word of God, according to the Second Helvetic Confession. Preaching remains prior and basic in all these confessions. The sacraments are "mystical symbols, or holy rites, or sacred actions" which God "from the beginning" has added to preaching to seal and confirm the spoken word. Baptism and the Lord's Supper are always seen as direct replacements for the sacraments of the old covenant—respectively, circumcision and the Passover. Although not mentioned in the confessions, the Reformed theologians often spoke of the two trees in the Garden of Eden, the rainbow in the time of Noah, and the like, as sacraments. Hence, the sacraments are seen as ancient and continuing in the church, although taking various forms.

Sacraments have only one author, God. God not only originally and exclusively instituted the sacraments but still today makes them effective. "The faithful, when they receive them from the ministers, know that God works in his own ordinance, and therefore they receive them as from the hand of God." This offers another parallel made in the Second Helvetic Confession between preaching and sacraments. In both cases the true word is offered even if the preacher or presider is personally unworthy. Further, the word is received in both instances only by the Spirit's work in the faithful hearer, not by everyone within earshot of the sermon or everyone who receives the physical elements during the sacramental ceremony.

The three parts which make up a sacrament are the external sign (water, bread, wine), the thing itself or the substance of the sacrament (new birth, Christ's body), and finally, the word of God which binds together the other two sacramentally and makes them effective. The function of sacraments is to bring remembrance and renewal of God's grace toward men, and to "seal" (our translation says "assure") by an outward act God's work of salvation.

Baptism is the initiation ceremony by which persons are "enrolled, entered, and received unto the covenant and family" of God. That which is sealed is the cleansing from sin, the adoption as sons, the union with Christ, and numerous other gifts or benefits that come with entrance into the people of God. It is particularly important in the Reformed confessions that children be baptized. On this score they differed not only from the "believers'" baptism of the sectarians but from the infant baptism of Rome.

The Roman Catholic sacrament of baptism with water was regarded as bringing about just one thing, forgiveness for the inherited guilt of original sin. The haste to baptize a dying infant which has no place in Protestantism results from the view that this is the only way the child might enter heaven. Subsequent to baptism the constantly repeated sacrament of penance is necessary to deal with sins committed after baptism. By contrast, the Reformed teaching is that baptism is the sign of the forgiveness of all sin, not merely original sin, and as such it needs no further supplement. Also, it is a sign of grace already offered in the covenant to the members and their children. The effectiveness is not dependent on the ceremony with water—"although it is a great sin to . . . neglect this ordinance" (Westminster Confession, Ch. XXVIII, Sec. 5)—and thus the accidental or unavoidable omission of it does not exclude the individual from salvation.

Among the baptists of the Reformation period the view was held that the ceremony means nothing unless accompanied by free intentional belief. Only those who had reached an age of discretion were baptized. Catholic or Protestant infant baptism counted for nothing; hence, adults had to be rebaptized (as it appeared in the eyes of the orthodox) to join the baptist societies. In the Reformed confessions, baptism is the external sign of the covenant people as circumcision had been for those under the old covenant. The baptism of a helpless child was the most dramatic and precious symbol of God's freely given grace. If the child were required to respond, salvation would be dependent upon a work of the individual. To repeat the process once carried out was a high insult to divine grace. The Heidelberg Catechism is especially lucid on the gracious character of infant baptism (Q. 74).

We turn now to the other sacrament.

Common meals provide the nourishment without which life cannot go on. The sacrament of the Lord's meal or Supper has to do with the spiritual food on which life eternal depends. It is called the "Lord's" because it was he "who first consecrated it to his Church." The same consecration or blessing "still remains among all those who celebrate no other but that very Supper which the Lord instituted" (Second Helvetic Confession, Ch. XXI).

The nourishment of eternal life comes from Christ's sacrifice, his body given and his blood shed, which are "received spiritually by true faith" in all who believe. This reception of Christ's body or union with Christ through his body is the substance or thing signified by the sacrament of the Lord's Supper. Some of the greatest sacramental struggles of the sixteenth century concerned the relation between or the identity of literally eating the bread and wine of the sacrament and receiving the body of Christ. We present here only some aspects of the problem as it is posed particularly in the Reformed Church.

The Second Helvetic Confession distinguishes three kinds of eating. (1) "Corporeal" eating or literally consuming a food has no direct relation to receiving the body of Christ. (2) "Spiritual" eating is faith. Or, more fully, it is the union of the believer with Christ in faith. "By spiritual food we do not mean some imaginary food..., but the very body of the Lord given to us.... And this eating of the flesh and drinking of the blood of the Lord is so necessary for salvation that without it no man can be saved." Clearly this conception, derived from the sixth chapter of John's Gospel, is the most important in the Confession. It is an eating, however, that is not linked essentially with the sacrament. It goes on "as often and wherever a man believes in Christ." (3) "Sacramental" eating refers to consuming the elements of the Lord's Supper by one who at the same time participates in the "higher spiritual eating" already mentioned.

The key term in the Reformed doctrine is "spiritual." By this term it hoped to avoid what it regarded as the material or physical presence of Christ represented both by Rome and by the Lutherans. Rome held that with the recital of the words, "This is my body" a miracle took place by which Christ's body became really or substantially present, although the appearance of bread and wine remained so far as the ordinary sensibilities of men were concerned. Luther held for the "ubiquity" of Christ's body, not replacing the substance of bread and wine, for this would abolish the sign which is a necessary part of the sacrament, but present "in, with, and under" the signs in the course of the whole liturgy. In either case, reasoned the Reformed Churches, the integrity of Christ's literally ascended body and thus the human nature of his incarnation, are compromised. The answer, according to the Confessions we are now analyzing, is that Christ's presence is the work of the Spirit. "In the Supper rightly used," reads the Scots Confession, "Christ Jesus is so joined with us that he becomes the very nourishment and food of our souls. Not that we imagine any transubstantiation . . . ; but this union and conjunction which we have with the body and blood of Christ . . . is wrought by means of the Holy Ghost, who by true faith carries us above all things that are visible, carnal, and earthly, and makes us feed upon the body and blood of Christ Jesus, once broken and shed for us but now in heaven. . . . Notwithstanding the distance between his glorified body in heaven and mortal men on earth, yet we must assuredly believe that the bread which we break is the communion of Christ's body. . . . The faithful . . . do so eat the body and drink the blood of the Lord Jesus that he remains in them and they in him" (Ch. XXI).

The motive in each case—Roman, Lutheran, and Reformed— is the same: to show the Supper as a means or instrument of the union of the believer with Christ. The first seems to sacrifice the signs, the second to endanger the humanity of Christ, and the Reformed view is sometimes said by its opponents to present the "real absence" of Christ. When, however, the teaching about the Holy Spirit is fully understood, it becomes clear why the writers of the Reformed confessions found that there is nothing unreal or absent in the living work of the Holy Spirit.

The greater problem for the older Reformed confessions was to relate the sacramental act to the ongoing participation of the believer in Christ. If the true participation is that of faith, then the sacrament seems to be expendable. That it is observed at Christ's command is certainly to the point but does not of itself explain the function. The Second Helvetic Confession teaches that the something more which the sacrament offers is progress, growth, refreshment, and increase of faith. It also teaches along with the Heidelberg Catechism that the remembrance of Christ's sacrifice is strengthened by the sacrament.

One more observation in this extremely brief glance at sacramental teaching: the believer is throughout the recipient. In accord with the teaching about the grace and love of God that come to man apart from his own initiative, both sacraments are sheer gifts of God through Christ. Man prepares nothing, brings nothing, offers nothing. The church does not offer up Christ (Westminster Confession, Ch. XXIX, Sec. 2) or itself or its tithes and services to receive them again in some other form. Hence, questions should be raised about the practice of bringing forward the elements for the Lord's Supper along with the offerings of the congregation in the Communion Service. At least none of the present confessional documents offers a basis for this practice.

Appendix

Appendix

A HARMONY OF
THE BOOK OF CONFESSIONS

A harmony is an arrangement of parallel passages side by side for convenient comparison. In the table that follows we list citations of parallel subject matter by chapter, paragraph, article, or catechism question number. Because of its fullness and its inherent value, the Second Helvetic Confession is used as an outline for the whole as it was in *The Harmony of Protestant Confessions* of the year 1581. The topics in the left-hand margin, thus, list most of the chapters of that Confession in approximately their original order. There is some rearrangement and omission in those cases where the sequence or subject matter is so unusual as to be awkward for the others, for example, Chs. 4, 5, 6, and 7. The Harmony is meant to be practical for the average reader rather than exhaustive; hence, it is limited to major topics found in the chapter titles and outlines of the various writings. The numbers given in parentheses indicate references where the topical word is not found or the citation is for some other reason not so direct as in the others.

Topic	Second Helvetic Confession Chapter	Scots Confession Chapter	Heidelberg Catechism Question	Westminster Confession Chapter	Shorter Catechism Question	Barmen Declaration Thesis	Confession of 1967
Scripture	I-II	XVIII-XX	21	I	2-3, 88-90	1	3, 27-30, 49
Trinity	III	I	25	II	6		5, 7
Creation	VII	II	26	IV	(1), 9-10		16-17
Providence	VI	I	1, 27-28	V	11-12		16-17
Covenant	XX	IV-V	19, 74	VII, XIX	20		18-19
Sin	VIII-IX	III	3-11	VI, IX	12-20, 82-85		12-14
Election	X	VII-VIII	26, 31, 52, 54	III, X	7-8, 20		(18-20)
Jesus Christ	XI	V-XI	29-52	VIII	21-28	1-2	3, 8-11, 15, 24, 32
Holy Spirit	III, etc.	XII	53-64	XXXIV			Part I, Section C
Law	XII	XIV-XV	3-4, 92-115	XIX, (VII, XIII)	39-81		
Gospel	XIII	IV-V	19, etc.	VII, XXXV			6, 7, 18, etc.
Repentance	XIV	(XII)		XV	87		21

Justification	XV	(XV)	31-34, 60-64	XI	32-33	2	22
Faith	XVI	XII	1-2, 21, 32, 53, 60-61, 74	XIV	86, (30-38)		10, 21
Christian Life	XVI	XII-XIV	Part III	XIII, XVI, XIX-XX	35, 39-82	2-3	21-26, 41-47
Church	XVII-XVIII	V, XVI, XVIII, XX to XXII	54, 85	XXV-XXVI, XXX-XXXI		3-4	20, 22, 25, etc.
Mission				XXXV		6	31-33, 41-47
Sacraments	XIX	XXI-XXIII	65-68	XXVII	88, 91-93		
Baptism	XX	XXI-XXIII	69-74	XXVIII	94-95		51
Lord's Supper	XXI	XXI-XXIII	75-85	XXIX	96-97		52
Worship	IV-V XX-XXVII			XXI-XX	45-62		36, 49-52
Marriage	XXIX	XXIV		XXIV			17, 47
State	XXX	XXIV		XXIII		5	17, 25, 45
Consummation	(XI)	XVII, XXV	57-58	XXXII	37-38		11, 26, and Part III